Midge Magic

MIDGE MAGIC

Don Holbrook
Ed Koch

STACKPOLE
BOOKS

Published by
STACKPOLE BOOKS
5067 Ritter Road
Mechanicsburg, PA 17055
www.stackpolebooks.com

Printed in China

10 9 8 7 6 5 4 3 2

First edition

Cover design by Wendy A. Reynolds
Front cover photo of Penns Creek by Norm Shires; fly photos by Don Holbrook
All interior photos by Don Holbrook, except pages 69 and 77, by Norm Shires

Library of Congress Cataloging-in-Publication Data

Holbrook, Don.
Midge magic / Don Holbrook, Ed Koch.— 1st ed.
p. cm.
ISBN 0-8117-0996-5
1. Flies, Artificial. 2. Fly tying. I. Koch, Ed. II. Title.

SH451 .H58 2001
688.7'9124—dc21

Library of Congress Control Number: 2001020089

Editor's Note

This book is a collaborative effort between Don Holbrook and Ed Koch, who, through decades on the stream together, developed the art of midge fishing shared here. Most of the text, except where noted, was written by Don, and it is his research and patterns represented in the body of the book and his voice in the narrative. Ed wrote the preface, along with parts of chapters 2, 11 and 13. We would also like to acknowledge the work of Dave Breitmeier and Ken Yufer, who contributed the text for chapter 13.

CONTENTS

PREFACE

In 1971 a young man walked into the Yellow Breeches Fly Shop. He had recently moved from West Virginia to Pennsylvania to work for a local water company. Wanting to learn to fly-fish for trout, he purchased a 6½-foot Fenwick rod, Cortland line, leaders, tippet material, reel, and a few flies. It was midsummer, so the flies I sold him were terrestrials and midge patterns. A short time later, he returned to buy a fly-tying outfit. Thus began a twenty-eight-year career of trout chasing, pattern development, success and failure at trout catching for Don Holbrook.

I sold the shop in 1974 and over the years saw Don occasionally on the stream, at club meetings, or at fly-tying classes held over the winter. In 1991 several of the old-timers told me to have Don show me his flies, a bit of sarcasm in their tone. I sat down next to Don and asked him to show me what he'd been fishing lately.

Reaching into his tying kit, he pulled out four boxes crammed full of dozens of size 18 midge nymphs. The flies were all tied the same way, except for color. There had to be at least two dozen different colored nymphs. They had no tails, no thorax, no wing case, no throat, and no collar. Each fly had the body wrapped flat, starting just down the bend and forward to within a few millimeters of the eye. A bulbous head was tied at the eye of the hook. All were tied with some kind of yarn. Half were tied with one color on the body and head, and the other half had a contrasting rib of a lighter or darker color than the body and head. The other patterns were tied with a yarn body and head and ribbed with fine tinsel. There had to be fifteen or twenty different color combinations.

"What are they?" I asked. "Do they work? How long have you been using them?"

I've learned over the years not to put anyone down or to make light of their flies until I've had a chance to fish them. Over the years, I've met many great fly fishermen and been introduced to numerous patterns that I've been thankful for many times over.

Don was an instructor at the fly-tying class that night and had two youngsters to work with him. He suggested that we meet for breakfast. What Don told me that morning and many times since over the years is retold in the following chapters.

Don had been fishing Big Spring, a limestone stream not far from Carlisle, Pennsylvania. One evening, he was fishing his way downstream to the parking lot. He'd been casually fishing a nymph on the way down, not paying much attention to what was going on. He'd made a cast with a nymph and taken a few steps downstream, when he hooked something. A short time later, he guided a nice brown trout into his net. It was getting dark, and he had to use a flashlight in order to release the trout without losing the fly. Holding the tippet in his right hand and the flashlight in his left, Don shone the light in the trout's mouth. He couldn't believe, much less understand, what he saw. "The fish's mouth looked like a Christmas tree with hundreds of lights in it," he said. "No matter how I held the light, his mouth twinkled and glistened all over."

At that time, anglers were allowed to kill one trout over 14 inches. Don removed his nymph and let the trout lie in his net. The trout measured 15½ inches. Don headed for the car. As manager of a local water company plant, he had equipment on hand, such as a microscope and camera, that he could use to record and try to identify what was

Big Spring Creek near Newville, Pennsylvania. One of the classic limestone streams in Cumberland County.

in the trout's mouth. He cleaned the trout's mouth and stomach, emptying the contents into petri dishes to inspect and photograph under a microscope. There were hundreds of tiny nymphs. Don had never seen anything like it. The nymphs ranged in size from 5 to 15 millimeters, with the average size being about 10 millimeters. There had to be twelve to eighteen color phases. At home that night, he tied up a dozen nymphs in size 18 and in six different solid color variations—cream, tan, black, olive, brown, and gray. He tied the bodies of dubbed rabbit fur, starting at the bend of the hook and wrapping forward to the eye. A small, oval head or collar finished off the imitation. They looked much too simple, though so did the real specimens.

The next evening found Don back on the Big Spring by 7 P.M. From the parking area to the head of the spring was about 400 yards. Don decided to test the new patterns in this stretch. Tying the gray nymph to the 6X tippet, Don stood searching the water upstream. If the trout hadn't been spooked within the last hour or so, they could always be found close to either bank out of the faster middle current.

It didn't take Don long to locate several feeding trout. Kneeling in the grass so as not to spook his quarry, Don observed the trout for several minutes. "OK," he thought to himself, "it's time to find out whether I'm even close to figuring out what's going on with that trout from last night and the hundreds of tiny nymphs in his mouth and stomach."

Don made several false casts to be certain of the distance, then let the line go. The leader turned over smoothly, dropping the little nymph several feet in front of and just to the left of the trout. The little gray nymph broke the surface film and began to sink as it drifted toward its quarry. But the current began to pull the tiny imitation toward midstream, away from the trout. Don waited until his leader and fly were well behind the trout, then picked the line up off the water.

The second cast placed the nymph about 2 feet in front of the trout, directly in their feeding lane. The little nymph sank and drifted toward the trout. A brown saw the fly and moved to his left to inspect the imitation. He refused it and turned back to his feeding station. Again Don waited until his fly was well behind the trout before lifting his line from the water and catching the tiny nymph in his hand.

Don watched for several minutes to determine how the current would carry the nymph to the trout. His next cast dropped the fly 2 feet in front of his quarry and a little to its right, closer to the bank. The little gray nymph began to sink. This time the trout turned slightly to the right, opened his mouth, and softly inhaled the imitation. Don struck, hard enough to set the hook but soft enough to protect the tippet. The brown felt the sting of the point, turned to his left, and headed for midstream and the cover of the weeds. In just a few minutes, a plump brownie slid into Don's submerged net. Ever so gently Don slid his fingers down the delicate tippet, grasped the little nymph, and released the fish. The trout flipped once and was gone—left to test another nymph another day. Working upstream, Don took two more trout on a cream nymph, another on a tan, and two on an olive. He was extremely pleased with the results of his new midge patterns.

For the remainder of that season and two seasons following, Don fished at least twice a week, often three or four times. The new patterns consistently produced trout, from midsummer right through fall, and even into the winter months. All color variations worked well. Don added ribbing to the basic colors he started with. The ribbed patterns took more trout than the nonribbed. Don took one trout every other month for eight months—four trout a season. He checked the stomach contents and found that the size of the midge larvae remained consistent, but there were as many as thirty-six color variations over the eight-month period of monitoring. Many were solid colors, but over time, there were an increasing number with ribbing in both lighter and darker colors. The more Don observed the nymphs, the more he became convinced that a smoother body material than the dubbed fur would be more effective. He began experimenting with dozens of different materials from the local fly shop. Some worked, and some didn't.

One weekend, while reading the Sunday paper, he saw an ad for cross-stitch yarns on sale at a local craft shop. He stopped at the store the next evening on the way home from work. There had to be 100 or more different colors and shades of yarn hanging on the pegboard display. He purchased two dozen different colors, enough for forty-eight different nymphs—twenty-four solid and twenty-four ribbed. The yarn came in three- and six-strand twist. Each pack would tie hundreds of flies at a cost of about 60 cents. For several nights, he tied dozens of solid and ribbed nymphs with the new yarn. And to his delight, they outfished the fur patterns about six to one. Over the years, he continued to experiment with color variations, and today his yarn patterns number in the hundreds. The only change made from the original patterns was to rib some of them with very fine silver or gold tinsel or wire. These patterns work as well as the yarn-ribbed originals.

He gave me several dozen different patterns to try, and over the next several seasons, I fished them hard on a number of my favorite streams. They did extremely well. Then I decided it was time to fish with Don.

We met and fished a feeder to the Yellow Breeches that originated in a spring-fed lake in

The "Little Run" flowing out of Boiling Springs Lake into Yellow Breeches Creek, a short stretch of fly-fishing-only water filled with trout.

the village of Boiling Springs. Locals call it the "Little Run." The feeder is only about 30 feet wide and 400 yards long, at best. It gets an unbelievable amount of pressure twelve months a year and can be very difficult to fish. In about an hour's fishing, I had two trout, and Don had seven. "Enough," I said. "Let's go down to the main stream." There I caught five, and Don eleven.

I was convinced that Don was on to something.

—Ed Koch

INTRODUCTION

Fishermen are curious fellows when it comes to midges. Most won't fish them until they are convinced there is no other way to catch a trout at that particular moment. But in reality, it's probably the most likely way to catch trout at any moment.

Looking back over twenty-five years of fishing midges almost to the exclusion of everything else, I am amazed that most of the published patterns are mainly suggestive in nature. As I was drawn more deeply into studying these insects over the years, first through simple observation, then with photography and microscopy, more questions arose with each discovery. Could trout really tell the difference between these thousands of insects? If so, was there any way to reasonably imitate them that was worth the effort put forth in studying them?

I am now convinced that this is the case. There is still plenty of room for suggestive patterns, and many of the patterns in this book are just that. They work too well not to use them, whatever their attraction. Nevertheless, I firmly believe that the closer your fly appears to be the trout's natural food, the more likely they are to take it.

I like simple fly patterns. I see no point in tying fifteen materials on a hook when three will do the job. If you like to use more embellishments, feel free to add all you wish, but first ask yourself why.

October 1, 1974 - *Allenberry on the Yellow Breeches. Ed Koch recommended using a #18 herl midge pupa with a gray body. Caught four fish the first night (about 7pm)—one was a 17" rainbow. Caught several the next few nights, drifting the fly to the top of the middle dam.*

This entry, in my nearly thirty years of fishing notes to date, was the start of fishing with size 18 or smaller flies. My success at fly fishing to this point had been mediocre at best. I fished mostly in the fly-only section of the Yellow Breeches Creek at Allenberry Playhouse near Boiling Springs, Pennsylvania. There were always trout in this section of the stream, due to periodic stockings by the Yellow Breeches Anglers Club. Fishermen were plentiful too. The occasional fly-fishing school was held here, and I would try to fish there on those days, edging as close as I dared to try to learn something.

July 22, 1975 - *Stopped by Ed Koch's fly shop to buy some materials, and asked for suggestions. He tied a #20 black midge and told me to try it in the little run below Boiling Springs Lake.*

July 23, 1975 - *Boiling Springs, Little Run, about dark, many small trout, caught 2 on #20 black midge, missed many.*

These were the first fish I had caught on midge drys. I had bought a copy of Ed's book *Fishing the Midge* the previous fall but had used only the subsurface patterns. Small hackles were hard to come by, and I was still pretty much fishing the standard patterns and sizes that I had been taught at the local fly-tying clinics. Most locally available necks were selling for $2 to $5 each, and I invested the princely sum of $25 for a grizzly neck that some of the local tiers were starting to breed. Thus armed, I began tying Ed Shenk's No-Name Midges with a passion. I was fascinated that trout would take these tiny flies, even though my equipment and technique were still somewhat on the crude side. I was one step closer to becoming a midge fisherman.

Yellow Breeches Creek near Allenberry Resort, Pennsylvania.

The Carlisle Fish and Game Association, near Carlisle, Pennsylvania, started a winter fly-tying clinic of ten weeks' duration around 1970 or 1971. Even though I worked on the Yellow Breeches Creek for the local water utility, the significance of this area was unknown to me. Being raised in more southern climes, I had never seen a trout before I moved here and had fished very little. How amazed I was to find that this was a limestone valley of great importance to the fly-fishing world, and that many of the innovations, techniques, and writings of the sport came from here. And these same people came to the fly-tying clinics as speakers, tiers, and friends. Talk about being in awe! The local game warden, Gene Utech, had the unenviable task of teaching someone left-handed (me) how to tie. He made me sit across the table from him so he could tell what I was doing. Vince Marinaro was a frequent visitor who impressed on me the importance of observing and then logically reasoning why something happens.

Local tiers, too numerous to name, whose tying skills I will never be able to equal, freely shared their knowledge with beginners. But the one who impressed me the most was John Shollenberger. He was a guest tier for several years at the winter clinics and, among other patterns, tied intricate midge drys down to size 32. Years later, at a dinner auction, I bid on a small glass dome with seven of his midges mounted inside. I intended to own it regardless of cost. It still resides on my tying table as a reminder of how far I yet have to go.

Boiling Springs Lake is fed by giant limestone springs that sustain a vast amount of insect life.

Big Spring Creek, near Newville, Pennsylvania, was closed to fishing in the area of its headwaters for several years in the late sixties and early seventies as part of a Pennsylvania Fish Commission study. The area was opened to fishing in early 1976, and I was there on the first day. By now I knew the stream was famous for its strain of wild brook trout. There were more people there than any opening-day crowd I had ever seen. There were also more trout than I had ever seen in one place, other than a hatchery. No matter where you stood, there were fifty trout within 20 feet of you. This later became my test area for new fly patterns.

January 1, 1976 - *Big Spring Creek, catching a few on #16 mole fur nymph, #12 red wool, #20 ant, #16 otter fur cress bug. Heard fish are feeding on small black flies. See fish taking mostly under, some on top. Caught no flies.*

Fascinated by the number of trout in one location and the apparent difficulty in catching them, I returned here to fish every weekend through April, a round-trip of some 60 miles. I tried many patterns and had some success, especially with a little size 18 olive-brown fur nymph with a silver rib. I knew enough (or thought so) by now to understand that small midge patterns were used by many of the regulars who fished here—in particular, midge drys. Diving right in, I soon acquired every hook made down to size 28, furs of every color available, and anything that even remotely looked like it would be useful. I tied fly patterns based on "by guess and by gosh." Many of them worked at times. Many didn't work at times. Most worked sometimes. I just didn't know why.

June 5, 1976 - *Big Spring Creek, caught one, missed four, on #16 brown w/ latex wing case, caught 15" rainbow on gold wet with white wing. In stomach: midge pupae #24 yellow or olive, ribbed brown, brown wing case, #20–#22 white larvae with gray rib.*

Back in those days, I occasionally kept a trout to eat. I don't anymore, mainly because I prefer the taste of smallmouth bass, for which this area is also decidedly known. I didn't know much then about collecting the insect life of the stream. Oh, I would pick up rocks along the shallows, looking at the general size and color of mayfly nymphs and such, as I had read about in books. But this time, when I cleaned the fish, which I didn't do until I got home, I cut open the stomach and spread everything out in a little white dish. This was the first time I had ever seen actual midge pupae. I decided, right then and there, if this was what the fish ate, this was what I was going to tie.

I really don't remember what led me to finally choose the materials I ended up using. Most likely, I stumbled over them in one of the local sewing shops. (So much for keeping good notes.) Regardless, I tied some midge pupae on #24 hooks using a piece of pale yellow embroidery floss for a body and ribbing it with a reddish brown 6/0 tying thread. And it actually worked:

June 6, 1976 - *Big Spring Creek, caught 15+ on #24 midge yellow floss, ribbed brown thread, used one piece of lead on leader, many missed. Caught 1 on #14 reddish yellow wet with white wing, 1 on #16 sulfur nymph.*

I tried to imitate the white larva with a gray rib next. Unable to find a close match, I dyed some white floss a very pale shade of gray. It was so close to white that I cut the dyed strands longer than the white ones in order to tell them apart. I ribbed a white floss body with the pale gray floss. This turned out to be the most successful pattern to date of them all. Years later, I found out that the larvae I had found in that first trout's stomach were the larvae of a member of the blackfly family. I soon came to the conclusion that the ribbed effect of the body was the number-one feature that the trout keyed on. Twenty-five years later, I still remain convinced. I could be wrong, but somebody has to prove it to me.

Let me state right up front that I've never seen a midge pattern I didn't think would catch fish. The difficulty is where and when. Little has been written in angling literature on midges. Dave Whitlock has written several times on midge life cycles and behavior, most notably in *Dave Whitlock's Guide to Aquatic Trout Foods,* which you would be well advised to read. W. Patrick McCafferty's *Aquatic Entomology* perhaps is a little too scientific for a lot of readers, but it will really open your eyes with its detailed descriptions. And my coauthor, Ed Koch, has written the only book totally devoted to midges to date. It is as applicable today as it was when he wrote it.

Color is the number-two feature trout key on. If your imitations are a few shades off in color, you may still catch fish. If you hit the exact shade of color of the naturals, you will catch more fish. A lot more fish. I have never given up on the premise that if I can match the naturals exactly, I will catch every fish in the stream. I realize we don't really know exactly what a fish sees. I sometimes wonder if we are really sure of what *we* see. Since I have gotten more deeply into macrophotography, I now have to also worry about what the film sees. Regardless, my ultimate aim has evolved into matching every midge that I encounter. I should live so long.

As far as size goes, if you're going to imitate a size 22, use a size 22. Enough said. Luckily, the vast majority of midge pupae, at least in my area, are size 18. Unfortunately, they do grow down to size 28 (and some I've seen would probably be labeled as size 50—I don't even think about these), but tying them is really not that formidable a chore.

What has resulted from twenty-five years of tying and fishing midges probably 95 percent of my fishing time (for your own sanity, I don't recommend that you follow this regimen) is a style of tying that is simple yet effective, emphasizes what I believe are the important features of the insect, and is presented in a manner that is reproducible by anyone. There have been a great number of successes, a great number of failures (yes, there are days I catch nothing when everyone around me is hooking up), and many side paths I have taken in my patterns as ideas led to ideas. They are all presented somewhere in this writing.

CHAPTER ONE

Fishing the Midge

I depend 99 percent on my patterns for success, to the exclusion of other factors. I think that's why I've put so much effort into them over the years. I'm not the worst fisherman around, but you're not going to see me being hired to give casting clinics or stream strategy sessions. I'm not a very good wader, I now wish I had paid more attention to tackle over the years, and I have this blind faith that trout can be anywhere in the stream.

That said, I'm still going to reveal to you how I go about fishing with small flies, be they wet, dry, or anything in between—not with the idea of telling you what you should do in order to be successful, but hinting that there are lots of things you really don't have to do.

To put things in perspective, I guess I should tell you about the waters I fish so you can relate or modify my experiences to fit your own situation. I've been lucky enough to have lived in the Cumberland Valley of Pennsylvania since 1969. This area is famous for its limestone waters and the vast amount of insect life and fish they can support. In less than thirty minutes, I can be fishing on the Yellow Breeches, the Letort, the Big Spring, and many others, including their

The Allenberry dam on the Yellow Breeches.

tributaries. Not much farther away, I have access to many mountain freestone streams. Among them are found many types of stream conditions, including deep pools, shallow riffles, pastoral stretches, and tumbling waters in close cover. A good bit of the Yellow Breeches is wadable, except for those portions above the many old mill dams still in existence. It probably averages 50 feet in width and is the biggest water in the valley, other than the Susquehanna River. The rest of the streams are, in general, fished by necessity from the banks or just off the edge, most being 10 to 20 feet in width on average. I guess the only kind of streams I haven't fished are the bigger, heavier waters, and I've also never fished a lake, in which I know midges are an important food source. You'll have to adapt these methods there.

TACKLE

Ed Koch sold me my first fly rod at his shop in Boiling Springs nearly thirty years ago. He loaned me my present rod a couple years ago. In between, I've owned three other rods: one my wife bought me for Christmas, one I bought myself, and one I won at the local Trout Unlimited dinner one year. The point is, I never had much interest in acquiring new rods, there always being some fly-tying purchase to be made. For twenty-some years I successfully used a 7-foot, 6-weight rod to fish midges. Ed finally got tired of seeing me use such a heavy outfit and loaned me a 7-foot, 4-weight rod, which I still use today. I was a little amazed at how much easier it was to cast. But if I had to go back to the 6-weight, I know I could catch fish with it.

There are proponents of both longer and shorter rods. I have used neither, due perhaps more to a lack of knowledge than anything else. I used a fiberglass rod for most of my early years. After switching to graphite, I went through a long learning period where I missed a lot of strikes. Even now, if I haven't been on the stream for a while, it takes a bit to get my timing back. Fishing subsurface, as I do 95 percent of the time, a rod with a little slower action may be of benefit. However, the ease of casting drys improved drastically with the faster rod. The point is, you can successfully fish midges with whatever you own, but also be aware that something more suitable may be out there. It's a good idea to check out the various options. I hope to do so in the near future. Ed is threatening to take his rod back.

As far as reels go, I hate to admit to it, but basically, if it fits on the reel seat, I'll use it. My reels are usually a little large for the rod. I just don't pay them any mind.

I'm a bit more careful about leaders, and I do tie my own. Since I almost always have weight on the leader above the fly, leader design may not be as important with midge pupae as for dry flies. (I won't go as far as to say that you are actually lobbing the fly and weight, as opposed to casting it. It's more like you're trying to cast too large a fly with too light a leader. Casting midges takes a slightly different touch, but you'll quickly pick it up on your own.) Over the years, I've settled on a 5½-foot leader consisting of 20 inches of .019 hard mono; 10 inches of .017; 8 inches of .015; 6 inches of .013, .010, and .008; and finally, 12 inches of .006 (5X). To this, I attach 5 feet of soft 7X tippet material. I think this extralong tippet section absorbs some of the shock of the initial strike, which can be anywhere from very light to nearly violent. Don't think that all midge takes are nearly imperceptible.

When the tippet section gets down to 2 feet or so, I add a 3-foot section. The shorter this section becomes, the more you'll tend to break fish off. I always use a soft mono for the tippet. Close your eyes and try to visualize your fly in the water right next to a real insect. Tumbling, gently rolling, floating, whatever. The trout sees it. Put yourself in its place. See what it sees. React as it will react. Hooked! It's amazing what you can see with your mind's eye. That's why I use soft mono;

it allows the fly to drift more naturally, to appear unattached to the line.

The long piece of 5X is there only so I'll be able to tie on an entire tippet if necessary. When the 5X is too short to work with, replace the leader. I admit that I sometimes simply add a piece of 5X, maybe even two. Lately I've been using some of the new tippet material on the market, which is available down to 10X. Some of it is stronger than some of my older 7X. If I'm going to go down this light, I add a short piece of 7X onto the 5X as a transition.

Tippet size ultimately depends on the water you fish and your confidence in your technique. I haven't used tippet heavier than 7X for more than twenty years, because I'm convinced that I will catch more fish with it than if I used 5X or 6X. But you shouldn't take my word for it. Once you know that your fly will catch fish, try different tippets. Test, test, test.

Although it goes against common wisdom, I use the same leader for fishing on top with dry flies. It actually works pretty well, as I'm generally not casting more than 15 feet, often less. I like to get close to rising fish if I can. I will shorten the tippet somewhat because I can now see the take and have some control over the force of the strike when I raise the rod tip. I also clean and silicone grease the tippet, an old habit. Leaders pick up a lot of dirt in use. Pull it through a fold of your shirt, if nothing else. Plead ignorance when your wife asks what the black streaks are that won't come out.

Eagle Claw makes a little nylon piece called a Leader-link, which I've used for years to attach the leader to the fly line. I've only broken two of them in fifteen or twenty years. One just plain broke, and the other I hung up in a tree and stupidly tried to jerk it out with the rod. I'm lucky the link broke first. I find no difference in casting these over any other attachment, even when fishing drys. The choice is yours.

I use weight on the leader 95 percent of the time, but I never weight a fly. It's just one of those things I visualize as being completely wrong. Again, test, test, test. The amount of weight depends on your particular water, so you'll have to experiment. I normally use only very small amounts, but I've never been able to pinch one of the supersmall split shot onto a tippet without dropping quite a few of them. I finally discovered weights made of lead wire of various diameters, each piece with a lengthwise slit to lay the tippet in and then pinch each end shut. I'll cut the larger ones into pieces with my clippers, but again, this depends on the type of water you're fishing.

A size 32 White Emerger (left) and a size 10 Cahill shown at actual size illustrate how small a midge pattern is compared to a traditional dry. Hard to believe, but big trout are actually hooked and landed on these tiny flies.

Small, curved-jaw hemostats are handy for removing small hooks that are not right in the edge of the mouth where they are easy to get out. Small, flat-jawed electronic pliers can be used to bend down barbs on the smallest hooks. I've used weight-forward lines the last few years because they feel better to me on the smaller streams. Sometimes only 1 foot of line is out of the top guide. I have no scientific basis for this choice. If I can put the fly where I want it, I'm happy.

The rest of your gear is personal. I happen to like chest fly boxes. Two trays carry enough for me and are not cumbersome. Ed recommends wearing drab clothing. Gene Shetter, the local chicken guru who raises birds for genetic hackle, gave me a camo T-shirt after I showed up one time too many in a white one. I really should pay more attention to these things. I did finally paint my white wading staff flat black.

TECHNIQUE

Finally, we're ready to get on the stream. Alas, here is where I could really take lessons. I've never been as good at spotting fish as most people. If I see one, that's the one I'll fish for. I guess I'd be classified as one who fishes the water. The smaller streams I most likely fish from the bank.

I prefer to work upstream in the hopes that I'll be able to spot any fish before they spot me. You *can* work the water by wading downstream. It depends on how skittish the fish are, how much room you have to work, and whether there are any pools or riffles.

Work every pool from the bottom up, casting farther on each cast. Fish every eddy behind a rock, if you can, and in front. Work every outside bend, which usually has an undercut area, especially those on your side of the stream, if you're fishing from the bank. Cast upstream while you stay hidden. Try any place you think a fish could hide while it waits for food to drift by. Riffles can be a problem on the mountain streams if you're fishing with weight. The amount I use to get down quickly in the pools may be too much for the riffles. If so, I'll just skip over them on the way up and maybe fish them on the way back down after removing some weight.

The little, slow-moving limestoners around here have lots of hiding places. They tend to be choked with watercress and elodea a good part of the year. Many times the fish are highly visible and the trick is to get the fly to them without spooking them or hanging up in the vegetation. Other times you have to fish every patch of open water you can find, even if it's only a slit inches wide. It takes patience. Spotting fish is an art form here. Many people fish drys for this reason.

In the bigger, wadable water, I look for current breaks—those places where two different currents exist side by side, be they fast and slow, fast and faster, or any other combination. I still look for the same things as on the smaller streams, but inside of those things, I look for the current breaks, and they are where I'll try to put my fly on the first cast.

Given a choice, I'll probably try to work the faster water first. Any fish here are likely feeding and have less time to examine a fly. You have a good chance to catch one here and pump its stomach to see what the fish are presently feeding on. But don't think they can't be selective in the faster water. How many times has someone caught fish in a riffle you just worked through, or vice versa? You can fish a riffle either upstream or down. Upstream, I'll cast a little more straight upstream and lengthen up and across as a pattern. Downstream, I'll cast more across and let the drift carry farther down with each cast. Follow the drift with the rod tip. A little slack doesn't hurt, but not too much. Watch the line, but don't stare at it. It can mesmerize you. You could lose your footing, and you'll miss the birds and trees and other nice things around you. In other words, relax. You're here to enjoy yourself. Use the right fly in a reasonable place where there are fish, and you'll catch one. Learn from this one, and you'll catch two, and so on.

I don't use a strike indicator. Maybe all these years of nymph-style fishing has given me a sixth sense of when a fish has taken the fly. But I've watched a lot of fish pick things out of the water as they drifted by and quickly spit them out faster than lightning. I have to wonder if these aren't the fish the indicators are catching. Let's face it. There's only one reason we know for sure that fish pick up our flies: They think they're food. Sometimes the fish give the fly a quick examination with whatever senses they use and either accept or reject it immediately. Other times, the fish are convinced it is food before they pick it up, and a hard strike results. Therefore, the more realistic the imitation appears to the fish, the more likely a take and hookup with less effort on your part.

As you move up- or downstream, look ahead. Don't just wade aimlessly. As in deer hunting, you try to move in a manner and to a position that will give you an advantage over your quarry. You must learn where the fish like to spend their time, where they watch for danger, and where they escape to. All of these things will help you locate, catch, and then land the fish. Watch for current breaks ahead of you, and wade to the side of them so you can cast into them. Watch for fish ahead. It's not uncommon to wade up on one. Fish around those big rock eddies. Little rock dams, common around here, always have fish above and below them. In the pools, fish will tend to lie just off the main current or under it waiting for food. Figure out where that is, and deliver your fly to them. Fish tight along the deeper banks. Fishing the water involves a lot of trial and error. But as you catch fish over time, patterns will develop in your fishing subconscious. Let them lead you through the stream.

I have a few rules I try to fish by:

• *Change flies after ten casts if you can see fish.* This is hard to do, and sometimes I stubbornly refuse, but I know better. If they don't take it in ten casts, the odds say they won't ever.

• *When in doubt, go deeper.* Although you should try to use the amount of lead on your tippet that you think will run the fly at the exact depth at which most of the fish are holding, if you're not hooking up, add weight until you finally hit the bottom, then back off slightly. If they're not taking at their own depth, I think they are more likely to take food below them than above.

• *Run your favorites first unless you know what they're taking that day.* You're likely to fish them harder than other flies because you have confidence in them. When all else fails, I run the different colors of Diamond Midges to try to find a starting point. Try floating a midge pupa when fish are rising.

I said at the start I wasn't going to tell you how to fish, only how I do it. Now you know.

ED KOCH ON GEAR AND TECHNIQUE

Gear

I like to call what I do light-line fishing, a fast-growing trend in the United States. I have an assortment of rods, including four Scott, two East Branch, one Orvis, and an old Garcia Lee Wulff 5½-foot. My Scott rods are an 8-foot, 4-inch for a 3-weight line, a 7-foot, 2-inch for a 2-weight, a 6-foot for a 2-weight, and a 5-foot, 6-inch for a 2-weight. This last one is, without question, the finest small rod I've ever owned. It has a medium-soft action, and in use, it flexes from the tip to the grip. Casting is effortless. With only about 6 feet of line in the air—great for really small streams—the rod will turn over beautifully a 6-foot, 7-foot, or 9-foot leader. Casts of 40 feet or more are no problem. The rod is designed for small streams, 10 to 20 feet wide. In testing it, however, I found that casts of 40 feet are as effortless as casts of 20 feet. It's a three-piece model with internal ferrules, which make for the effortless casting ability. Its tip will protect tippets to 10X. My East Branch rods are an 8-foot for a 2-weight and an 8-foot for a 1-weight. The Garcia is a 5-foot one-piece rod made back in the sixties for a WF5 line.

Today I use a nylon cord line made in England during the fifties. It's the most extraordinary line I have ever owned. Lines for most of the light rods are double-tapers. On the Orvis rod, I use a weight-forward line. The double-tapers allow for a gentle turnover and soft presentation for the 6X to 10X tippets and small flies I use for 85 percent of my year-round fishing on streams varying from 15 feet to 70 feet in Pennsylvania, Virginia, West Virginia, and Tennessee. Varivas, a Japanese company, makes the tippet material, which is some of the best I've tried in a long time. They also have fluorocarbon tippet material down to 7X. Look for it in your favorite tackle shop or contact the company at e-mail

The Knot

During the second day of the Fly Fishing Show in 1999 in Salt Lake City, a father and son walked into the Varivas booth to see the new leader material being shown. The father suggested that I take a look at a knot his son had developed for attaching leader to fly. I gave the young man a piece of tippet material and a hook. He tied a knot while I watched. Then we tried pulling it as hard as we could. The knot never slipped. We pulled even harder, until finally the tippet material broke. We tied the knot on different-size trout fly hooks and saltwater hooks. The knot never slipped. Tying this knot is simple, and there's only one turn of mono on top of the hook eye. It's a real boon for midge fishing as well as standard dry-fly fishing. Follow the steps in the illustration.

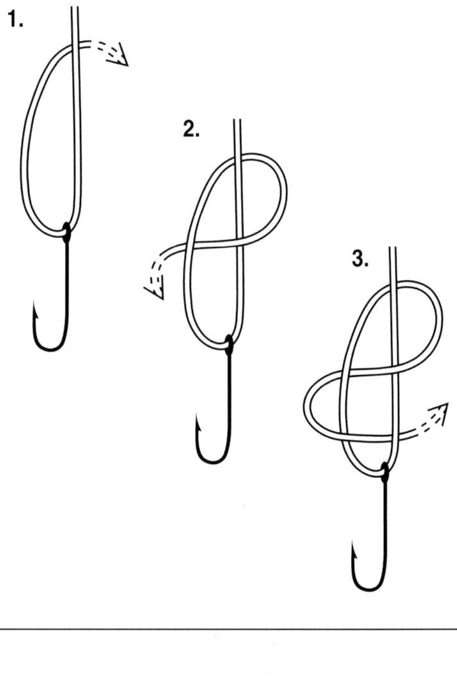

address sales@varivas.com for the nearest dealer. My leaders range from 6 to 8 feet.

Casting

People tend to make casting difficult. It's too fast, too slow, too much power, not enough power, or whatever. If you are a beginner and are having problems, find someone you know who can help you, or go to your local fly shop or the shop where you purchased the rod. Shop owners are ready and willing to help. Trout Unlimited chapters and Federation of Fly Fishers groups regularly give instructions. Numerous fishing shows held across the country have been helping beginners for years. And dozens of videos by many of the country's best casters are available.

The problem I've encountered most over the years is that beginners tend to try to cast the entire fly line. Believe it or not, if you can learn to cast 40 feet of line accurately, you will catch more trout than most anglers. Stop and think for a minute. Whether you are fishing the water (90 percent of anglers do this), working trout you can see, or working feeding trout is important. Working to rising trout, the number of casts you have to make to place your fly in his feeding circle will determine your rate of success. More casts mean less trout; fewer casts, more trout.

What and how a trout sees is critical. A trout watching the surface sees what is on the water surface in a V or cone shape. The deeper the trout is in the water the narrower his view is in the cone. The closer the trout is to the water's surface, the wider his field of view. That's why it's so critical to be able to drop your fly in that 10- or 12-inch circle (plate) you have been practice casting to.

What I do when I locate a trout in a feeding lane looking for insects, or a trout actively taking flies during a hatch, determines how successful I might be on any given day. Rather than making my first cast directly to the trout, I cast off to the side, right or left, to determine the exact length of the cast needed to reach him. Only then do I attempt to drop the fly in the feeding lane, from 2 to 3 feet to as much as 6 or 8 feet ahead of the trout. The amount of time you've practiced on the lawn will now determine your success on the stream. Make your cast so that your line and leader turn over and straighten out at least 3 feet above the water's surface. This will allow your fly line and tippet to drop softly to the water to avoid spooking the trout. If you don't get a look on the first cast or two, keep trying. If the trout looks but refuses, keep trying. If you get a take but miss the strike and the trout doesn't spook, try again. Keep working the fish.

Seeing Trout

Before you can see trout, you have to get close enough to them in the stream. With a little common sense and practice, anyone can master these techniques.

I always fish upstream. Wading upstream gives me advantages over other fishermen, as well as the trout. Light and the position of the sun determine which side I fish. My home stream is the Yellow Breeches, a limestoner near Boiling Springs, Pennsylvania. The stream flows north to south, which means the sun coming up in the east hits the right-hand bank in the morning hours and going down in the west hits the left-hand bank in the afternoon. So in the morning I fish the bright right bank, and I fish the bright left bank in the afternoon. On an overcast day, I can work either bank first. A cloudy day makes it a little more difficult to spot trout, but not enough to keep me off the water. The Breeches is wooded its entire length along both banks, so I'm pretty well camouflaged when approaching the water.

Before entering the water, stand about 5 feet back from the water's edge and look into the water toward midstream about 10 feet. Look through the water at the stream bottom so that you are seeing the gravel and stones. Polaroid glasses are a must, as is a cap with a brim or bill. Wear a long-sleeved shirt in a neutral color. Light-colored arms waving in front of a green background of leaves will send trout scurrying for cover. It may take several minutes for your eyes to adjust to looking into the water at the streambed, and not just at the surface film. Slowly scan the gravel on the stream bottom, from the bank where you are standing toward midstream. The stream bottom will be either gray to white stones (limestone) or tan to brown or yellowish (freestone).

The first few times you try this, you may not see trout right away. Don't give up. Stand and watch for several minutes. If you see no movement, raise one arm in the air, and wave it from side to side. Any trout you did not see will dart away immediately. They will be easy to see when moving. Watch them until they stop. Usually they will not go out of eyesight. When they stop, watch them for a while and get used to the look of their shape, color, and moving fins underwater. Study their shape for a few minutes. Then look away. Look back at the stream bottom and find the fish again. Do this about a half dozen times.

When you can pick out trout fairly easily, step into the water, wade out 5 to 10 feet from the bank, and turn to face upstream. You need to be far enough out in the stream that overhanging brush will not hinder your casting. Begin searching the water 10 to 20 feet upstream, looking for the shape of a trout. Don't be in a hurry to move until you're certain there are no trout about 15 feet in front of you. Take two or three steps upstream. Stop and start looking for trout again about 15 feet ahead of you. If the water is knee-deep or less, trout will be easy to spot from just a few inches below the surface and down to the gravel on the stream bottom. At first you likely will see only trout that you spook, darting for the stream bottom. Watch them and hope they settle down close so that you might have a chance to try for them. Search the water from the bank out to where you are standing, slowly. Don't look just once, but scan three or four times. Often I stand in one spot five minutes just watching for trout to resume feeding. I move upstream very slowly, searching for trout. I may move only 5 yards in fifteen to thirty minutes. If it happens to be a day when midges are plentiful and trout are gorging themselves, it is not unusual to fish only 100 yards or so in two or three hours in a morning.

In faster-moving, broken water, it's much more difficult to spot trout. Here you need even more patience. You have to move more slowly and watch the water longer. When you're first learning to sight-fish, you may want to wait until you build confidence in your trout-spotting ability before fishing fast water. Don't give up on fishing fast water completely, though. Once you've learned to spot trout and work them in fast water, you'll be amazed at how many more trout you take, especially larger trout. Some of the wiser, larger trophy trout live in the fast, broken water of the stream, avoided by 60 to 70 percent of the trout as well as most fly fishermen.

When you find a trout in a given location, he will be there for the rest of his life unless his food supply dries up, a larger trout moves him out, or an angler kills him. As you learn to spot fish, your confidence level will rise with every trip you make astream, and the number of trout you catch will also increase.

Wading

Wading techniques are few but important. Once you enter the water and begin moving upstream, don't lift your feet out of the water until you're ready to leave the stream. Each time your foot comes out of the water, you send out waves and noise, which spook the trout. When you take a step, lift your foot off the stream bottom just enough that you don't roll any stones or gravel. When you plant your foot again, do it slowly, easing your boot foot down until you feel it touch the stream bottom. Then carefully put your weight on it. If done correctly, you will not send any noise or vibrations out to your side or upstream. This is critical in slow, quiet water. In faster-moving water or riffles, any noise you make will be carried downstream away from the trout. When wading upstream, stay as close to the bank as possible. And even if you think you are moving slowly enough, slow down!

I've spent as little as five minutes to as much as a half hour on a single trout. Your technique when finding trout, wading, casting, and hooking the fish determines how successful you will be. If a trout looks at your fly three or four times and doesn't take, change flies. Often resting a trout for a few minutes will help. Watch him for five minutes or so. Is he taking something on top or in the surface film? It's difficult at times to tell the difference between a subsurface and a surface take. This often happens when small flies, midges, or tiny spinners are on the water. To find out just what is on the water, I carry a small aquarium net, 3 x 5 with superfine nylon netting. It's excellent for collecting surface or subsurface insects, as well as kicking gravel and picking up drifting nymphs near the stream bottom. Don't give up, and don't hurry—relax, have fun. All the spotting, watching, changing flies, and checking insects improves your skills and eventually will pay off.

CHAPTER 2

Matching the Midge

To start with, I'm not going to tell you that you have to do this. If you'd like, pick out some of the patterns in this book that appeal to you for whatever reason, tie a few to carry, and fish them when the moment strikes. You'll soon find favorites that you've been successful with and have confidence in. But I will tell you this. Seeing a light-colored midge in the air does not mean that it is light-colored, and the same goes for dark-colored. And catching one and looking at it with the naked eye does not tell you much more. And if you're thinking of fishing a pupa during a hatch, it tells you even less.

At some point in time, you may decide that you want to know a little more about the insects you are trying to imitate. Small aquarium nets or rectangular ones with handles that you can roll up are useful during an emergence of midges, at least in flowing water. The cloth mesh has to be fine, especially for the size 28s. Cloth from a fabric store can be used for this.

Seining stream bottom material or disturbing underwater vegetation upstream of you is sometimes useful. But the quickest method I've found is to pump the stomach of the first trout I catch and examine the contents. Some fishermen decry this method as being injurious to the trout. I've pumped dozens of them in the last twenty-five years and don't think I've abused one. However, there are concerns about handling trout, overly playing them, and so forth. I honestly don't know the absolute answer. The best I can do is describe my methods as clearly as I can, and you can take it from there as you see fit.

To do this, catching a trout is a prerequisite. I'll leave this part entirely up to you. (I almost always use either a black-fly larva or a flesh-colored shrimp, no matter where I am.) As far as equipment, I strongly suggest that you use exactly what I do. Laboratory supply firm catalogs have an item that looks like a long, plastic eyedropper in different sizes. These are called disposable plastic transfer pipets, or something similar. The photograph below shows what I'm referring to and the modifications I make to them. The most useful size is approximately 9 inches (22.5cm) long, with a body diameter of about 3/16 inches (5mm). I use this for all fish up to 16 inches in length. The second one I carry is approximately 12 inches (30cm) long, with a body diameter of about 3/8 inches (9mm). I rarely use this one, but I carry it just in case I need it for a very large fish. As you can see in the photograph,

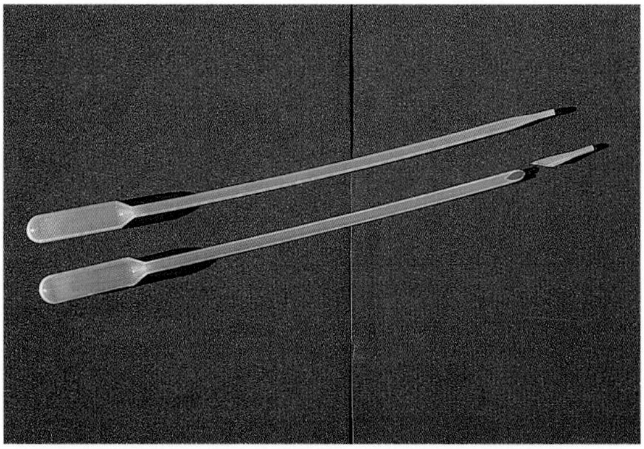

A plastic disposable transfer pipet. Make absolutely sure you smooth all rough edges to prevent injury to the fish.

I cut the tip back within the tapered section, so the opening is large enough for the insect that is being recovered. The shallow cutting angle and the taper help the tip to enter the trout's throat easily. The sides of the pipet have a mold line that tends to be rough, and the tip will feel sharp after cutting. I sand these areas with 400-grit sandpaper until they feel smooth to the touch in both directions. Remember, you will be inserting *and* removing it from the trout, and you want to lessen the chance of injury to the fish as much as possible.

A small container is needed to hold the insects that you remove from the trout's stomach. I like the clear or translucent plastic canisters that some brands of 35mm film come in. The lids are easily removed with one hand yet do not easily come off on their own. Most camera stores will give you some if you ask.

I don't like to handle a fish, if at all possible. The more they are handled, the less their chance of survival, I think. Whether you can avoid handling them depends on your location in the stream, more than anything. If you're midstream in heavy current or deep water, you'll have to net the fish and handle it more. Closer to the banks, you can perhaps lead it into a shallow or sheltered spot. Just keep in mind that it is a delicate creature, and treat it so. I won't pump the stomach of a fish that fights it too much. You'll learn when to quit and let it go.

It's important to first fill the pipet with water. Then gently insert the pipet into the trout's esophagus about 3 inches or less, squeeze the water into its stomach area, and withdraw the pipet while simultaneously releasing the bulb, which will allow it to suck out the contents without damage. Once is enough. Whatever I get, from nothing (if the fish wasn't feeding at the moment) to a full pipet, I release the trout immediately. Squeeze the bulb to empty the contents into your container, and rinse the pipet with a fill or two of stream water. It's all really simpler to do than it is to describe. Now you're ready for the process of discovery.

Just a quick glance into the container may at least give you a clue as to what general coloration and size is predominant at that moment. With some experience (and record keeping!), this may be enough to let you pick two or three probables out of a dozen or so possible patterns you might expect for the current time period and stream. How far you wish to go after this point is entirely up to you. Midge patterns are still a wide open field in the sport of fly fishing. What Ed and I have done probably only scratches the surface.

After collecting the insects, my examination methods ranged from simple observation when I

Sample containers come from many sources.

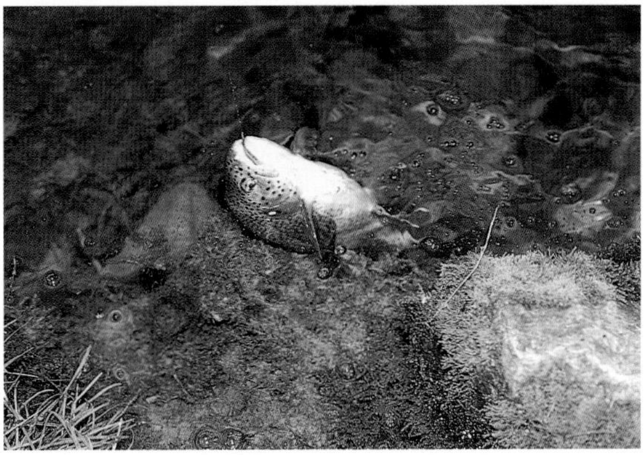

Sometimes the hard part is catching the first fish. That's a midge pupa in his lower jaw.

Gently, gently, gently. Let him go if he protests too much.

Results of a trout stomach pumping. Once is enough.

A closer view.

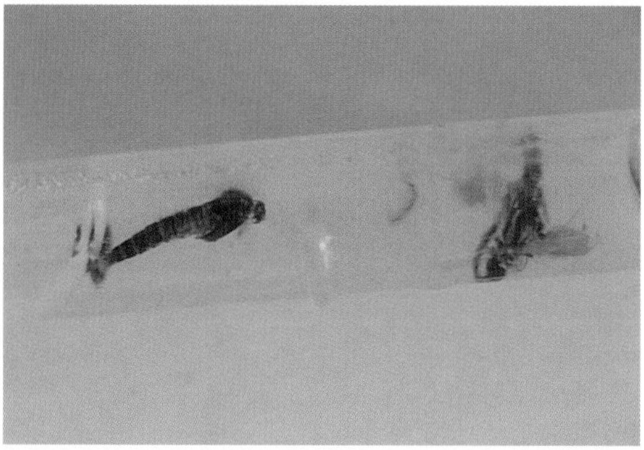

An even closer view.

first started out, then to microscopic studies, and finally to photography as a means of recording them. I have only a layman's knowledge of entomology, which is defined as the study of insects. My background in the laboratory, although not in biology, is an asset of sorts, simply because I have an idea of where to look for relevant information on methods and equipment. I hesitate to advise anyone on photographic methods, as I am strictly an amateur who has probably spent more time and money than the small returns would justify. I am forever grateful to all those who

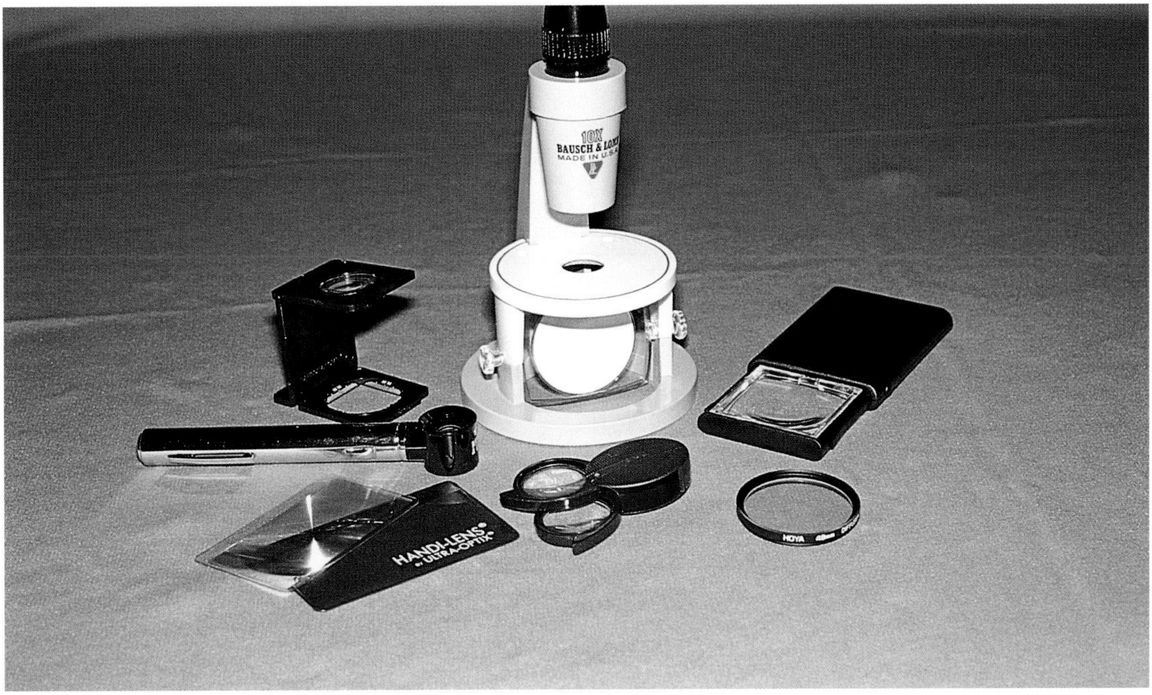

A collection of magnifying instruments. Some are small enough to carry in the field.

offered advice along the way. Regardless, I'll tell you what I did, and you can take from it whatever you may find useful.

Observations of insects in this size range with the naked eye would give you little useful information. This is because the human eye is very easy to fool. Sometimes we even see what we want to see rather than what we are really looking at. Magnification brings out more detail for the eye to pick up or resolve and transmit to the brain for evaluation. Hand-held low-power magnifiers, from about 5X magnification up to 10X, are available in a variety of styles from various sources. The photograph above will give you an idea of what to look for. Industrial supply houses, office supply stores, camera stores, toy stores, craft stores, and laboratory suppliers are all possible sources.

A common magnifying glass about 5 inches in diameter isn't too bad. Fold-up pocket magnifiers are used in a number of fields and are usually available in several powers. Small, lighted magnifiers are available for those with failing eyesight. I even have a credit card size piece of plastic that magnifies due to the pattern etched on it. Thin close-up adapters for camera lenses usually come in sets of three—1X, 2X, and 4X—that can be screwed together. These are often available used for a reasonable price. Many of these items are small enough to be carried while fishing and used streamside.

In the field, this equipment will give you a little more information to aid you in selecting a pattern that has a greater chance of success. I don't use it to do anything other than determine more accurately the actual color of the insect, be it larva, pupa, or adult, and whether it has a rib color. If you're looking at a size 24 or smaller, even the head color can be an important piece of information. And the same equipment can be used to get a closer look at your fly, which is just as hard to see as the insect you're trying to match it to. To observe an insect, use your pipet to remove it from the container, and just put it in the lid, or even in your hand. Carry an extra container if you think you'll be collecting any adult midges, either from the air or floating on top of the water.

Depending on your success rate, or the lack thereof (yes, there will be fishless days), you can carry in your vehicle some equipment that is a touch more sophisticated but not prohibitively expensive. Admittedly, this is one more level up the ladder and may not really interest you at first, but hand-held magnifiers tend to make the whole operation just a bit clumsy. You can find magnifying equipment that stands on its own, allowing you to keep both hands free. Small, one-lens, or monocular, microscopes are commonly available in powers from 10X to 15X. Another option is a lens with a built-in base or a tripod type of support, such as those used for examining film or jewelry. Craft and toy stores are possible sources, and I've found used ones in excellent condition at yard sales and swap meets. They are not quite as useful as the microscopes due to the limited area underneath the lens that you have to work in. The advantage to this type of magnifier is that once adjusted, it is forever focused on the subject (your insect), unlike a hand-held unit. This allows you to pay closer attention to details such as color shading and ribbing.

I usually carry such a magnifier in my truck, along with a white plastic lid from a butter tub or something similar to put the insects in. I can dump the whole container into the lid and, by moving the lid around, look at many insects very quickly. This will tell you whether there are several types and which one is most abundant, and let you quickly compare many of the same species for any minute differences. You can even add your selected fly patterns to the mix for a better look at just how close they are to being usable imitations. This all takes you another step closer to being a full-fledged midge fanatic. You could even tie matching patterns streamside if you wanted. I haven't met many people who do this, even for the larger insects like mayflies. I did it a few times. Once it even worked.

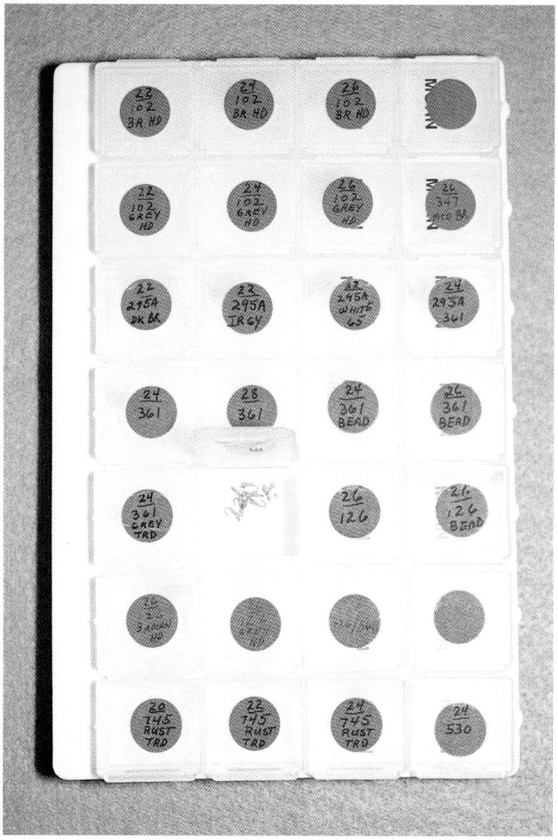

A seven-day pill holder is perfect for carrying midge patterns. Pattern numbers can be written on small round stickers and put on the lids of the compartments. It's a good idea to put the boxes in Ziplock bags.

Unless I'm forced into it by necessity, I'd rather take the insects I've collected home with me, where I can examine them in a more relaxed manner. Plus, I have better equipment there to examine them with, and my tying table and photographic equipment are at hand. My own little world. I can go as far with this insect sample as I want or feel is necessary.

At home, you can use whatever equipment you already have, be it a magnifying glass or a microscope. The important thing is that you are satisfied with the results. One drawback to the

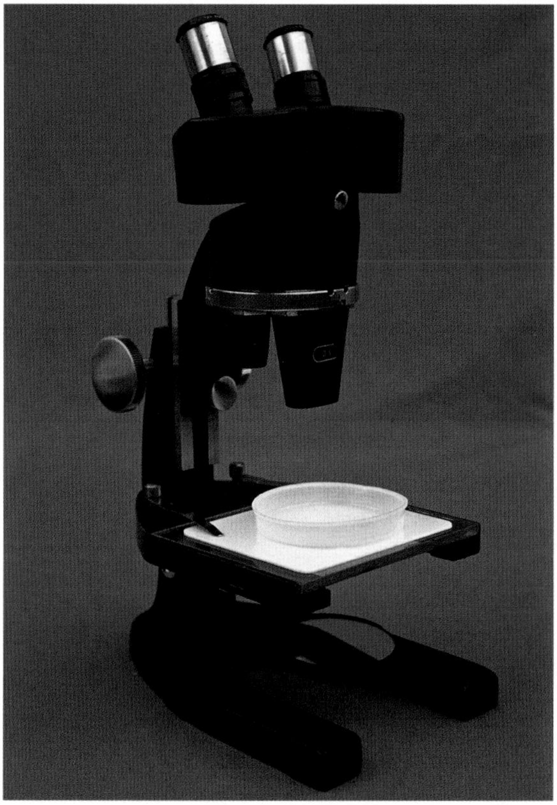

It's a good idea to talk to an expert, such as a local science teacher, before investing in magnifying instruments. Magnification is like horsepower—expensive. But a nice little 10X–30X binocular scope is a joy to use.

monocular magnifiers is that they are tiring to the eyes. There is nothing quite as nice for this kind of investigation as a binocular microscope. Human eyes were meant to see in a binocular fashion, and I wonder whether the brain isn't more efficient when interpreting binocular data. The photograph above shows the one I am presently using. It's an older Bausch and Lomb unit with 10X eyepieces and a revolving objective lens turret holding 1X, 2X, and 3X lenses. I most often use the 3X, which gives a final magnification of 30X (3X objective times 10X eyepiece). This suits me, but you might like something a little different. You don't need equipment this sophisticated to

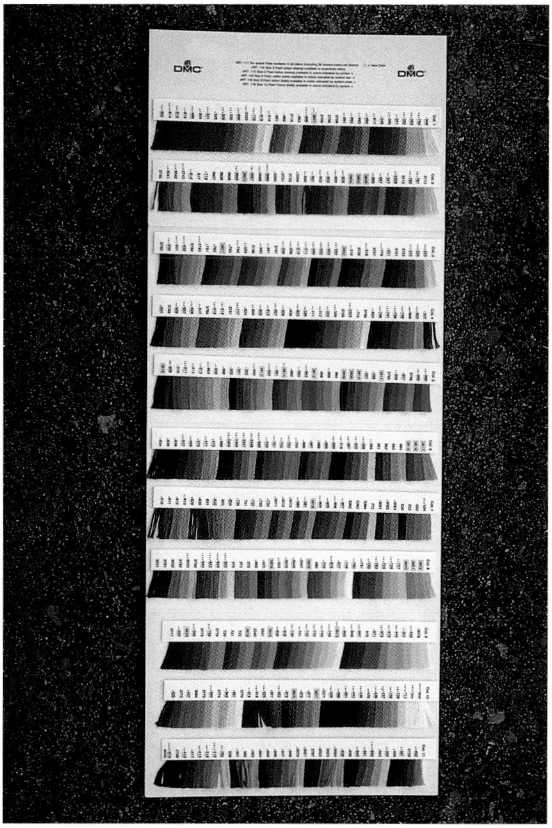

A DMC embroidery floss color chart of actual samples is available in craft stores.

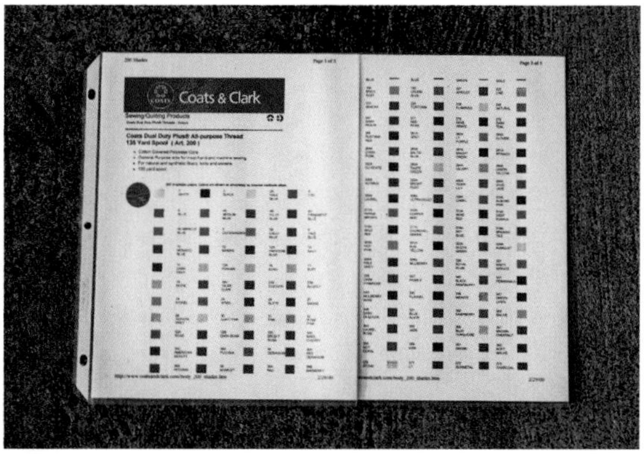

The color chart for Coats Dual Duty Plus thread is available in full on the Web at coatsandclark.com. Printed color charts are not 100 percent true to color, but they are a useful reference.

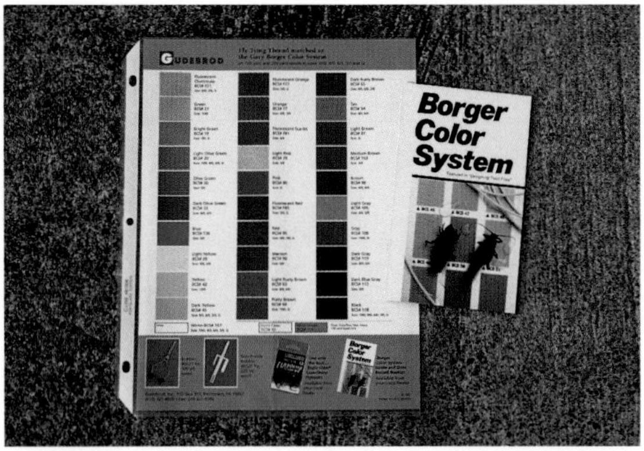

Not all fly-tying thread makers produce color charts, but they all list descriptions of their colors. To lessen the confusion somewhat, this book describes colors as closely as possible to the Borger Color System chart available in most fly shops.

do what I do; it just makes it a little easier. A new one is rather expensive. You can find them used, but you'll have to hunt for them. Big flea markets are sometimes a source, as is government surplus. Large cities are more likely to harbor one somewhere. Expect to pay $100 to $300, unless you're very lucky.

The kind of light you use to view your collected insects makes a difference in what you see. White light is made up of colors—all the colors. For our purposes, it is roughly equivalent to midday daylight. Light bulbs, on the other hand, do not emit white light per this definition. They exhibit a color shift, which can alter the way the colors of your insects and the materials you will use to imitate them appear to your eye. What appears to be an exact match for a certain color may not look that way under a different light source. This property of light is known as its color temperature and it is measured in degrees Kelvin. All you need to know at this point is that daylight is usually considered to have a color temperature of about 5,000 degrees Kelvin, incandescent bulbs are about 3,200 degrees, and halogen bulbs run around 3,400. Fluorescent bulbs are too variable to be measured but are known to have a strong greenish cast. This will be important to you if you plan to photograph your objects later, but for now you just need to realize that the light source can make a big difference. Just remember that the trout sees everything somewhere in the 5,000-degree range. I use a daylight fluorescent lamp most of the time, simply because I like it.

Once you've found a nice, comfortable spot and have everything arranged, pour the insects you collected out of your container onto a white plastic lid or dish that will fit under your chosen magnifier. Leave enough water in the lid or dish to reasonably cover them, but not so much that it's likely to spill every time you move the lid.

From this point on, write down, in a legible, organized manner, everything you see. This information will be worth more than you realize right now. Trust me on this one. I learned the hard way.

First, just take a slow, general look at the entire collection, slowly moving the lid around and using the bodkin needle from your tying bench to occasionally move something about or separate things. You are gathering general information, such as the types of insects—larvae, pupae, midges, mayflies, caddisflies, or whatever; their relative numbers (which kind is predominant, which kind is most scarce); their sizes and whether any certain ones come in more than one size; their general coloration, especially that of the most numerous one. Write all of this down. Down the road, you'll begin to see general trends, and it can lead to developing your own hatch charts, maybe even writing a book if you are so inclined. Include the name of the stream, the date, every fly pattern you tried, and its success or lack thereof. It may seem like a lot of trouble and easy to forget or put off, but you'll regret every entry that you leave out. I did.

Now pick out a good representative of the dominant midge and separate it from the rest. You may even want to transfer it to another plastic lid so you have room to work. It can be removed with your bodkin needle or an eyedropper, which I prefer. Now take a more detailed look at the specifics. Determine the size again—accurately. Drop a hook in beside it, if necessary. Look at the shape of the insect and its various body proportions. Does the body appear to have a ribbed or banded appearance? How wide are the bands in relation to one another? Is the head area the same color as one of the bands? Write it all down. The more midges you look at, the more things you'll see.

Next, pick several pieces or strands of body material that appear close in color to the insect under magnification, and place this material in the viewing lid, either alongside the insect or across it. Both ways have their advantages, as you will discover. Continue trying various materials until one matches the dominant color, which is normally the darker of the two if the midge is banded or striped. Write it down. If it's not an exact match, note whether it's lighter or darker or even between two existing shades. Be specific. Don't write "medium olive" or some other nondescriptive term that you will not be able to match five months down the road, much less five years. I use the manufacturers' code numbers. If I tell you to use a certain color by its code number, you can be assured that your fly will match mine in every respect. Repeat this process for the other color, if there is a rib or band. This could end up being the tying thread color. Similarly, match the head/frontal area if it's a different color.

If you can't find a match, either do the best you can or get out the dye pot. Or start on the second most predominant insect in the sample. You may be wondering if it's worth all the trouble to do this. I'm convinced that the right color will catch ten times as many trout as one that's a shade off.

Now tie the fly. Then toss the finished fly into the lid with the insect. Happy? Tie more. Write down all the details.

Many pupae such as this size 18 can be imitated using basically one color. You could tie a thin black rib to imitate this one but it's probably not worth the trouble.

Set a pupa in water and view it through a microscope. Select several strands of body material (floss, thread, or whatever) close to the color of the natural and lay them across its body. (It helps to pre-wet the material with your thumb and finger so it sinks into the body.) This will allow you to see the colors as they'll appear in use and to pick the one that best matches the natural.

The photos on the following pages show naturals and my imitations of them. As you can see, some match more closely than others.

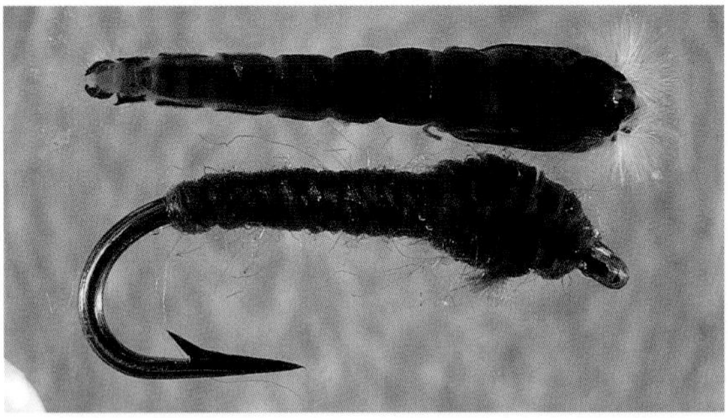

Tie a fly with the chosen material, wet it, and place it next to the insect. Here's an example of a good match tied with DMC 3787 floss.

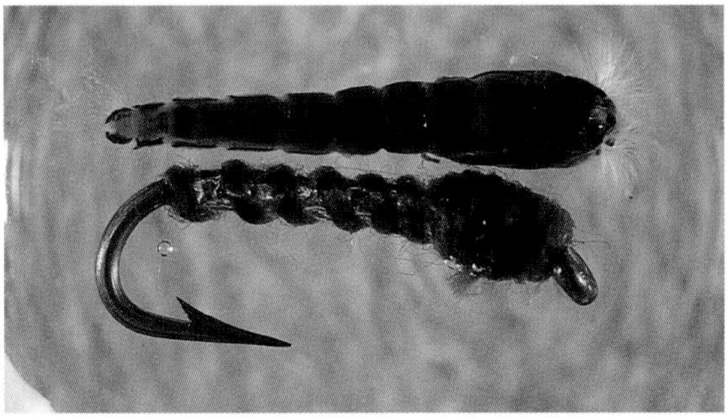

An emerger Diamond Midge, also with DMC 3787 floss.

This one's a little more difficult; it needs a rib color, too. Keep trying until you find a pair of colors that match.

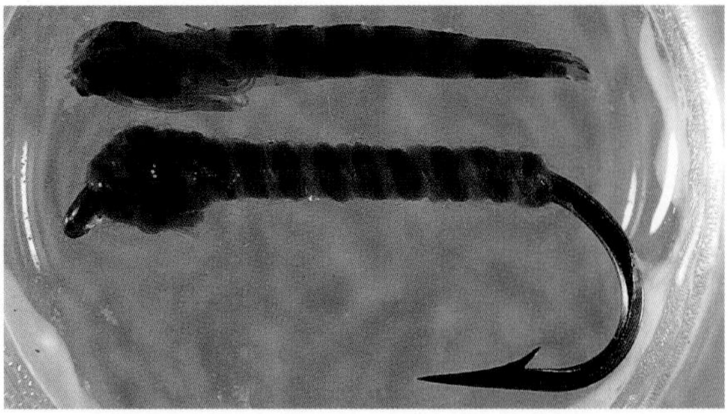

That match in this case is provided by DMC 840 and 841 floss.

Here's a size 18 pupa, followed by three intrepretations of its rib width and color.

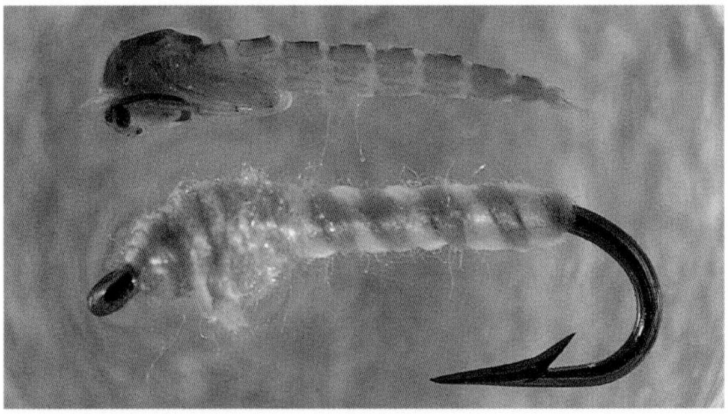

18 - DMC 3827/DMC 739. The rib in this imitation is wider than that of the natural, but we'll let the trout decide. If you're unsure of the exact color, try several. The top two patterns on the facing page are two more variations.

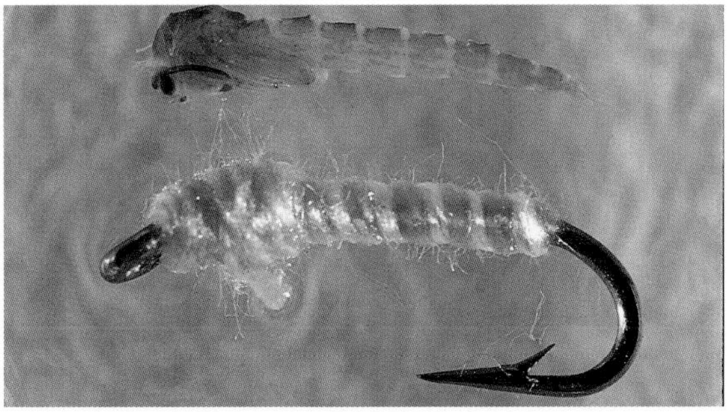

18 - DMC 3827/DMC ecru.

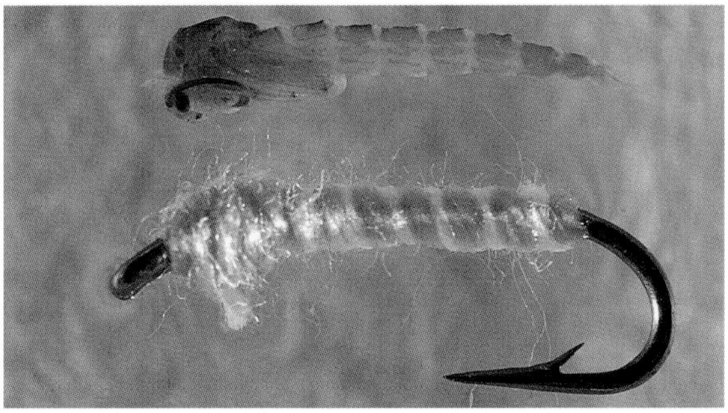

18 - DMC 3827/DMC 712. Take your pick or let the trout do it.

The insect here is not a true midge, but this 24 - C&C 54/47 pattern matches it almost exactly and has proven to be one of the author's most effective flies.

Not a bad imitation, but the gray head color is not exact.

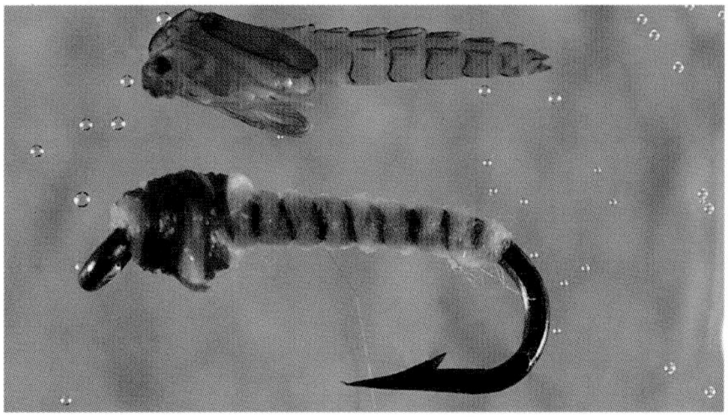

The brown head color is a closer match, but the body wraps are a little too loose, making the bands look wider and too dark.

26 - DMC 3022/C&C 361. In this pair, the darker strand has been varied. A floss strand has been mixed with a thread strand for the body.

26 - DMC 3023/C&C 361, a slightly lighter version of the previous pattern.

22 - C&C 347 with a gray head.

22 - C&C 361 with a gray head. The body color is a good match but the head should have been brown. Head colors can be difficult.

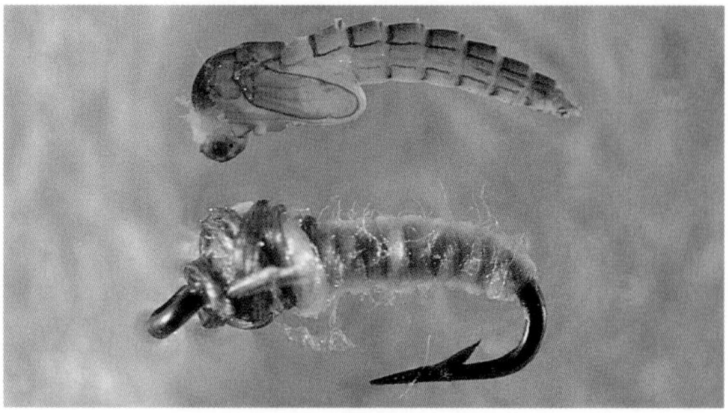

26 - C&C 102 with a brown head.

26 - C&C 347 with a brown head. The head color is right, but the body color is off. Keep in mind that film sometimes interprets colors differently than the eye. This particular pattern has been problematic.

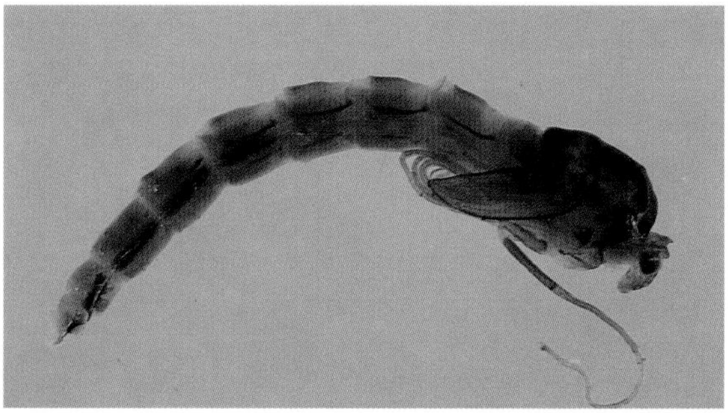

How would you interpret this one? Rib or no?

A rare mottled color.

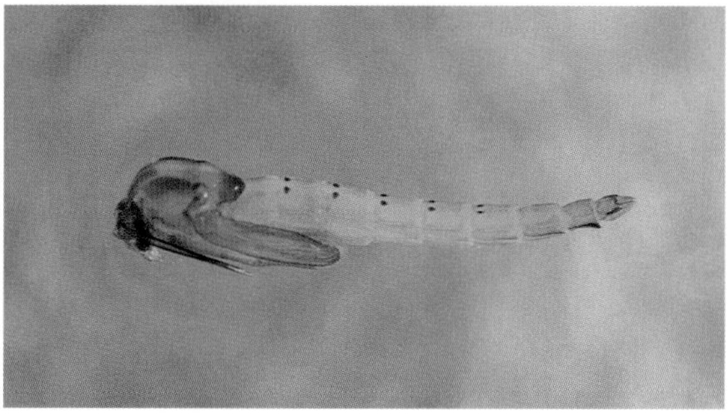

An interesting pattern.

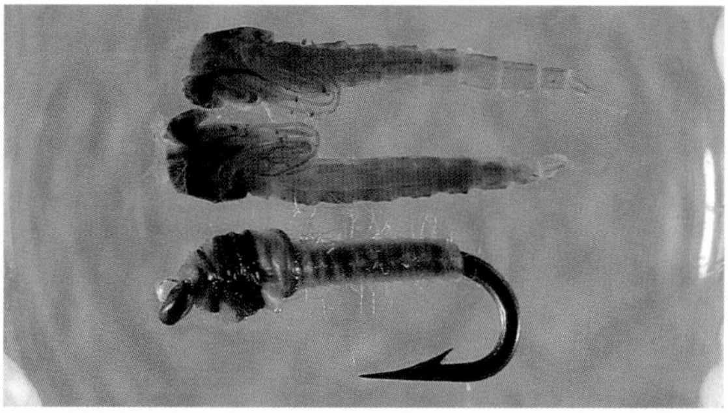

Very nice color, but the rib is too prominent. Should have just overwrapped the head.

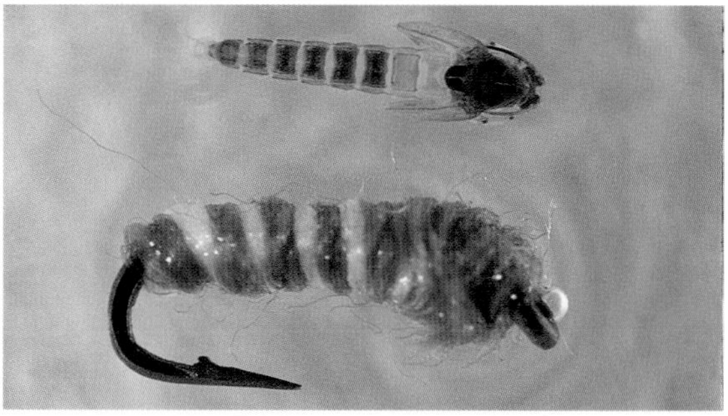

26 - C&C 127A/C&C 116.

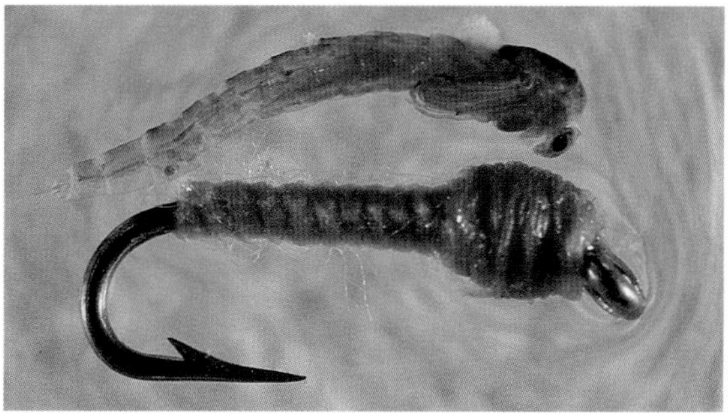

18 - DMC 733/Unithread camel brown head. A fairly decent match.

26 - C&C 309A/dark brown head.

If you wish, you can record your flies—and even the naturals—in photographs. The feeling of seeing the image of your creation on paper for the first time is akin to the feeling you got when you caught the first trout on a fly you tied yourself. Both can give you a lot of personal satisfaction.

I started photographing midges and midge flies as just something I thought might be interesting. I had little equipment and even less knowledge. The results showed it. My subject matter looked almost like little specks, but if I looked really close, I could make out some details. Even so, like most beginners, I was proud of my work.

Gradually, I learned more about macrophotography and started buying equipment one piece at a time, upgrading as dollars allowed, and becoming more excited as each piece produced better information than the last. I also relearned the old adage that "you get what you pay for." Top-grade photographic equipment costs money, sometimes a lot of money. It also gives superb results. Go this route if you wish, but only if passion tells you to.

I finally got to the point where my passion was to photograph every midge I could, with its matching imitation in the same frame. I should live so long! Little did I realize the difficulty—no, make that the near improbability—of doing this. First I had to actually collect the insect, which meant I had to find the time to do this and still make a living and have a life. Next I had to imitate it near perfectly and, when magnified, pick out the only too obvious errors and correct them somehow. Then I had to actually photograph them together, knowing that camera and film probably don't see things exactly as the human eye. And after all this, I wondered if the fish saw yet something else.

Macrophotography equipment is available from several manufacturers. If you're new to this field, I highly suggest that you spend some time researching and gathering information before you purchase. Some publications are available from manufacturers, such as product catalogs, and Kodak and other aftermarket publishers offer manuals on close-up photography in general and guides to particular cameras. Don't overlook out-of-print publications available from various sources. Your local camera shop or camera club should be able to at least point you in the right direction. Most equipment you would want is available used, and with a little knowledge and judicious care, an outfit can be assembled for a lot less than the price of new equipment. As with anything used, however, caution is advised.

I use Olympus 35mm single-lens reflex equipment, mainly because that's what I got started with, but also because they have an extensive line of macro equipment. I use OM-2N bodies (no longer available new), which are fully automatic with through-the-lens light metering. I don't recommend manual cameras unless you're an experienced photographer, because of the exposure calculations involved. I've always let my camera decide when to cut off the exposure. Let your local camera dealer advise you on your results, be they slides or negatives, and adjust the camera to slightly under- or overexpose accordingly. He or she has seen a lot more film than the average person.

A bellows is necessary to obtain the necessary magnification. It should be mounted vertically on a small copy stand, which you can either buy or make if you're handy. Lenses can be either standard macro lenses or enlarger lenses with a special adapter. I use a 38mm macro lens for the bulk of my work, going to a 20mm macro lens for hook sizes 26 to 28. Other methods have their own special set of problems. Standard focusing screens inside the camera can be dark and difficult to focus properly under these conditions. Interchangeable screens are almost a necessity at these magnifications. I find a clear one with

Don Holbrook's setup for photographing midges.

crosshairs to be the most usable. Attachments can be added to the eyepiece of the camera to magnify the image slightly and improve focusing ability. I use off-camera flashes with the appropriate cable hookups rather than existing light for consistency. One is located 10 inches on either side of the subject and slightly above.

The bellows extension determines the magnification of the subject and allows you to fill the frame with the image. The distance of the entire unit from the subject controls the focus. All of my photographs are made with the subject in water. This keeps it from drying and distorting, as it might in the air. It also solves the problem of whether the fly materials look different wet or dry. At present, I am using a 1/4-inch-thick glass slide, with a 3mm-deep circular well in the center. These are used in biological laboratories and can be quite expensive. A cut-off small, clear plastic container or something similar should be just as suitable.

I mostly use various colors of felt as a background. Experiment to see what satisfies you. Whatever you use, raise your specimen container about 1/4 inch above it so it will appear as a blurred or out-of-focus background that won't distract from your subject. You'll learn soon enough about the shallow depth of field in macrophotography.

After composing and focusing your shot, turn off any room lights, which will be the wrong color, and trip the shutter using some sort of re-

The author's setup for photographing flies. The macro stage moves left and right, forward and back. An 80mm macro lens with 1:1 adapter and an Olympus T10 ring flash were used for most shots in this book. A light gray foam background was placed four inches behind the fly. All photos were taken on manual at 1/30 second, f11, and the flash set to manual guide #4. Ektachrome EPN100 film was used for most of the shots, including the Hatch Chart.

Store samples in isopropyl alcohol and date the containers.

mote release. Don't forget to stop the lens down and turn the camera on. It's very easy to forget, trust me. Experiment with various films. They can make a difference. At present, I am using Kodachrome 64 Daylight for slides and Kodak Royal Gold 100 for prints. Keep a record of each frame: the date, a description of the insect, and the camera settings. It will pay off.

CHAPTER 3

Diamond Midges

Diamond Midges are flies that are so named because they sparkle like diamonds. Since the beginning, fly tiers have added pieces of wire and various tinsels to their patterns to give a bit of flash or a suggestion of nymphal gases, or just because they thought it looked nice. I did the same thing for years because it worked reasonably well. I just didn't know why.

Twenty-five years ago, I fished the Big Spring Creek in the Cumberland Valley of Pennsylvania quite regularly. I was just learning to fly-fish at that time and occasionally had some moderate success. The upper section of the stream had been closed for a number of years and had only recently been reopened to public use with, I believe, a daily limit of two fish over 15 inches. There were so many fish in this section that a single drift of 15 feet of line plus leader would swing your fly through twenty or more fish. Not having anyone to fish with or learn from at this time, I considered this to be an ideal fishing school where I could see every fish's reaction to my flies, leader, and presentation. For the first couple summers, I fished here four or five evenings every week, a round-trip of some 60 miles from my home. During the other seasons, I rarely missed a weekend here.

I was using standard nymphs and streamers. The instructors at the Carlisle Fish and Game fly-tying classes had marked appropriate patterns in my copy of *Noll's Guide to Trout Flies.* I also had copies of Art Flick's *Streamside Guide* and Ed Koch's *Fishing the Midge.* I'd picked up on some of the local patterns as well: a size 12 red wool, Ed Shenk's cress bug in size 16, and a flesh-colored sculpin for night fishing. Occasionally a fish even took a dry fly. But something was missing. So many were fish there, and yet I caught so few. Some of the standard patterns worked at times, and in talking to other fishermen, I knew that some of them fished flies all the way down to size 28, but I really had no idea why, though. I guess I had an inkling that midges were one of the staples of these fish's diets. I'd seen midges hatching at various times, caught some, and tried to tie something resembling them with various furs and poor-quality hackle. I was more successful at tying size 18 nymphs of various colors, my best one being an olive fur with a silver rib, wood duck tails, and a turkey wing case.

After one unsuccessful evening, as I pondered my failure while walking back along the creek to my car, I idly cast some nondescript nymph into the water. A large brown trout hit the nymph, and I landed it. At that time, I carried a large flashlight while night fishing, as water snakes abounded, and I did not proceed down a bank without checking things out. In order to unhook the fish, I placed the flashlight between my teeth. When the beam of light shone in this fish's mouth, I was fascinated to see that his mouth was full of what looked like sparkling diamonds.

Although I rarely kept a trout, I took this one home. By the time I reached home, it was after 10 P.M., and I sat on the back porch stoop under the door light and cleaned the fish. The large trout's mouth must have had at least fifty midge pupae in it, many of them still alive. As I picked them out of the trout and placed them in a little white dish, they still sparkled in the porch light as I moved them around. The majority of them were dark brown or olive, in size 18, with some smaller ones down to size 28. To the naked eye, the bodies appeared to have a striped or banded effect, along with the sparkle.

I immediately increased my output of size 18 nymphs made of various dark-colored furs ribbed with silver tinsel, and the number of trout I caught also increased. Though tying a size 18 was not a major problem, anything smaller was difficult to tie satisfactorily. Tinsels at the time were metallic, and very narrow widths were difficult to come by, as few tiers had a use for them. Occasionally I would run across a spool of Veniard English tinsel, which was a little easier to work with, but it just was not intended for what I was trying to make it do.

Finally I came up with a solution: I simply reversed the standard tying procedure, tying the body with tinsel and applying the body color as the ribbing. After trying many different materials, I settled on one strand of six-strand cotton embroidery floss for the color ribbing. It was near perfect in size, strength, softness, and range of colors. I originally used an embossed metal tinsel for the most sparkle, but I've since successfully used other types. The metal tinsel tended to tarnish after some time, dulling considerably, and after the mylar tinsels came out, the embossed type became more difficult to locate. I now use a brand of mylar tinsel called FireFly Tye, which has the same appearance as the old-time embossed tinsel and is fine enough to tie size 28s with no problems. It was originally used as skirts on bass lures, I believe, and is sometimes hard to locate in fly shops. I bought a lifetime supply, a trait I wish I had developed years ago, as so many things in life that worked well are no longer made, or so it seems. If you can't find this tinsel, there are others on the market that are similar, maybe even better.

Over the years, I've become a little more selective in the colors I use on these flies, trying to match them a bit closer to the actual color of the midge pupae I've collected. However, you really can't go wrong if you carry a small selection in black, brown, olive, and gray. These are the best searching patterns of all that I use.

DMC six-strand cotton embroidery floss can be used as body material for hook sizes down to 28. The color range is extensive and the dyeing is consistent from lot to lot. Colors can be changed easily with common dyes and a little white vinegar to set the color. Other brands are also available. Craft shops have cross-reference charts.

Tinsel is available from many sources. Look for a brand that makes you happy when you tie with it.

DIAMOND MIDGE

The basic style of tying that I developed for this pattern is also used for most of the other nymph or pupa type of flies in this book. It is simple to tie and represents the basic body shape of a midge pupa. It is constructed a little differently than standard ties, so pay careful attention the first time through. I know some of you will just have to add more pieces to the patterns, and I encourage you to do so if you like. Just be sure to send me some if they work better.

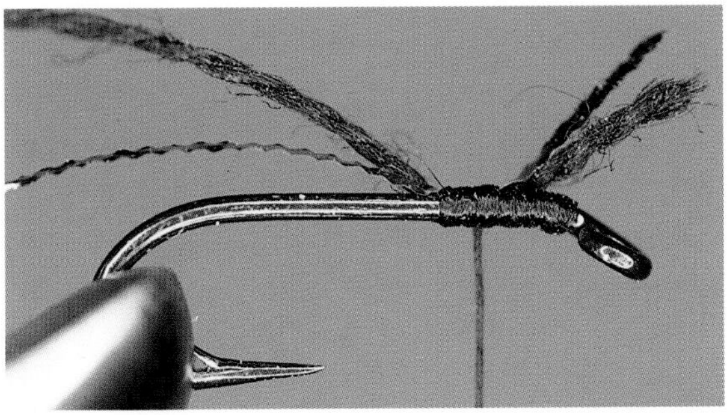

Step 1. Insert the hook into the vise, and attach the tying thread at the front. I use Mustad #3906B hooks for size 18 and #94840 for size 20 through 28, and Danville 6/0 black thread for all sizes. Select the color of floss for the body. I use DMC brand six-strand cotton embroidery floss, available at sewing or craft stores, and all the pattern colors are given using DMC color numbers so you will know exactly what color is being described in the pattern and Hatch Chart. For other brands of floss, color crossover charts are sometimes available where you buy it. Cut a piece of floss about 6 inches long, and separate the six strands. Cut a piece of tinsel about the same length. Tie the tinsel and the single strand of floss on top of the hook, about one or two eye widths back from the front and parallel to the shank.

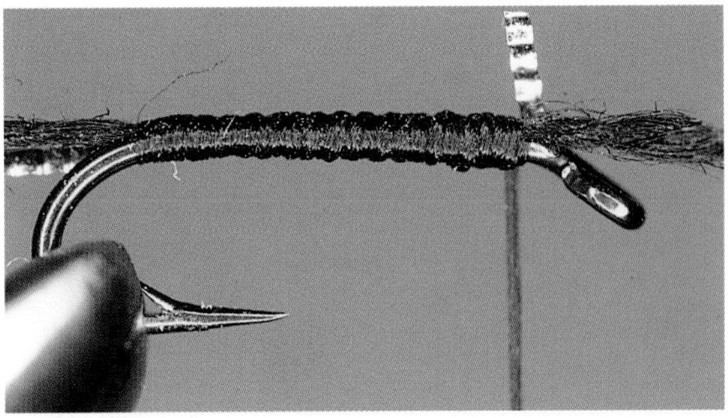

Step 2. While holding the two strands together along the top of the hook, wind the tying thread back to the bend and then forward to the starting point. Trim the excess floss and tinsel, and take a couple wraps to cover the ends. Your thread should end up about one eye width back of the eye.

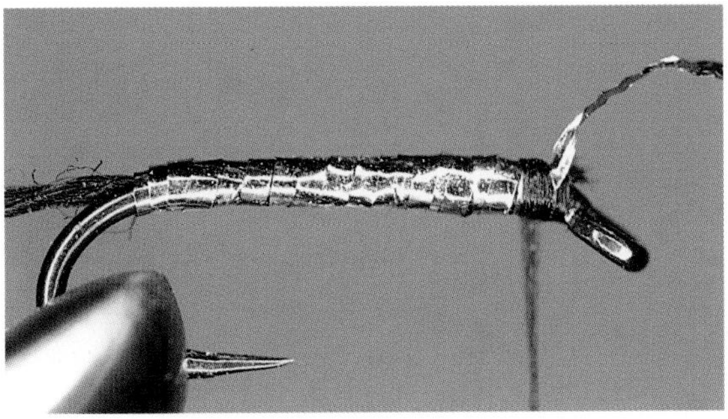

Step 3. Wind the tinsel forward in close wraps, forming a solid tinsel body. Tie it off where the tying thread hangs, and cut off the excess.

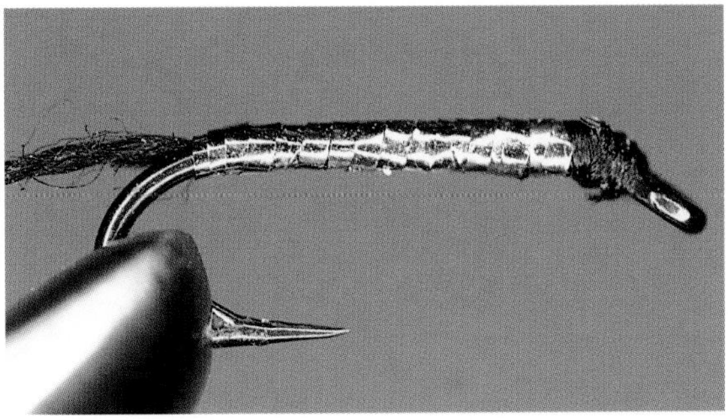

Step 4. Make a couple half-hitches, and cut off the tying thread. It is no longer needed.

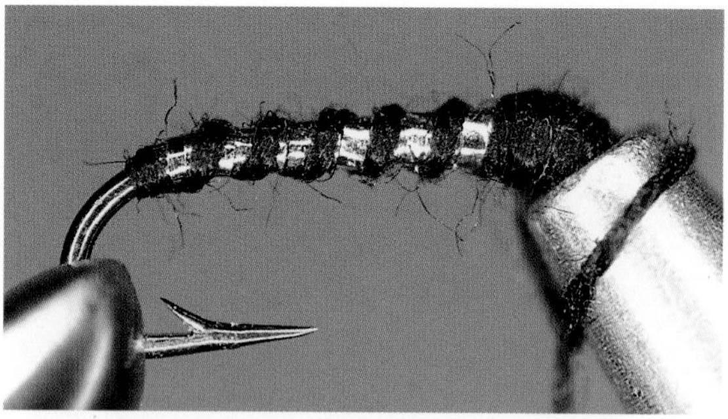

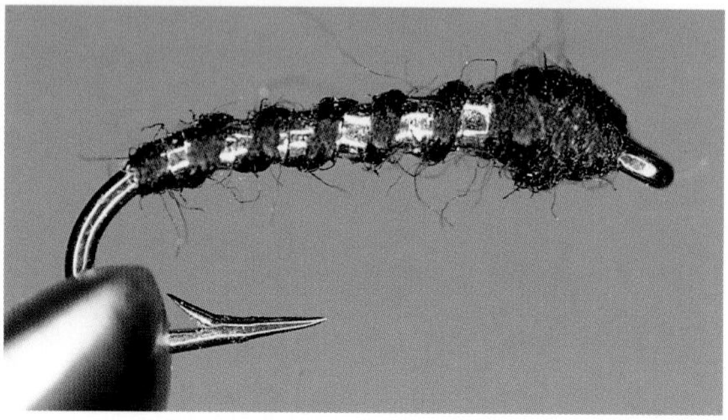

Completed Black Diamond Midge.

Step 5. Wind the floss strand forward in spaced turns (depending on hook size) to the end of the tinsel body. Wind close turns right to the eye of the hook (it should take about three), then five close turns to the rear, then two more forward. Then, using the proper size half-hitch tool, add two or three half-hitches with the floss. You're building up the head of the fly with the floss rather than tying thread. Try to make a nice, rounded head through the location and number of half-hitches. This actually represents the thorax/wing-case area of the pupa. Snug the floss by working it back and forth a little, and cut it off under the hook, leaving a little tag. This is to prevent the half-hitches from coming apart, as the floss material is very soft.

You *must* cement this area of the fly, or it will come apart. I prefer to use a vinyl head cement, which dries in a few minutes and does not get hard or glossy. Add thinner to it regularly so it will penetrate instantly. Thinned regular head cement can be used if you can't find the vinyl. Being soft, the head will sometimes slide down onto the hook eye slightly. Just push it back with your thumbnail a little, or leave a little space up front if it bothers you. Finally, bend the hook slightly while it's still in the vise to offset the point about 15 degrees. Vince Marinaro taught me to do this, and I have religiously done it on every fly from size 18 on down ever since.

FAVORITE PATTERN COLORS

In the pattern descriptions below, the first number is the suggested hook size. The second number is the color of the floss rib and head. The final color is the tinsel.

18 – 310 black/silver
18 – 829 olive gold, very dark/silver
18 – 831 olive gold, medium/silver
18 – 918 red copper, dark/silver
18 – 938 coffee brown, ultra dark/silver
18 – 415 pearl gray/silver
18 – 648 beaver gray, light/silver
18 – 611 drab brown/silver
18 – 841 beige brown, light/silver

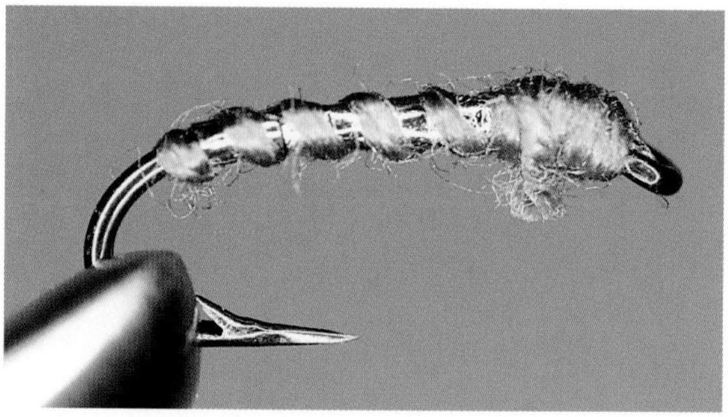

18 - DMC 831/silver.

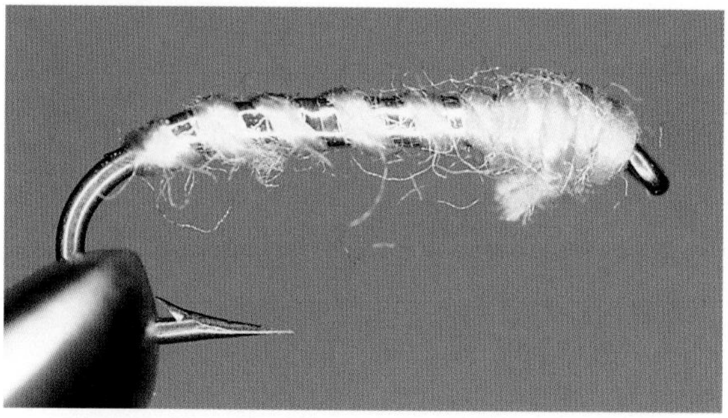

18 - DMC 415/silver.

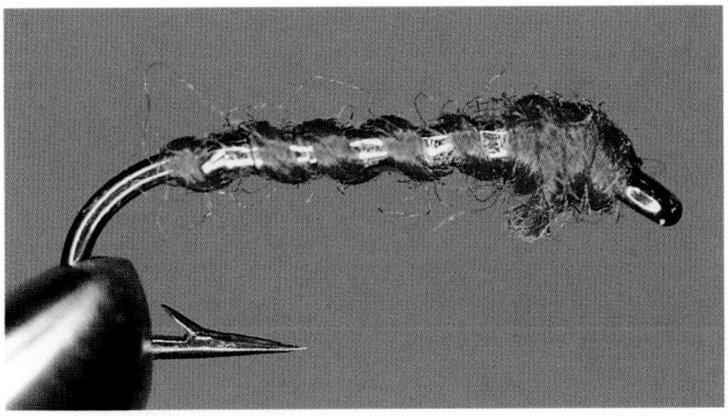

18 - DMC 918/silver.

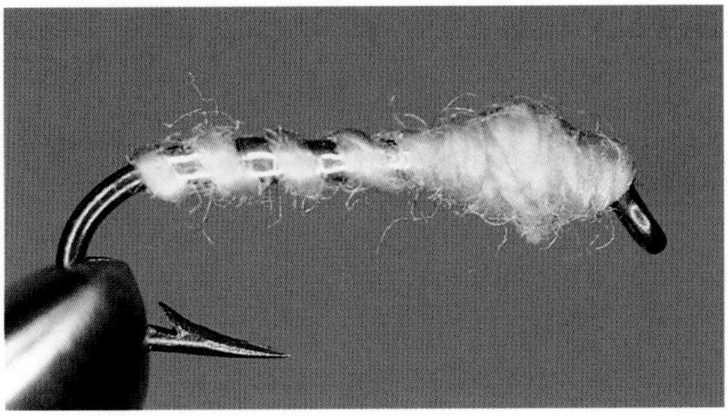

18 - DMC 842/silver.

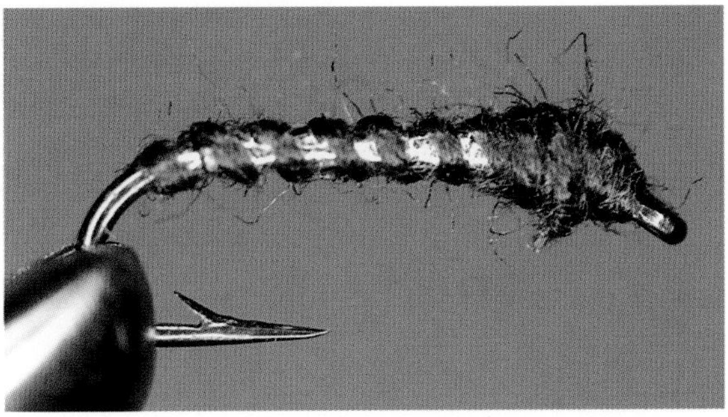

18 - DMC 938/silver.

An actual midge pupa and the 18 - DMC 938/silver that imitates it.

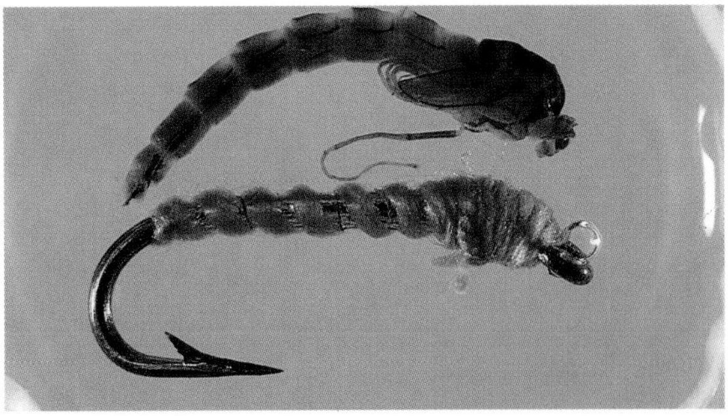

18 - DMC 3045/silver. (The air bubble in the hook eye was an accident.)

Try other tinsels. I tried blue once. It didn't work. But I might try it in a bigger size for bass someday. Lots of people have told me they think gold tinsel would work better, and I half-heartedly tried a couple. In the Hatch Chart, some patterns call for rainbow tinsel. It's the kind that changes colors as you turn it in the light. I think it's called holographic tinsel, but I refer to it as rainbow. Beware; not all brands work.

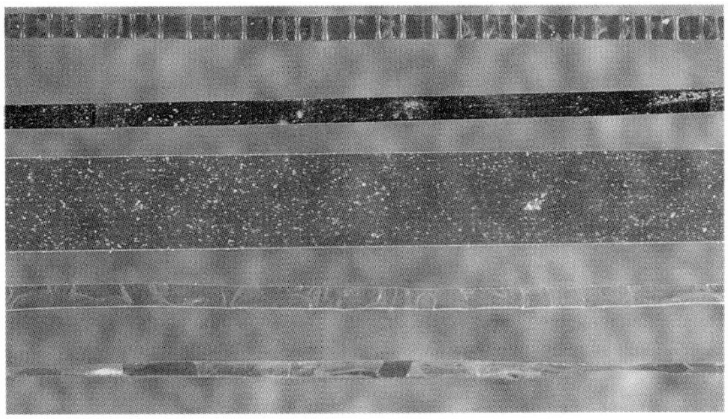

The various types of what I call rainbow tinsel, commonly known as holographic, look similar to the naked eye but differ under closer inspection.

CHAPTER 4

Rainbow Midges

Behold the beauty of Mother Nature's rainbow. The one I'm referring to here is not the one in the sky, but in the world of miniature insects, specifically those we fishermen refer to as midges. Once I began observing these insects with magnification, a whole new world opened up—a world of colors, subtle and striking, blended, contrasting, fading . . . endless possibilities. These seemingly unexciting little insects turned out to be intricately assembled life forms with a pattern to their makeup that might be the basis for a series of imitations.

Most of the specimens I examined appeared to have bodies of two colors, with a colored rib or band. The darker of the two colors was generally the color of the head/thorax area. I have come to believe that this effect is one of the major visuals by which a trout recognizes an item as being edible. Whether this appearance of a rib or band is caused by an actual color difference in body segments, a change in apparent color due to overlapping segments, or whatever, it is only important to arrive at a method of duplication.

To make the Rainbow Midges, I followed the general construction technique I had developed for the silver ribbed flies, using the same embroidery floss, but substituting colored thread for the silver portion. I selected one strand each of the two observed body colors, tied them on top of the hook shank, and wrapped them forward together to form a ribbed body. After cutting the lighter-color strand and the tying thread, I formed the thorax area by simply building it up with the darker strand and half-hitching it as if it were the tying thread. Thus the fly duplicates the natural in the three most important visual aspects: ribbing, color, and size.

This midge pupa shows the striped or banded pattern that influenced the author's early fly construction. His discovery of many variations in nature led to continual modification of fly bodies.

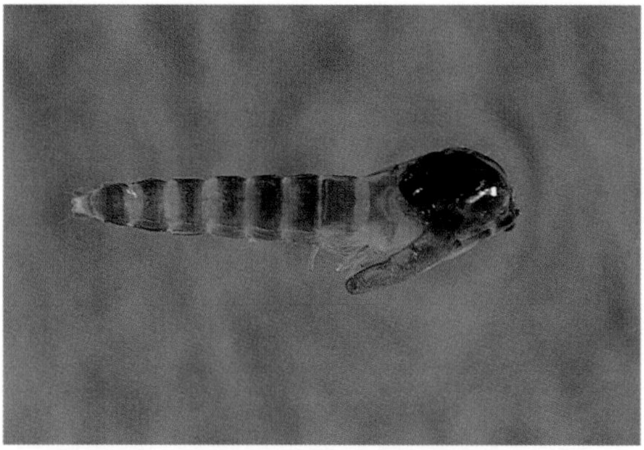

While to the naked eye, this and the preceding pupa appear almost identical, the coloration is slightly different. Although a generic pattern resembling either will surely take some fish, a closer match may take them all.

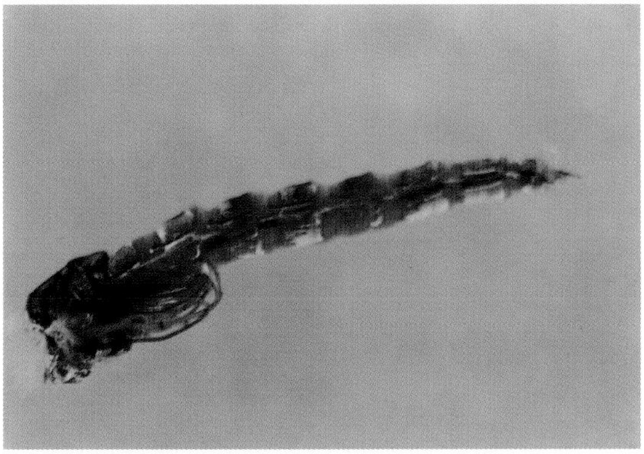

Another example with distinctive segmentation.

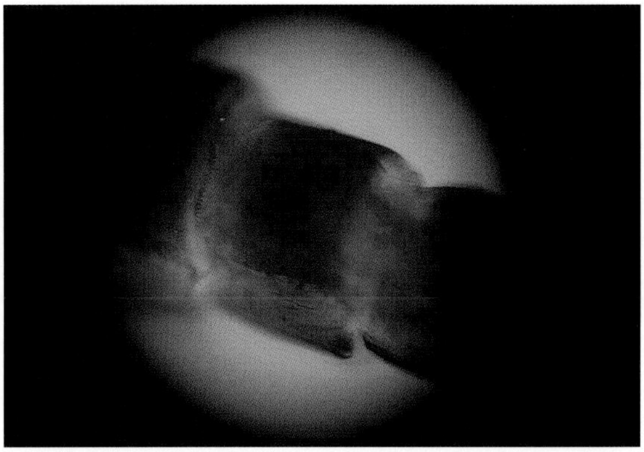

An enlargement of a pupal body showing the intersegmental area. In tying, simply try to imitate the visual impression it makes.

In twenty-odd years, I've had some duplicates work unbelievably, whereas other matches never caught a fish. But I guess it wouldn't be as much of a challenge or as fun otherwise, now would it?

RAINBOW MIDGE

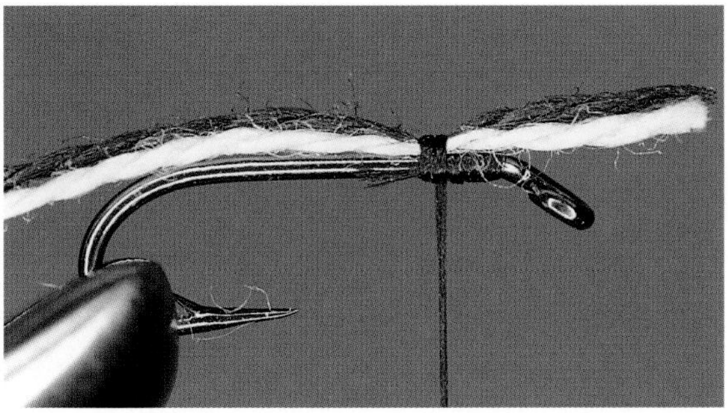

Step 1. Insert the hook into the vise, and attach the tying thread at the front. I use Danville 6/0, either white or black, as appropriate, for size 18 to 22. (See chapter 7 for size 24 and smaller flies.) Select the two embroidery floss colors either from your own observations or from the Hatch Chart later in this book. Cut the floss about 6 inches long, and separate one strand of each color. Tie these two strands on top of the hook near the front, parallel to the hook and extending out over the rear.

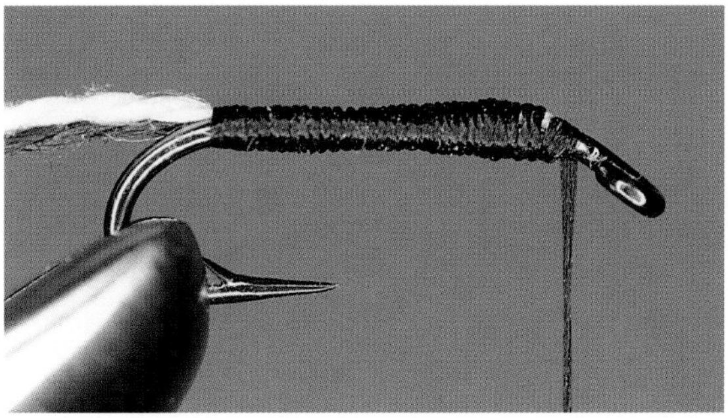

Step 2. While holding the two strands together along the top of the hook, wind the tying thread back to the bend and then forward to the starting point. Trim the tag ends of floss, and take a couple wraps to cover the ends. Your thread should end up about one eye width back of the eye.

Note: For size 18 flies, the author uses Mustad 3906B hooks. For all other sizes, he uses Mustad's standard dry-fly hook, 94840.

Step 3. Wind the two floss strands forward as a pair, forming a ribbed body. Tie them off where the tying thread hangs. Cut off the lighter-colored strand of floss and half-hitch a couple times. Cut off the tying thread; it is no longer needed.

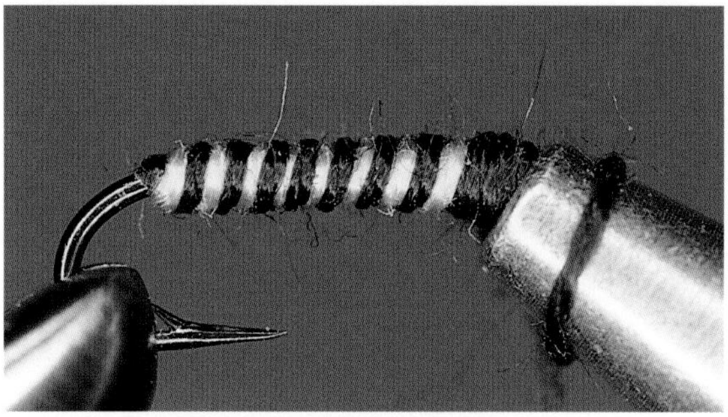

Step 4. Take the remaining strand of floss, and form a thorax/head area of about five turns in width. Then, with the proper size half-hitch tool, add two or three half-hitches with the floss. You're building up the head of the fly with floss instead of tying thread. Try to make a nice, rounded head through the location and number of half-hitches. Snug the floss by working the hitches back and forth a little, then cut it off under the hook, leaving a little tag. This is to prevent the half-hitches from coming apart, as the floss material is very soft. You *must* cement this area of the fly, or it will come apart. I prefer to use a vinyl head cement, thinned if necessary, to penetrate the head. Being soft, the head will sometimes slide down onto the hook eye slightly. Just push it back with your thumbnail a little. Offset the hook point a little as for the Diamond Midge.

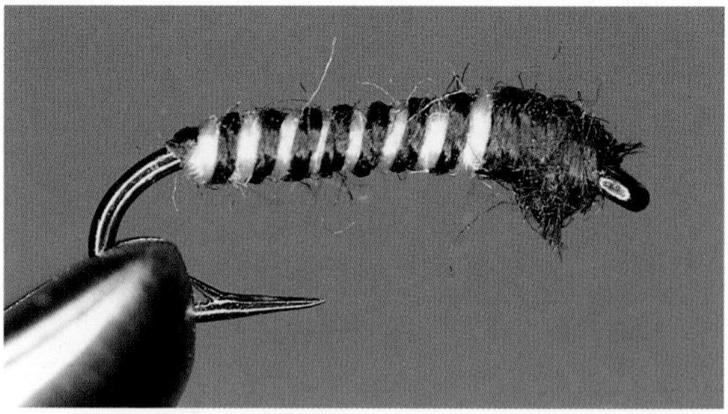

Finished Rainbow Midge.

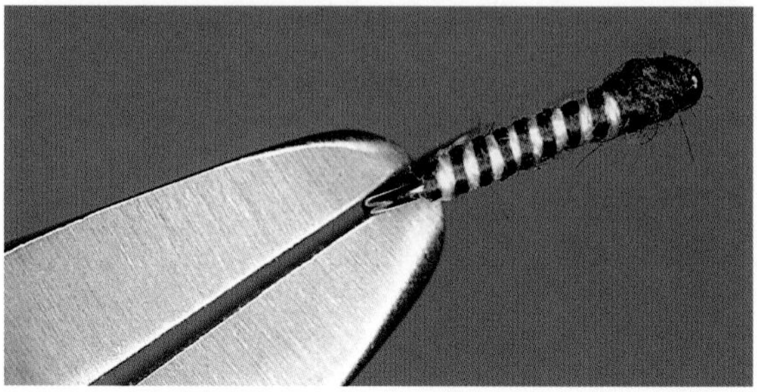

Top view showing approximately how much to offset the hook.

18 - DMC 842/white. This and the pattern below are two examples of the author's many Rainbow Midges.

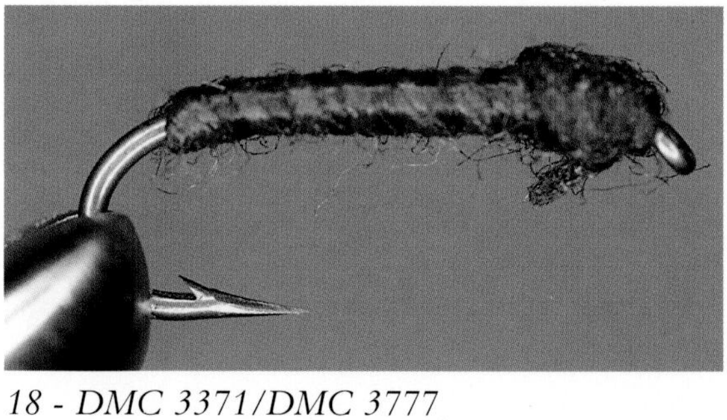

18 - DMC 3371/DMC 3777

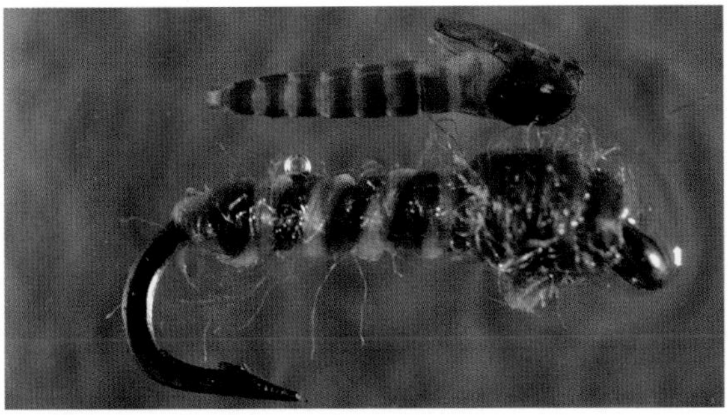

Not a perfect match, but getting there.

PATTERN NOTES

Although this pattern style was intended to imitate midge pupae, it can also be used for the larval phase, which you don't see imitated very often. One of the reasons is that larvae are not very available to the trout, a fact borne out by the infrequency with which I find them in stomach pumpings. However, they are still part of the trout's diet, and some patterns more suited to them are presented in later chapters.

One of their third cousins, so to speak, does exist in this form for the bulk of its aquatic life span and is very available to trout and sometimes constitutes the main portion of their diet. This happens to be the common black fly. This was the second pattern that I developed back in 1976, and it remains the most successful of all my patterns. Knowing very little at the time about the insects I was trying to imitate, I thought the specimens I found were midge larvae of some sort. My slides then were of low magnification and relatively poor quality. During a short paper I gave at a Harrisburg Fly Fishers Club luncheon, I put the natural up on the screen, and an entomologist from Penn State University, Greg Hoover, politely observed that it appeared to be a black-fly larva. An author and fly fisher in his own right, Hoover later sent me enough information that I was able to upgrade my knowledge and methods.

Although there are variations among black-fly larvae, this one has worked everywhere I have tried it. It is listed in the Hatch Chart as DMC 762/white. (DMC has no color number for white and labels it "blanc neige," which is French for "white snow.") While this is technically not a midge, the pattern style imitates it perfectly. If you tie only one pattern out of this whole book, make it this one. If you really want to make it work, dye some white floss a shade of gray so pale you can barely tell it from the white when it is dry. I use the #762 for the darker strand simply for convenience.

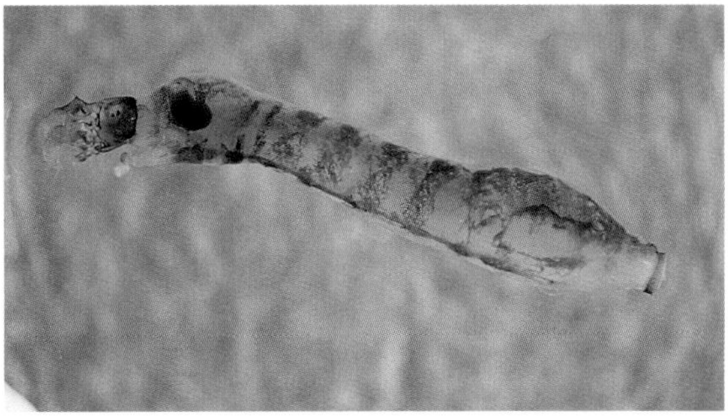

Side view of a black-fly larva with brownish markings. These larvae can be found in size 18 through 24 in various shades of gray to brown. They may be the most widespread small insects of interest to fishermen.

Top view of the same black-fly larva.

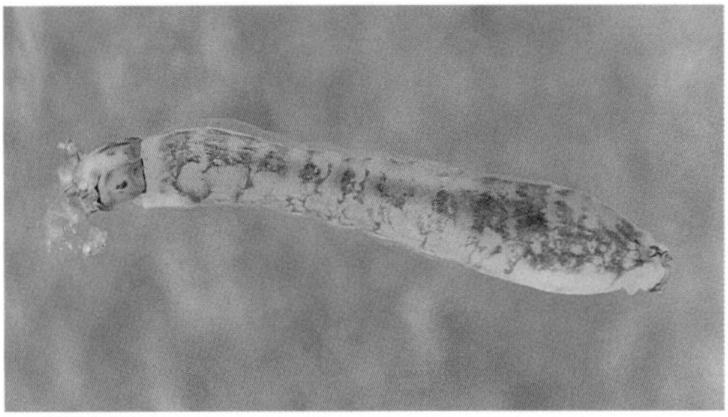

Black-fly larva with lighter and more grayish markings.

Black-fly larva with darker gray markings.

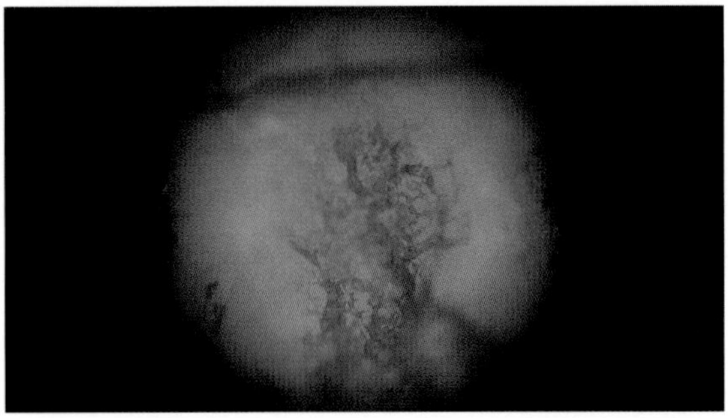

This enlarged area shows the markings to have a mottled appearance rather than a distinct banding.

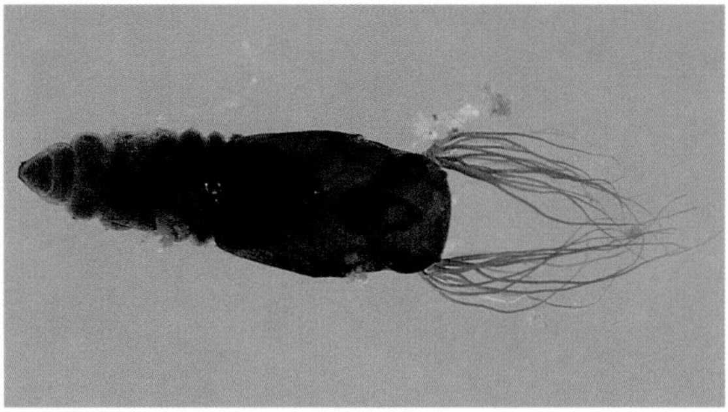

A black-fly pupa, the phase after the larval. Pupae attach to rocks where the fish can evidently pick them off. I sometimes find them in great numbers, but have never tried to imitate them.

Side view of a size 20 black-fly adult. I have never tried to tie a topwater imitation, although the trout eat them with abandon.

Black-fly adult, bottom (trout's) view.

Black-fly pupa and adult.

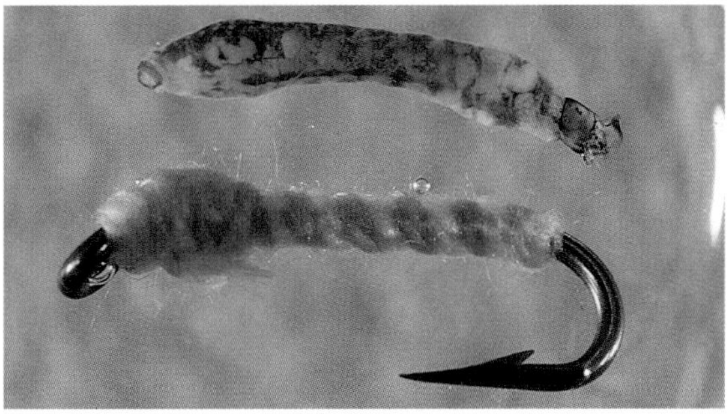

Black-fly larva with the author's original pattern, 18 - DMC 762/white, the lightest shade of gray available in DMC floss. You can dye the floss a lighter shade, which may give a better impression of the mottled shading. In any case, you can't go wrong with this pattern.

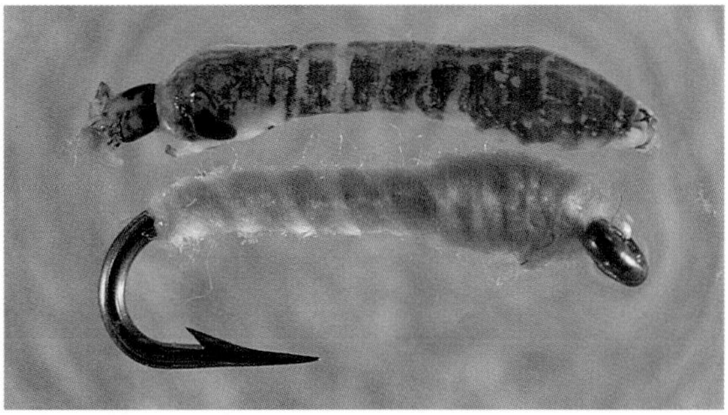

Another variation of black-fly larva pattern, 18 - DMC 840/DMC 543. There are five shades of beige-brown. At one time or another, they each excel.

CHAPTER 5

Clear Flies

Back in the early seventies, I fished Big Spring Creek near Newville, Pennsylvania, quite frequently. I liked going on weekday evenings, since the weekends were so crowded that it was difficult to test new patterns. A few locals were usually around, and one boy of about ten years old must have lived close by. He'd ride up to the stream on a fenderless bicycle, lay it down on the bank, and start to fish. He usually caught a few, and then got on his bicycle and left without saying a word to anyone. The odd thing was that I never saw him change a fly. One day, as I was fishing there with absolutely zero success, this kid showed up and started really catching fish. I could stand it no longer and finally eased over and casually asked what he was using that day. "A clear fly," he replied, and held it up for me to see. It was clear monofilament line of about 1X size wrapped around a size 16 hook and tied off with black thread. I thanked him, and shortly after, he left on his bicycle, never to be seen by me again. If I knew who he was, I would profusely thank him today, because this little revelation led me down another path of successful fly patterns.

The best I can figure is that this style of fly closely resembles in body shape the little midge larvae that abound in these waters and occasionally show up in trout stomach pumpings. I finally settled on a size 18 hook as the most common for this area, with a mono size of 5X. For years, I tied them with various colored threads in order to get different head colors and add a little tint to the bodies. I tied a few with colored mono used for spinning line but felt that dyeing mono was more work than I was willing to do.

I've recently rediscovered this technique. For a long time, I had been trying to match a particular midge larva with no success using my normal methods. It had an olive green color, but with a distinct rosy cast to it. These larvae were frequently found in late July in greater than normally seen quantities for this class of insect, and though fish could be caught on the usual patterns, it was obvious that the right one would be ten times better. While studying some of these larvae under the microscope one evening, I suddenly remembered how the thread underbodies on the old mono flies sometimes gave a little undercolor glow. I used red thread for an underbody, a yellow-green mono body sized to give nine wraps on a size 20 hook, and a head overwrapped with olive brown 6/0 thread. I caught fish the next evening that I hadn't moved in two weeks, except to avoid my leader.

THE CLEAR FLY

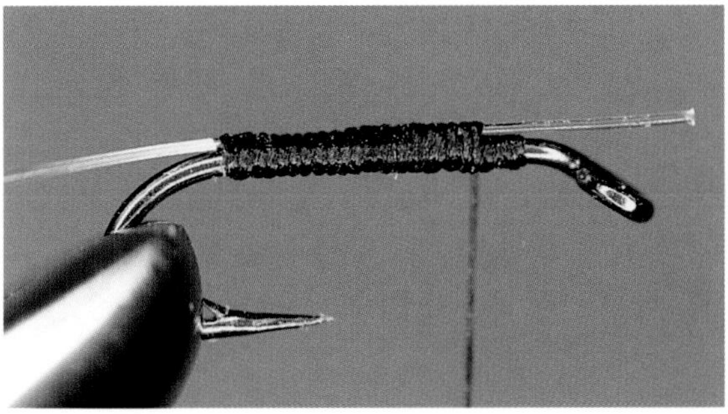

Step 1. Insert a size 18 Mustad 3906B hook into the vise. Attach the tying thread just behind the eye of the hook. Pick the thread color to suggest the inside or secondary color of the body, and the mono color to represent the outer or main color of the body. If you look at several of these larvae under magnification, it will be clearer to you. If you want to experiment, pick a colored mono, and tie several flies using a different thread underbody on each. This will give you an idea of the different effects you can achieve. I've used mono from 2- to 8-pound-test, or about 1X to 5X. Too large or too small won't look or feel right when you tie it. Trust your instincts. Cut a piece of the mono about 6 inches long, and attach it to the top of the hook near the front. Holding the mono parallel to the hook and pointing to the rear, bind it down with tight wraps back to the bend. Return the thread forward to about two eye widths behind the eye. Trim the excess mono.

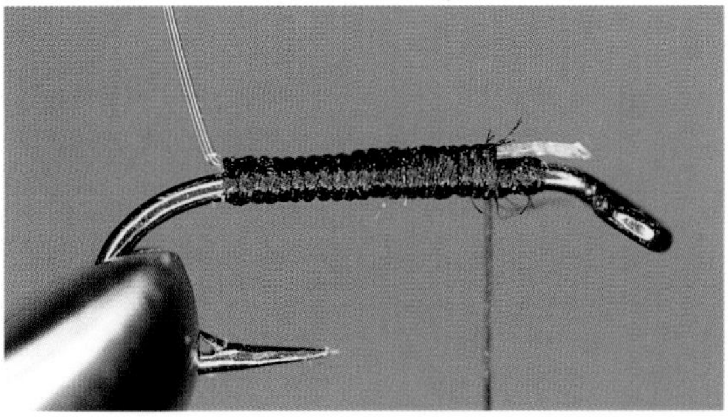

Step 2. Hold the mono straight up and bend it with your thumb where it exits the thread wraps. This will help it make an easier transition when you start the body wrap.

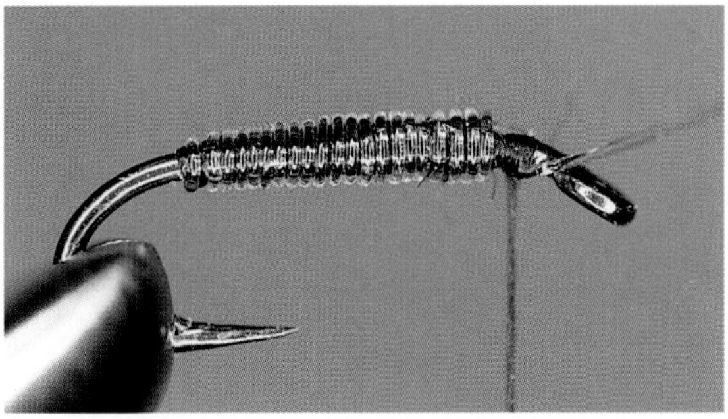

Step 3. Wrap the mono forward in close wraps to form the body. Tie it off on top of the hook at the point where the thread hangs. Trim the excess mono, and wrap the cut end down securely. Wrap a thread head just slightly smaller in diameter than the body. It should be a little longer than you're used to tying, and more cylindrical. Whip-finish or half-hitch, and cut the thread. Add a drop of cement if you used half-hitches. You'll often see these larvae with a different head color. If you want to match an actual larva, you can overwrap the original head with a layer or two of tying thread of the proper color.

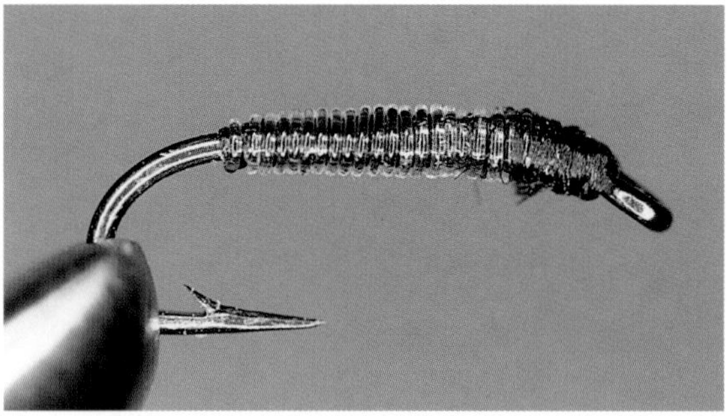

Finished Clear Fly.

FAVORITE COMBINATIONS

Clear monofilament is easy to obtain. This was the original pattern, and I like it with underbodies of black, white, red, and yellow tying thread. Colored mono is a little harder to obtain. Hundred-yard spools of spinning line will give you enough for one hundred years of fly tying, maybe more. If I see someone with a spinning rod, I often ask what color line the angler is using and whether he or she will cut me off 5 or 10 yards. Dyeing is another option. Hot water, Rit dye, and a dash of white vinegar will color any mono, but you've got to have a touch of fanatic in you. I've had exceptional success using Garcia Royal Bonnyl spinning line, which has a rich brown color and can occasionally still be found. Maxima brown leader might be a good substitute, but I haven't tried it. A yellow underbody is my favorite. The olive-bodied fly mentioned above was made with a Fenwick spinning line that I haven't seen for a while. I think it was called Riverline. Don't overlook fluorescent mono. Hoard samples of everything you run across. You just never know when you might need it.

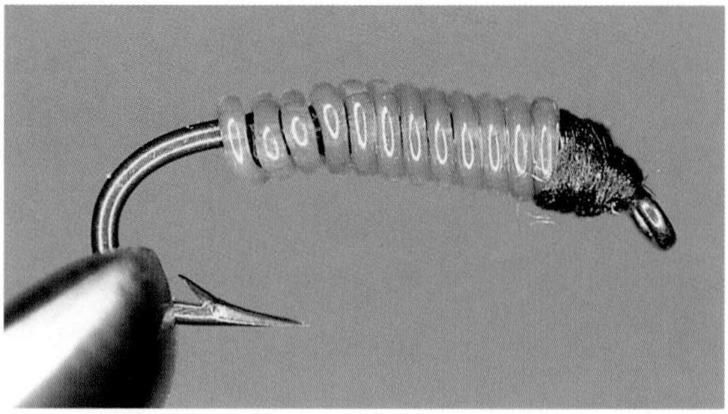

18 - olive mono/black thread. Monofilament thin enough to allow 8 or 10 wraps would probably look best, but sometimes you have to use what is available color-wise.

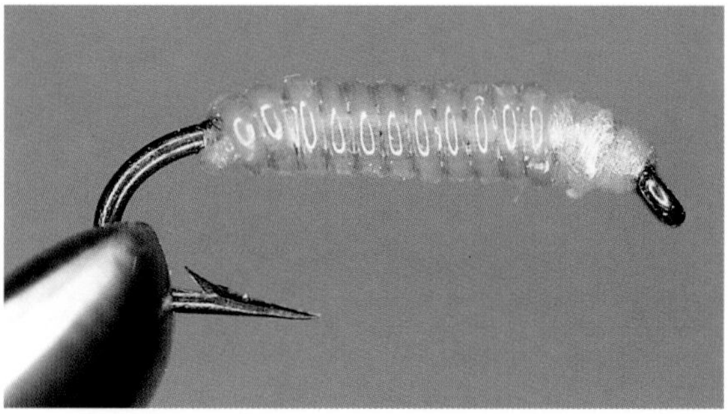

18 - olive mono/white thread. Same fly, different thread—a useful technique for creating a new fly.

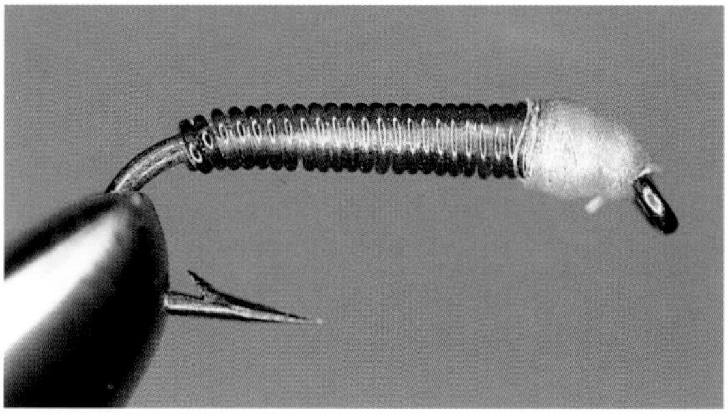

18 - brown mono (Garcia Royal Bonnyl spinning line)/white thread.

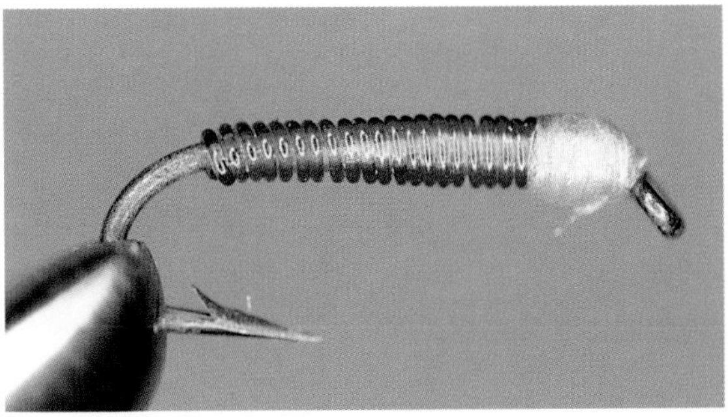

18 - brown mono/yellow thread

Typical midge larva. This pattern may be the answer to imitating these insects.

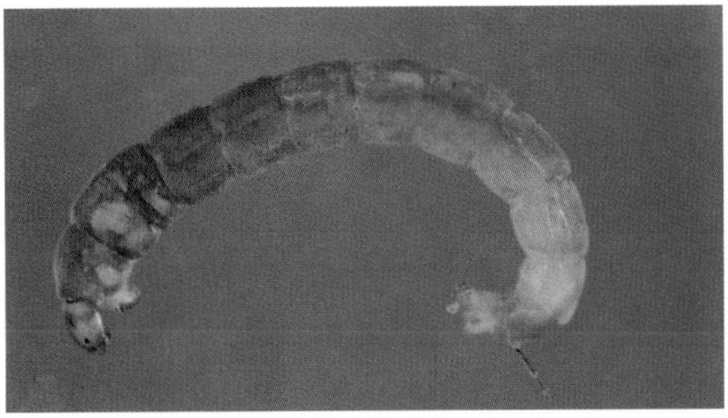

Another midge larva.

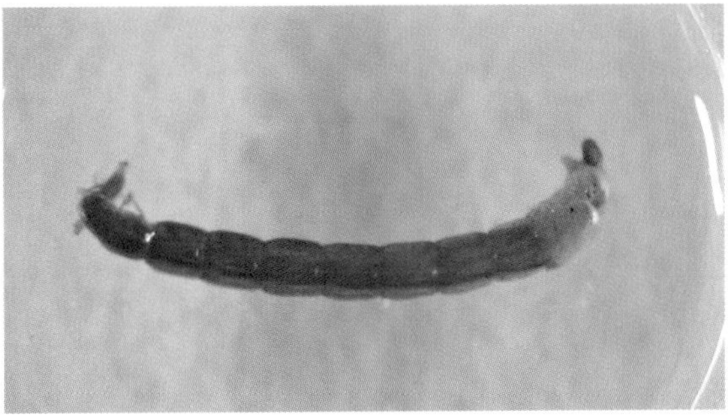

Yet another midge larva. See chapter 8 for another possible answer to imitating these insects.

CHAPTER 6

Metallics

I've always liked tinsel, especially silver. When I first started tying back in 1970, I invariably picked streamer and wet-fly patterns that had a tinsel-ribbed body. I think that's why I never became a dry-fly addict. Back then, the tinsel was still mostly made of metal rather than mylar. The embossed tinsel, with a pattern pressed into its surface, was my favorite. It seemed to make the light explode rather than simply reflect. I religiously ribbed most of my nymphs with it, little knowing that years later, when the Diamond Midges were developed, that would be half of their success.

With the advent of the mylar tinsels, the embossed variety became harder to find, especially in the smaller sizes. I used the spooled mylar silver tinsel for years, with about the same results as before. When they finally started making Christmas tree tinsel out of the same stuff, and in colors, I stocked up on it at the after-holiday sales to experiment with. A little red worm was common in our area streams, and most people fished a red wool nymph pattern to imitate it. I had been fooling around with some other ideas when I ran across the red Christmas tinsel. I simply made a tinsel body, as you would for a standard streamer, with a tying thread head that was also red. It wasn't that successful, really, and I soon learned that the cheap tinsel was very poorly made, with widths up to 1/4 inches in the same package. I did have some success with a bright silver one, but I soon let the idea and the materials lay dormant.

When a friend gave me some samples of a material he was using for skirts on bass lures, I couldn't believe my eyes. Here was a mylar tinsel that had the look of the embossed tinsel of old. Making some inquiries at the local sporting goods shop, I discovered that this material was sold under the name of FireFly Tye and was available in several colors. The material is very narrow, less than 1/32 inches wide, and never really caught on in most fly shops I've been in, for some reason. I guess most people just couldn't figure out what to do with tinsel that size. Oddly, I've found more of it in New York State salmon-fly shops than anywhere else. If you can't find this particular mylar, there are others on the market that are very close in appearance.

I sometimes tie things just for the sake of doing something different. I really can't remember what I was trying to accomplish, if anything. Perhaps the success of the clear fly was in the back of my mind, but I ended up tying a silver tinsel body out of this new material, and then started overwrapping it with a piece of 4X leader material, beginning at the rear of the fly. When I had wrapped the mono about halfway up, I was amazed. If the embossed tinsel had seemed to explode light, what the mono did was make it sparkle like it was alive. I don't know if it resembled a tiny minnow or what, but it quickly became one of my favorite patterns. I came to prefer a hard, shiny leader material as the overwrap. Dull leader material seemed to make the fly appear lifeless.

I have ideas for variations on these flies, such as colored thread wraps between the mono wraps, but alas, there is only so much time. I say this merely to suggest a direction you might take and save me the trouble. I tend to use the metallic patterns more when fishing the water rather than a particular fish, but don't discount this tactic. I also tend to fish them when the sun is bright, hoping the extra sparkle will attract the trout, and also when it's what I call dreary dark, again hoping the extra flash might help.

METALLICS

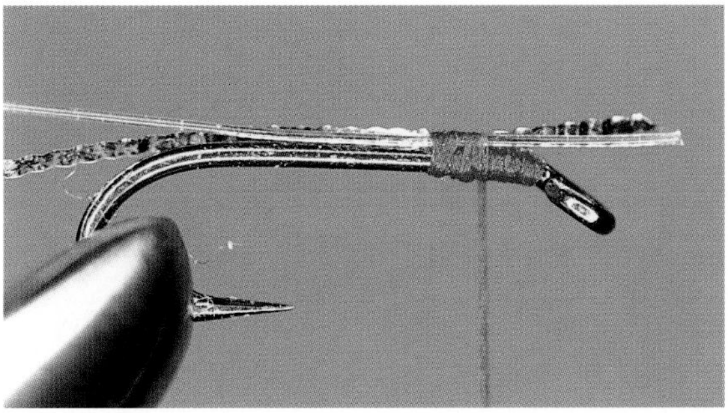

Materials tied on at front.

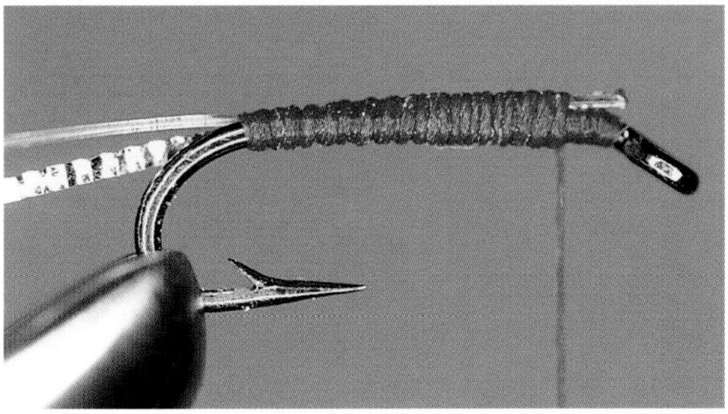

Tying thread wrapped back and returned.

Step 1. I usually tie these on size 18 Mustad 3906B hooks. You can tie them any size you want, down to a size 28. Insert the hook into the vise and attach the tying thread, your choice of 6/0 colors, near the front. Tie in the tinsel and a length of mono at this point and, holding them along the top of the hook, wrap them with thread to the bend, then return the thread to one eye width behind the eye.

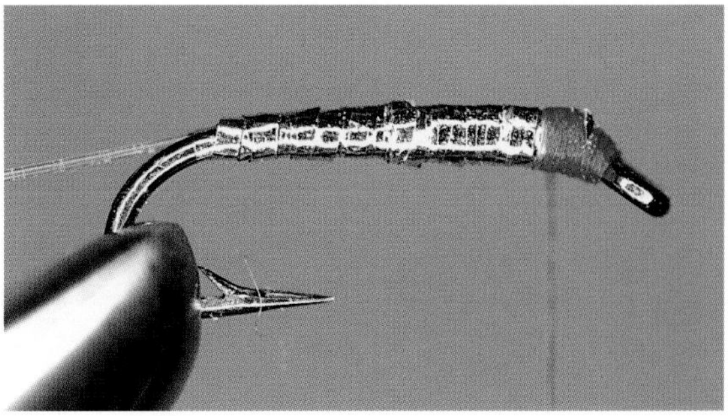

Step 2. Wrap a tinsel body, and tie off at the thread location. Cut the excess tinsel. Make sure no thread shows through the body between wraps.

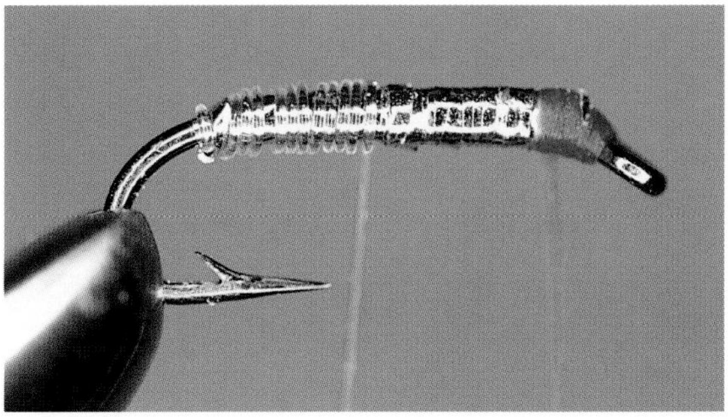

Halfway. Note the difference in the two halves.

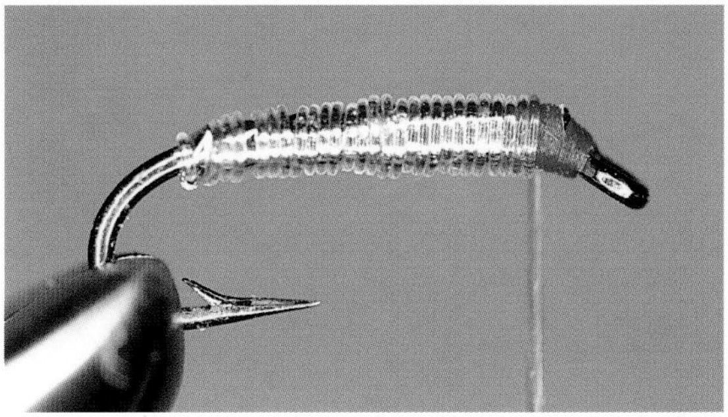

Completed.

Step 3. Overwrap the tinsel body in tight turns with the mono. Stop halfway up and look at the difference between the two body halves. If it doesn't sparkle, pick another brand of mono. If you're satisfied, tie off on top of the hook at the front, and cut the excess.

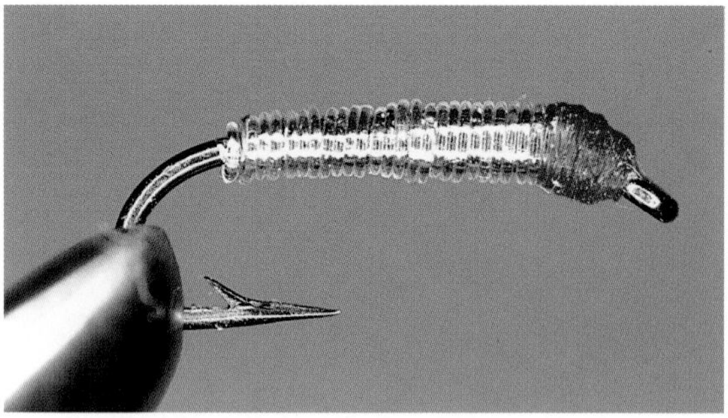

Completed 18 - silver/mono/red head.

Step 4. Wrap a nice head with tying thread to firmly lock down the mono end, and whip-finish or half-hitch. Cement if you wish, and offset the hook slightly.

FAVORITE PATTERNS

My favorite metallic pattern is silver, followed by copper, which I like early in the season. Green is next. We have a little green caddis locally, and when it's on, this fly is superb and outfishes any fur nymph I've ever used. I've had some luck with gold and really don't know why it doesn't work better. Last but not least is red, which can be used to imitate little red worms, but there are some beadhead patterns in chapter 8 that I found to be more successful.

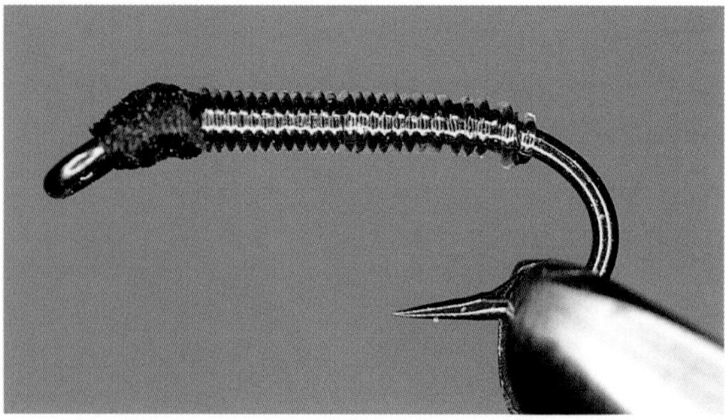

18 - copper/mono/black head. Perhaps not as good as the silver one overall, but when it works, it works!

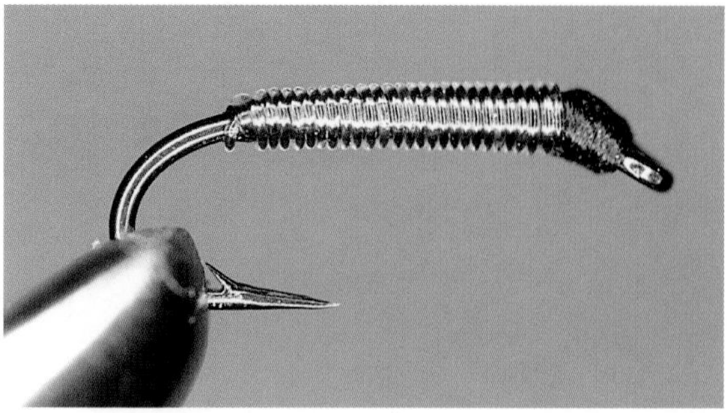

18 - green/mono/black head. Try it in late spring especially.

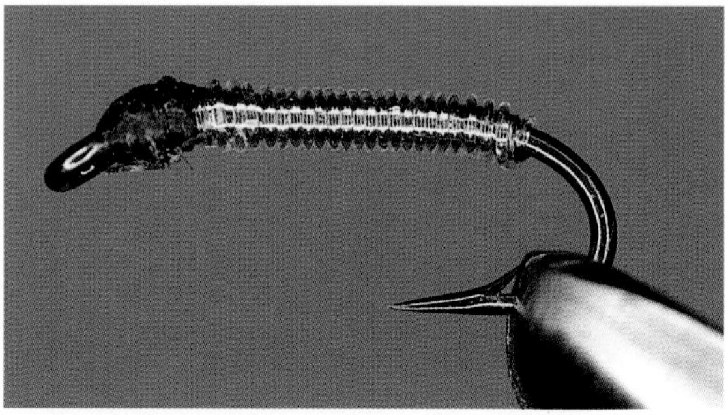

18 - gold/mono/black head.

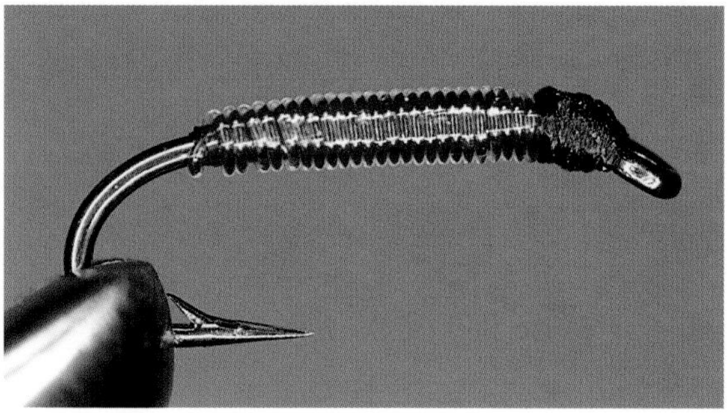

18 - purple/mono/black head. Just try it.

CHAPTER 7

Size 24s

Midges can range all the way down to size 40 something. That's when we mutter something under our breath, or get the streamers out, or the hot dogs, or whatever. I normally fish a size 18 midge pupa, on a Mustad 3906B hook, because that's the prevailing size year-round in our area streams. But there are times when a smaller size is not only advisable, but almost imperative, if you wish to pick up more than the occasional fish. Over the years, I've finally settled on size 24, on a Mustad 94840 hook, as the other prevailing size pupa. I can't see carrying all the patterns in sizes 18 through 28, although at times I've come close to doing just that. Why complicate life more than it already is? At any rate, you will have to decide your own approach.

Though I tied all the sizes for years using the same materials, they were not totally satisfactory under a size 22. The cotton embroidery floss was just a little too large in diameter and too soft and fuzzy. I put up with this for the longest time, until one day, while my wife was making a small sewing repair, I idly picked up her spool of thread and looked at it. Then, in a moment of inspiration, I broke off a piece, went to my tying bench, and wrapped it around a size 26 hook. At last—the qualities I was looking for.

Making a trip to the local sewing center, I came back with forty-some spools of Coats & Clark Dual Duty Plus thread. This thread has a polyester thread core covered with cotton fibers and is perfect for tying down to a size 28. Its specialized finish gives it what I call a hard shell coating, which overcomes the softness problems of the cotton embroidery floss. Although it comes in fewer colors than the floss, its advantages outweigh that shortcoming. If you can't find the exact color you want, you can always dye a spool of white thread to any color, which is more trouble than I care to go through, or you still can use the standard embroidery floss to tie the small flies. You'll just have to use a little more care. I fished them for years.

The tying instructions for size 24 and smaller are basically the same as for the Rainbow Midge series. Some recommended color combinations that I think will work most anywhere can be found in the Hatch Chart later in this book.

Although embroidery floss can be used for tying down to size 28, it does have its limitations. As the hook length decreases, fewer wraps can be put on the shank, somewhat limiting the visual effect you're trying to achieve. An alternative is thread. Coats Dual Duty Plus sewing thread has a cotton-covered polyester core and is available in 200 colors. You won't need them all but may use 80 or more if you're serious. It has the perfect size and feel for 24 to 32 size hooks. However, never forget — color rules. Use what matches.

SIZE 24s

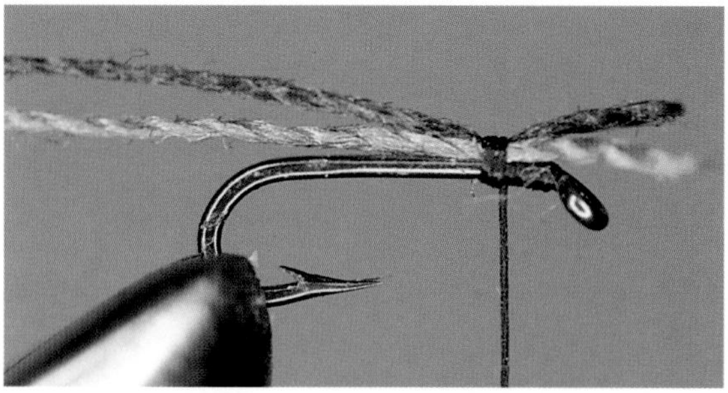

These are smaller than normal Rainbow Midges, just tied with a different material. The tying steps are repeated in this chapter for convenience.

Step 1. Insert a size 24 or smaller Mustad 94840 hook into the vise, and attach the tying thread near the front. You can use 6/0, but one of the newer threads like Unithread or one of the new 8/0 or 10/0 threads may be easier to handle. Use black for the dark-bodied flies and white for the light ones. Select the two body thread colors from the Hatch Chart or based on your own observations. Cut pieces about 6 inches long (only one strand if you're using floss). Tie the two strands on top of the hook near the front, parallel to the hook, and extending out over the rear.

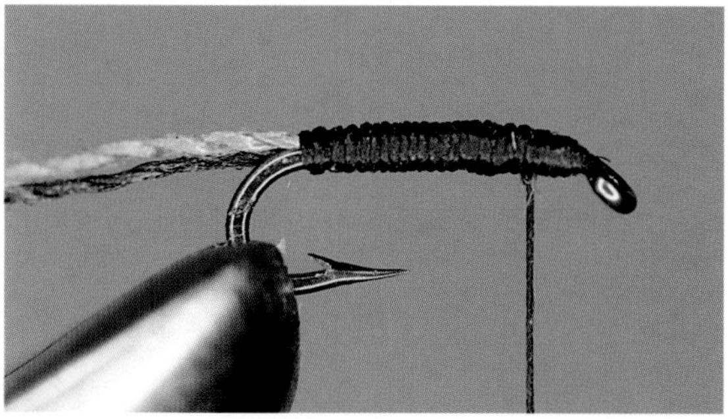

Step 2. While holding the two strands together along the top of the hook, wind the tying thread back to the bend and then forward to the starting point. Trim the tag ends, and take a couple wraps to cover. Your thread should end up about one eye-width back of the eye.

Step 3. Wind the two strands forward as a pair, forming a ribbed body. Tie them off where the tying thread hangs. Cut off the lighter-colored strand of body material and half-hitch a couple times. Cut off the tying thread; it is no longer needed.

Cut off the lighter strand after wrapping the body.

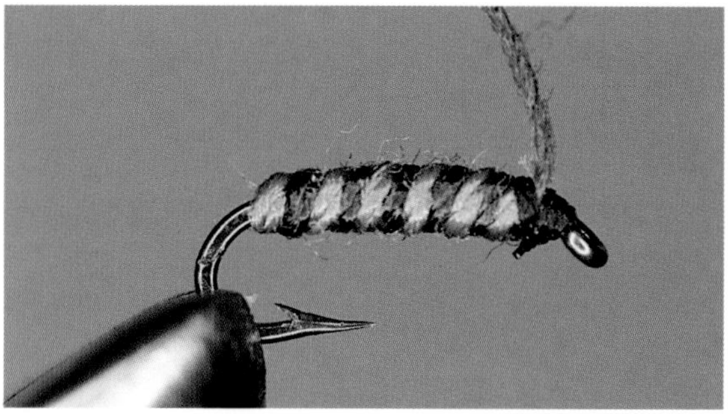

The tying thread is half-hitched and cut off. The remaining body strand will be used to form the head and finish the fly.

Use an appropriate size half-hitch tool to place each hitch in its location.

Step 4. Take the remaining body strand, and form a thorax/head area of about three to four turns in width. Then, with the proper size half-hitch tool, add two or three half-hitches with the material. You're building up the head of the fly with the body strand instead of tying thread. Try to make a nice, rounded head through the location and number of half-hitches. Snug the hitches by working them back and forth a little, then cut off the strand under the hook, leaving only the smallest tag. You *must* cement this area of the fly, or it will come apart. I prefer to use a vinyl head cement, thinned if necessary, to penetrate the head. Being soft, the head will sometimes slide down onto the hook eye slightly. Just push it back with your thumbnail a little. Offset the hook point slightly.

Completed size 24 Rainbow Midge.

THIN-RIBBED PUPAE

Over the years, I occasionally ran across pupae in this small size range that, unlike the larger ones, appeared to have bodies of only one color or had ribbing so narrow it was almost a faint stripe. I had seen various widths of color banding on the larger ones and had experimented with using more than two strands of body material. I didn't pursue this very hard and, after only moderate success, eventually pursued it to practically zero effort. But the narrow bands on these smaller pupae intrigued me. The effect seemed more subtle but, at the same time, seemed to have some measure of importance that appeared to be lacking in the larger pupae. At this point, I was taking photographs of the insects and their matching flies in the same frame, which gave me a different perspective than when I looked at them individually. These pupae had a head area color different from the main body color, but the same color as the thin ribbing. This precluded using another strand for this head color, as its width was too large to imitate the ribbing. For a while I tried using an added strand of tying thread, much as you would add a wire rib to a standard pattern by wrapping it forward after the body was formed. It just never looked right, and quite frankly, it wasn't too successful in the field.

I finally ran out of ideas and settled on tying the pupa with a single color body, and then overwrapping the finished head area with a thread close in color to the pupa head color. This immediately increased the success rate of the flies, and I was happy to tie them this way, as I discovered different ones for quite some time. I continued photographing them, especially if one worked particularly well. I occasionally had one of the photos enlarged to an 8x10. You can really pick out the tying errors when you see one this big. One day I was looking at an 8x10 of one of the size 24 imitations. I had used a darker thread underneath a light-colored body, and at first I chastised myself for being sloppy in my tying, as I could see the tying thread showing between the wraps of body material. But then I realized that I had inadvertently managed to imitate those superthin rib bands. I began buying tying thread in colors to match what I saw under the microscope. They don't all match exactly, but the end results are satisfactory.

The next thing I discovered was that the body wraps did not have to be spaced in order for the underthread to show. In fact, this proved to be a mistake. If you consciously try to leave a slight gap between each turn, you invariably end up with a rib that is far too wide. If, instead, you wrap the body strand as if you're trying to keep the thread from showing by wrapping it tightly, it shows through in precisely the right amount. Because the body material is round in cross section, the points at which the adjoining turns touch allow the thread, which is usually darker, to show through. I am absolutely convinced that the trout can discern this. A slight modification in the normal tying procedure resulted in the best size 24 and 26 flies to date. These are my number-three flies in the short list of patterns I would never be without. Fish them under or float them on top with a little silicone during a hatch. You're going to love them.

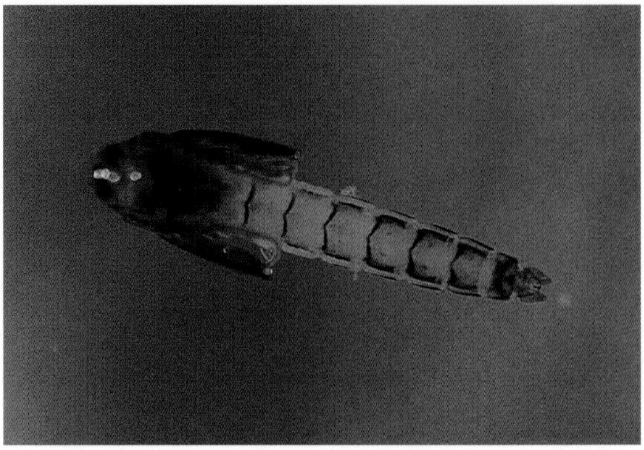

An example of a midge pupa with very thin bands of rib color.

Another example of a midge pupa with thin bands of rib color.

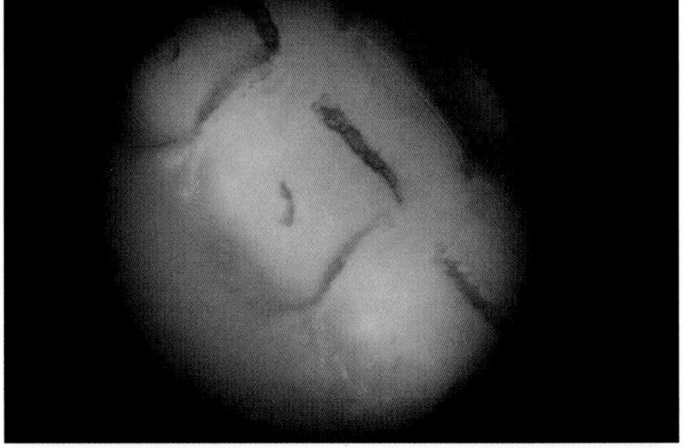

An enlarged view of the same midge pupa. Trout may, in fact, be able to distinguish this level of detail.

THIN-RIBBED PUPA

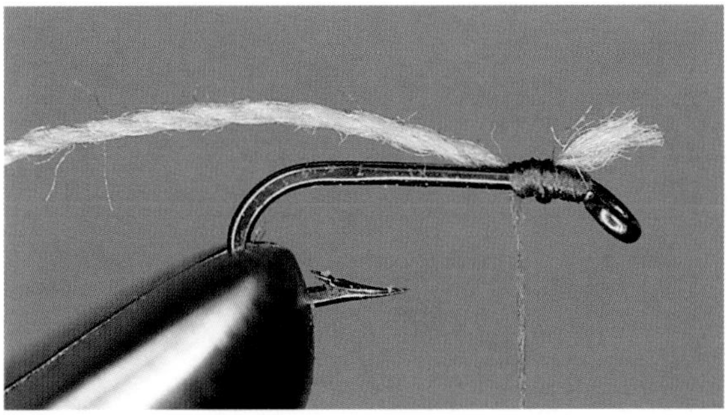

Step 1. Insert a size 24 or 26 Mustad 94840 hook in the vise. Pick your tying thread with care, because it will also serve as the ribbing and the head of the fly. Either choose one from the Hatch Chart or match an insect you have collected. Attach the tying thread near the front of the hook. Select the body color thread in the same manner. Use only the Coats & Clark Dual Duty Plus threads, as the floss strands will not give the same effect. Tie the body strand on top of the hook near the front, parallel to the hook shank, and extending over the rear.

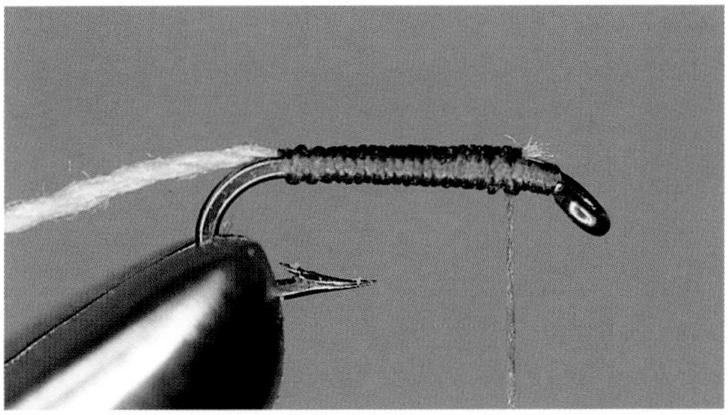

Step 2. While holding the body strand along the top of the hook, wind the tying thread back to the bend, and then forward to the starting point in tight wraps. Trim the tag end, and take a couple wraps to cover. Your thread should end up about one eye width back of the eye.

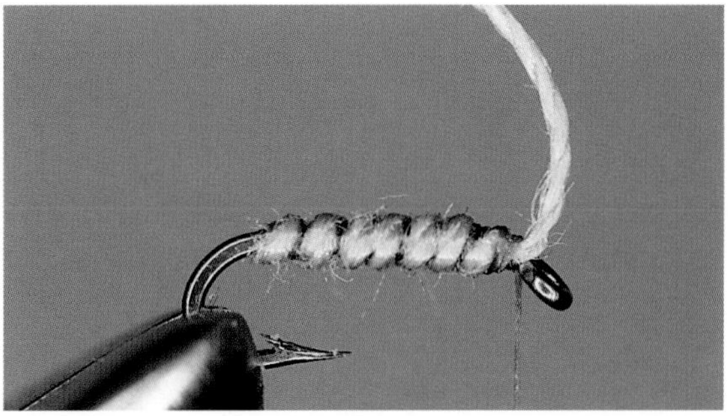

WRONG. Do not intentionally leave spaces between body wraps of tying thread on the underbody. This will make the thin rib color appear too wide.

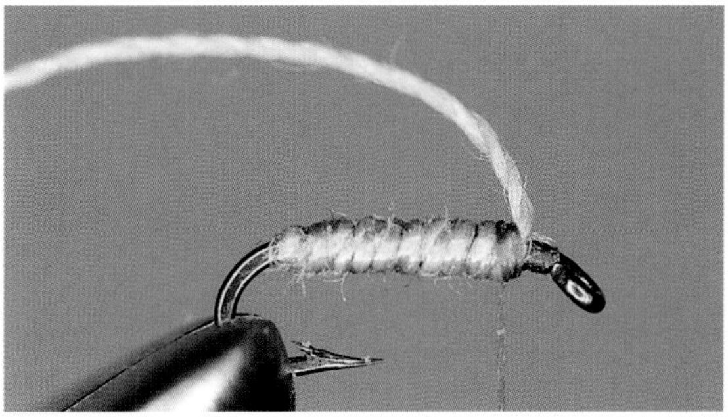

RIGHT. Wrap the body thread tightly and leave the thread at the rear of the head area.

Step 3. Wind the strand forward, forming the body. Tie off where the tying thread hangs. Do not cut the tying thread as in previous patterns.

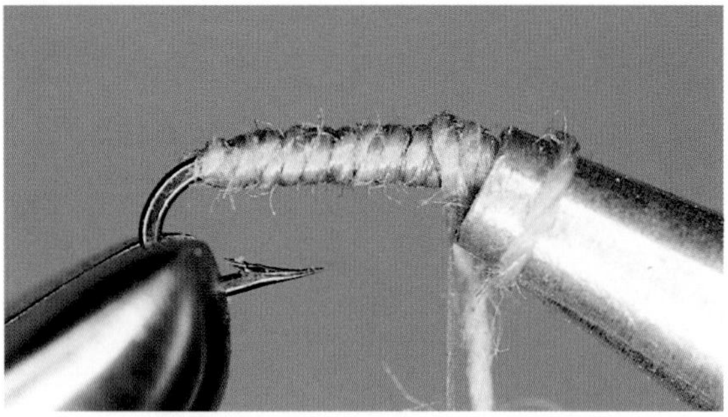

Form the head as you would when tying a Rainbow Midge.

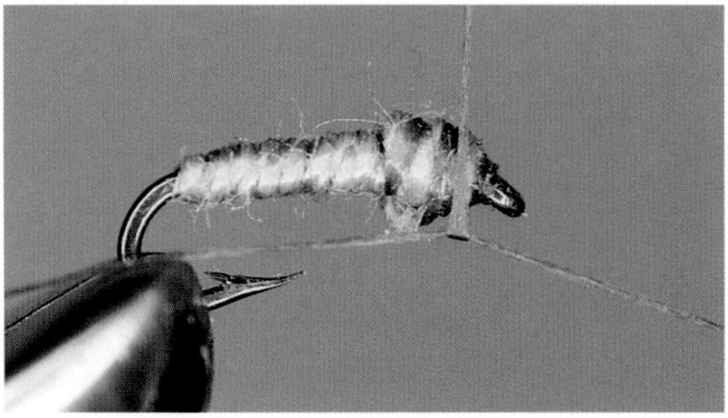

Use the tying thread to overwrap the head area. A whip-finish tool is the easiest way to do it.

Step 4. Take the remainder of the body strand, and form a thorax/head area of about three to four turns in width. Then, with the proper size half-hitch tool, add two or three half-hitches with the material. You're building up the head of the fly with the body strand instead of tying thread. Try to make a nice, rounded head through the location and number of half-hitches. Snug the hitches by working them back and forth a little, then cut off the strand under the hook, leaving only the smallest tag.

Now for the modification. Take the tying thread, which will be hanging at the rear of the head area, and overwrap the head to give it the proper color. Don't use too many wraps, or it will tend to slip off. Make just a few, and then whip-finish rather than half-hitch. Now you can cut the tying thread. You *must* cement this area of the fly, or it will come apart. I prefer to use a vinyl head cement, thinned if necessary, to penetrate the head. Being soft, the head will sometimes slide down onto the hook eye slightly. Just push it back with your thumbnail a little. Offset the hook point slightly.

Completed Rainbow Midge with a thin rib.

C&C 47/Unithread dark brown (BCS 98). An excellent fall pattern.

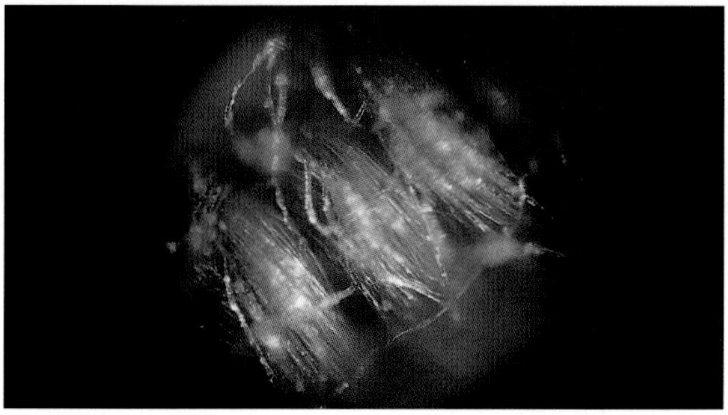

Enlarged view of C&C 47/Unithread dark brown. The tying thread underbody will show through where the wraps touch because the material is at its thinnest cross section at this point.

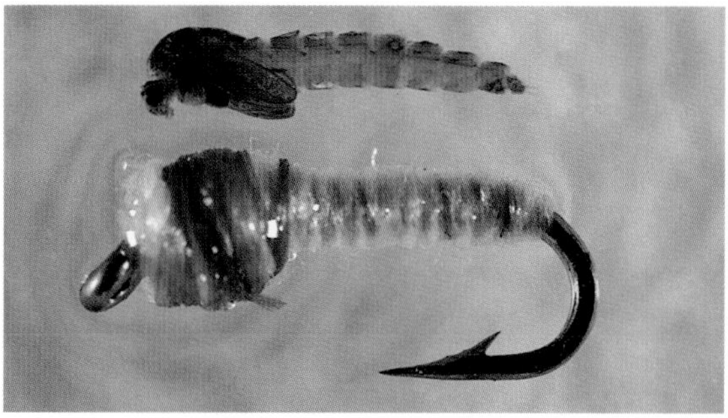

Size 24 midge pupa and a reasonable imitation.

CHAPTER 8

Beadheads

Beadhead flies have been in fairly widespread use for several years now. Magazine articles and fly catalogs have been touting them, some fishermen I know swear by them. Most everybody had some. Except me. I figured that all the beadheads were doing was getting the flies down to where they were supposed to be, and that they were nothing more than a fad. I wouldn't tie them or fish them.

Well, they're still here catching fish, and I'm not quite as dumb as I used to be. I'm not sure of the reason for their success, but it eventually got my attention. I bought beads, lots of beads. My favorites are the petite size glass beads found in craft shops.

When I first started fishing this area, one of the local patterns I was given was simply red wool wrapped around a hook as a body. I was told that there were little red worms in the stream, commonly called bloodworms, and that this was an imitation of them. Well, it worked and I used it and I was happy. But once I got interested in the insects themselves and saw these little red worms, it was an interesting revelation. They did not look at all like pieces of red wool on a hook. They were very thin and ranged from a size 18 on down. I started tying them with red thread for a body and built-up head. I used these for years, but something always seemed to be lacking. I knew what it was when I saw the bright red glass beads. I strung six of them on a size 18 hook, with a little red thread built up in the rear to hold them against the eye, and had instant success. I continued experimenting and eventually settled on a size 24 hook, with one red bead at the front and red tying thread as the body, as the overall most successful.

I've since tried some similar ones in other colors, khaki with a green bead being somewhat notable. I've added a gold bead just behind the eye of size 24 Diamond Midges. Some think that using materials like this pushes a fly toward the lure category. I really don't know what to say to that, but if something works, I like to use it, even if I don't understand why.

BEADHEADS

Step 1. There are some tricks to tying beadheads in the smaller sizes. The first one is *not* to start by putting the hook in the vise. The bead or beads have to go on before everything else. With sizes 12, 14, and 16 hooks and beads that have one end of the hole beveled, this is not too bad a chore, but with the smaller plastic beads, it can be a source of total frustration. First, bend down the barb on the hook, regardless of size.

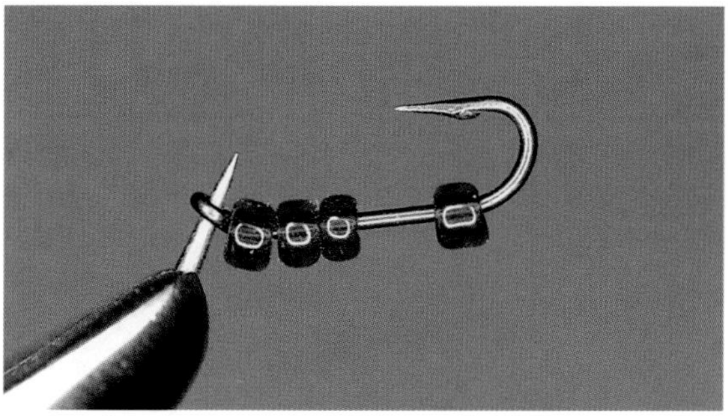

A straight pin held in a vise can be helpful when threading beads on a hook.

Step 2. Now you can do one of two things. Either hold the hook in one hand, while you place beads over the hook point with the other, or make something to hold the hook, giving you two hands to operate with. Whichever way you choose, work over a piece of soft cloth so any beads you drop will not bounce away to places unknown.

If you choose to hold the hook in your hand, hold it upside down by the hook eye, with the point lower than the eye. Pick up beads with a good pair of tweezers, and place them over the point. If you're making an all-bead fly, after putting two or three on, tip the hook and move the beads up against the eye. You'll then have to grasp it farther down the hook shank.

The other method is to place a piece of stiff wire, a straight pin, or a needle in the vise jaws, making sure it will go through the hook eye. Slide the hook onto the wire through its eye while holding it upside down, with the point lower than the eye. The beads will be a little harder to get on, but you can do it.

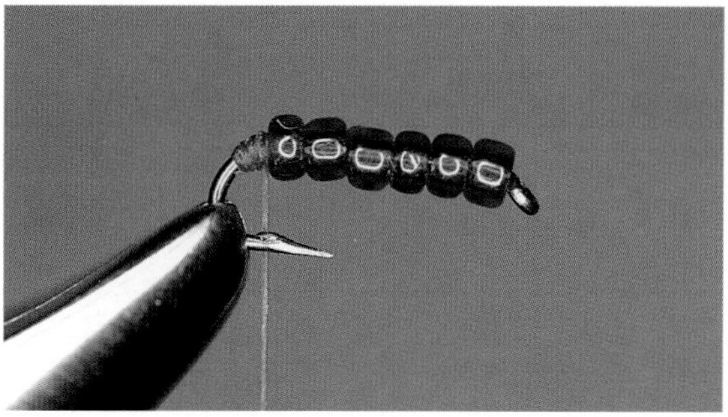

When tying an all-bead fly, use tying thread at the rear to jam the beads up against the eye.

Step 3. Once all the beads are on the hook, be it one or more, turn the hook right side up and insert it in the vise. Keeping the eye down slightly will keep the beads from sliding back onto the bend. If tying an all-bead fly, use an appropriate color tying thread to build up a little ball behind the rear bead to keep them tight against the eye. A whip-finish tool works well for this. If it's a standard one-bead fly, add a suitable body of whatever you like behind the bead. Finish with a half-hitch tool large enough to go over the bead.

LITTLE RED WORM BEADHEAD PATTERNS

Using a Mustad 94840 hook in size 24, add one red bead, and build a body with bright red tying thread. Start the thread right behind the bead, wrap back to the bend, return to the front, build up a little ball behind the bead to keep it tight, and whip-finish. This is the best pattern I've come up with for the little red worm, and it works pretty much year-round.

The second best is a Mustad 3906B hook in size 18, with six red beads for a body and a little ball of red thread at the rear to hold them on. You can also use a red floss or thread strand for the body.

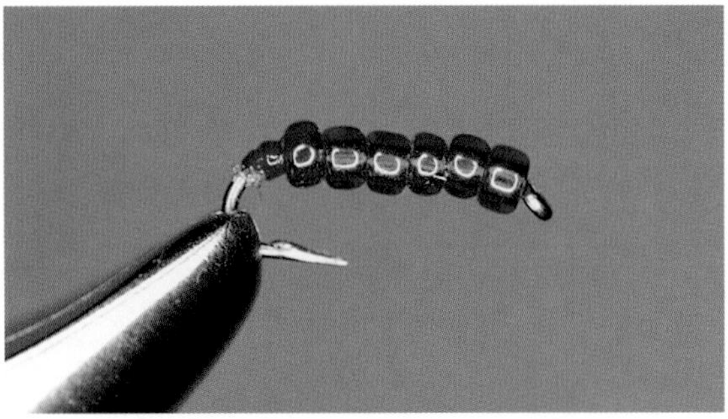

Completed all-bead fly. This pattern (which some might consider a lure) may be another answer to imitating a midge larva. The red one has been quite successful.

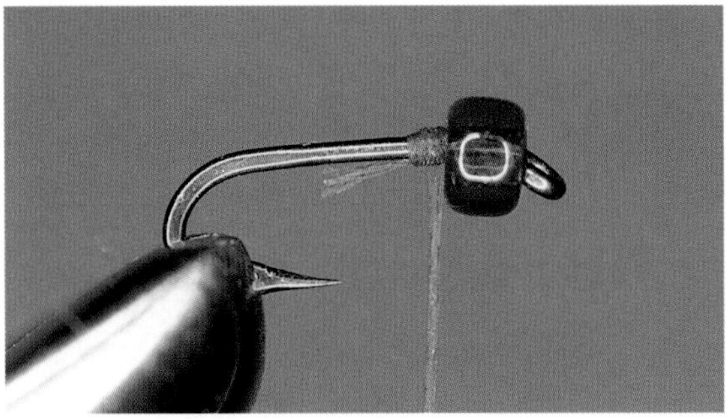

A single-bead fly.

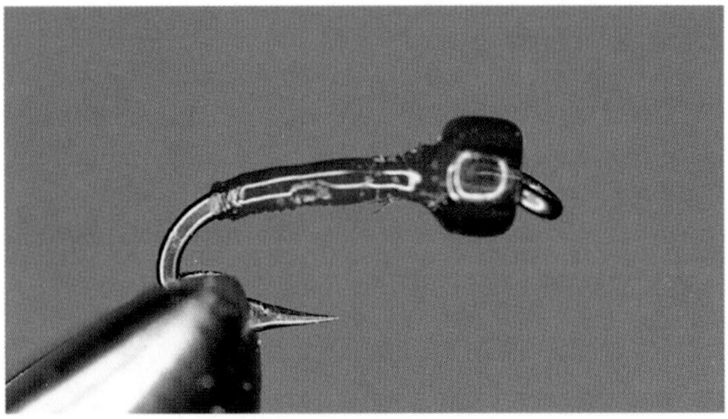

This version was completed simply by using tying thread to form the body.

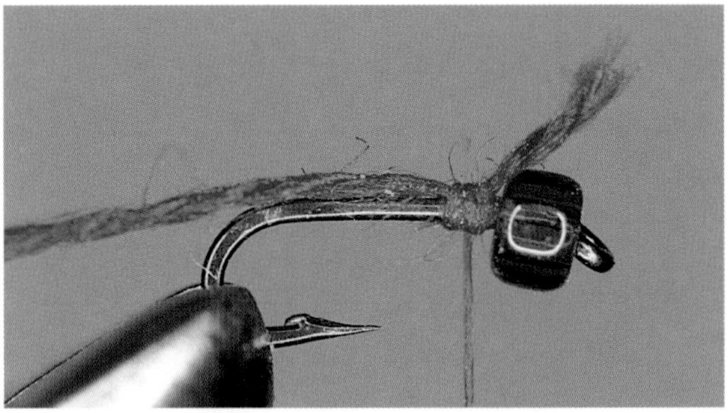

A strand of embroidery floss can be used as additional body material on a single-bead fly.

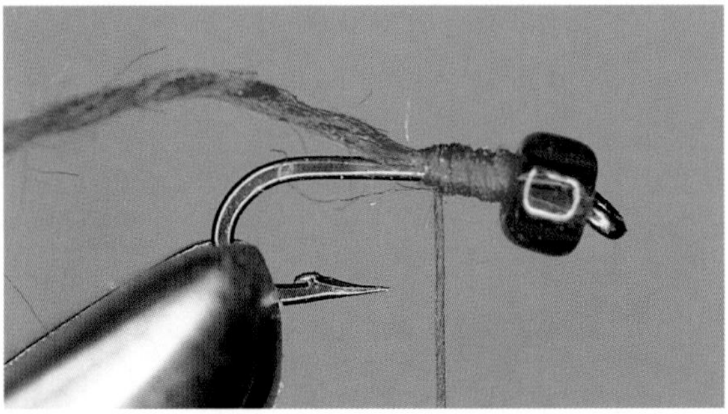

A little trick is to tie the body material in with two wraps and then pull it to the rear until the end is under the wraps. This is easier than trying to cut the end next to the bead.

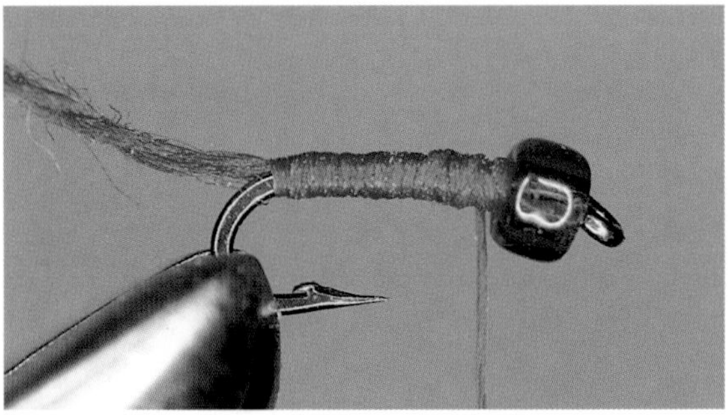

This step is similar to previous patterns. Simply run the thread back and then forward again. This makes a thinner body than if you wrapped the body material back and forth.

Wrap the body material forward, tie it off with the tying thread, and then, using a tool large enough to get over the bead, half-hitch the remaining body material behind the bead. Cement.

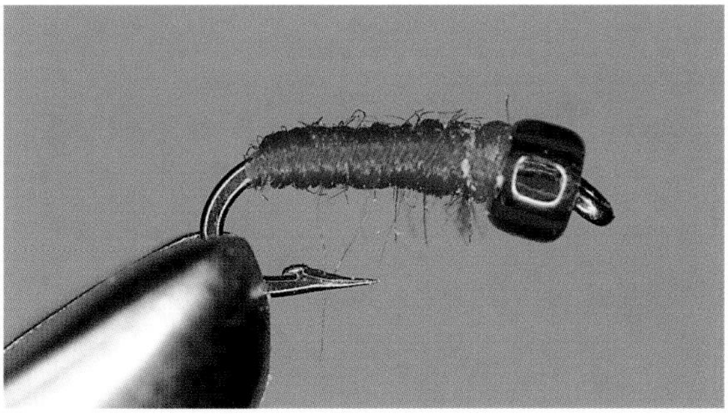

Completed size 24 DMC 666/red bead. One of the author's favorites.

26 - C&C 126/green bead.

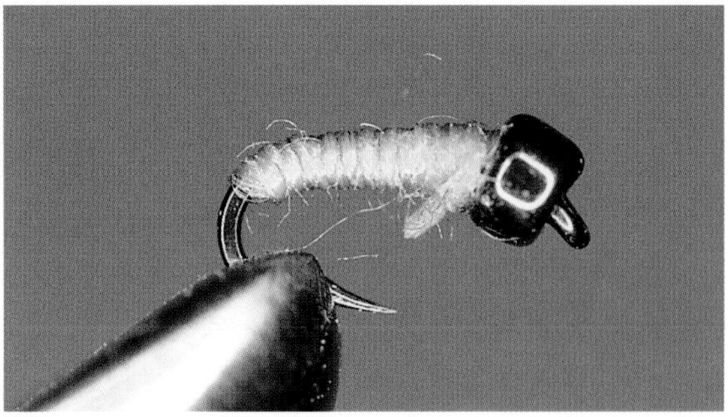

26 - C&C 361/iridescent bead.

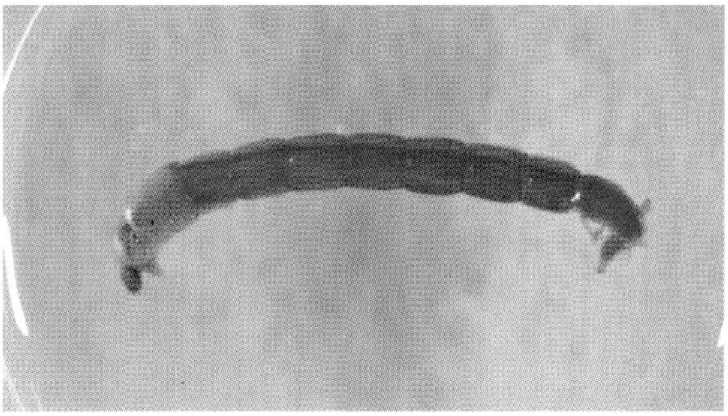

Many red patterns have been created to imitate this common midge larva, widespread in central Pennsylvania. Compare it to the all-bead flies and the larva photos in the Clear Flies chapter.

CHAPTER 9

Shrimp Patterns

Although they are not midges, freshwater shrimp are in the same size class as midge pupae, so I'm including them in this book. They're one of the most productive patterns year-round on the local streams, and not just for trout.

In 1977 I regularly ran across another fisherman who was generally quite successful, especially on the larger fish. He showed me a fly pattern one day with which he was doing quite well. The body was conventional spun cream or off-white fur, with little tufts sticking out of each end. These tufts were a topping of cream-colored feather barbules, laid on top of the body and held in position by spiraling (or palmering, if you wish) the tying thread along the body.

I used various combinations to try to duplicate this, the best having an off-white fur body with a flesh-colored topping spiraled with olive thread. Other colors have had varying degrees of success, one with a cream topping doing fairly well in the summer. Strangely, the one of this style that I thought most duplicated the natural olive shrimp coloration has been absolutely worthless. I've found some shrimp that were olive with an orange dot in the center of the back, so I tried tying one with an orange thread dot in it. I've also run across pale orange-colored shrimp in a size 20, but I haven't fished the imitation long enough to assess its long-term performance.

If I had to rate these shrimp patterns, the off-white one with the flesh-colored topping ranks at the top of the list. It's also the only one of my patterns in which I have not replaced the fur body with some other material over the years.

THE ORIGINAL SHRIMP

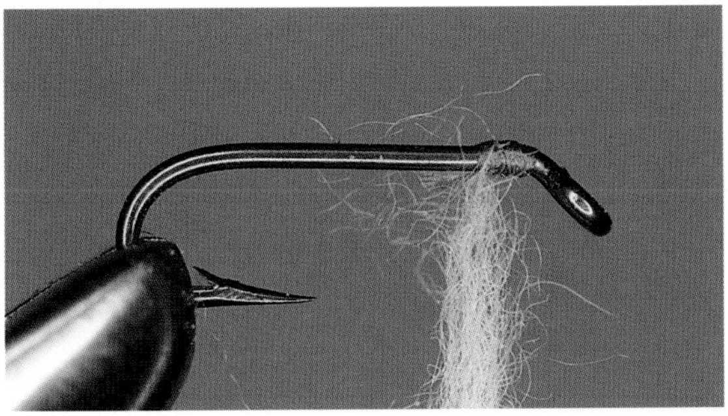

Step 1. Place a size 18 Mustad 3906B hook into the vise, and attach the olive tying thread at the front. Dub a layer of off-white fur onto the thread to form the body. I generally use a piece of bleached muskrat fur, available in all fly shops. They always seem to be the right shade, regardless of source, but if you want to check one, the color of DMC floss 746 is about perfect.

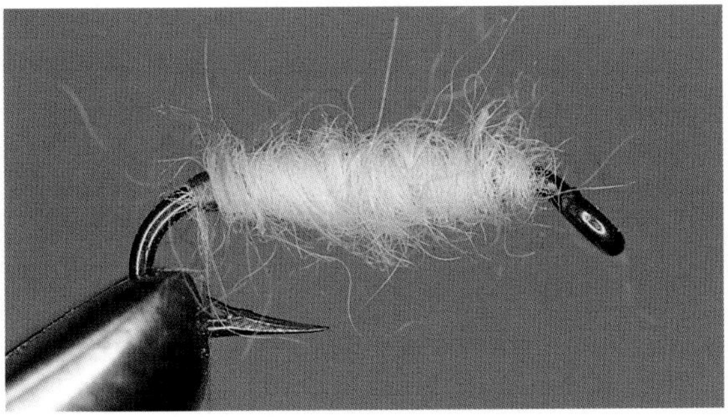

Step 2. Wind the dubbed thread from front to rear, forming a body just a little fatter than normal. You want it to be just a little wider than the topping. Leave the thread hanging at the rear of the body.

Step 3. Take a short length of DMC 950 sportsman flesh color six-strand cotton embroidery floss, and lay it lengthwise on top of the fur body and extending out over the ends. (I've also had success with DMC 712 cream color floss for the topping.) Tie it down on top of the hook at the rear of the body with several turns of the tying thread.

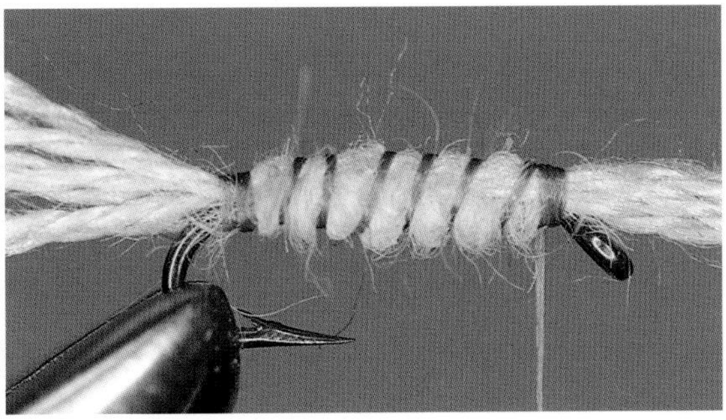

Step 4. Hold the strand by the front, and pull it tight along the top of the body. Spiral the tying thread to the front in about six turns, and tie off at the front of the body with several turns of thread.

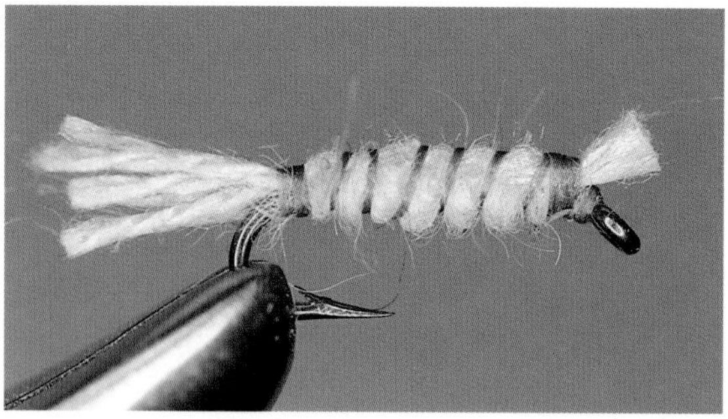

Completed Original Shrimp.

Step 5. Cut off the floss strand to a length of about 1/8 inch at the front and a little longer at the rear of the fly. Move the thread in front of the cut strand, and whip-finish the thread at the eye. Offset the hook slightly.

ORANGE DOT SHRIMP

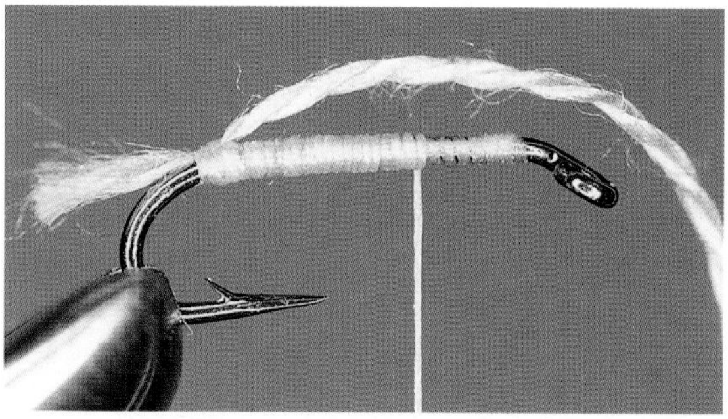

Forming the tail.

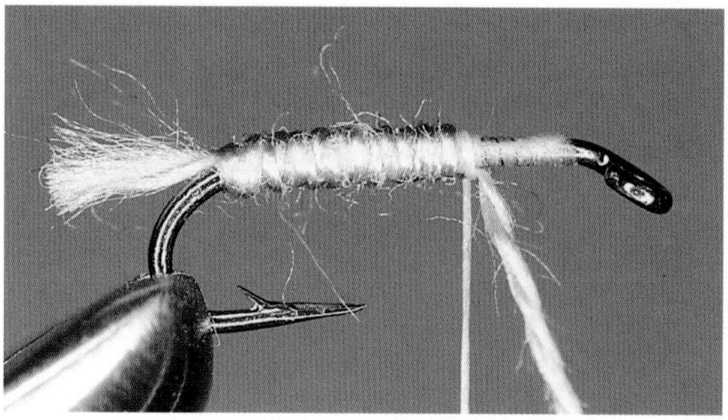

Wrap the body two-thirds of the hook length.

Step 1. Place a size 18 Mustad 3906B hook in the vise, and attach 6/0 white tying thread at the front. Wind an even layer of thread to the bend. Tie in one 6-inch strand of DMC 3013 light khaki green cotton embroidery floss on top of the hook, with one end extending to the rear about 1/8 inch. Wind the thread two-thirds of the way to the eye and let it hang. Wrap the floss strand forward in tight turns forming the body. Tie it off at the thread position.

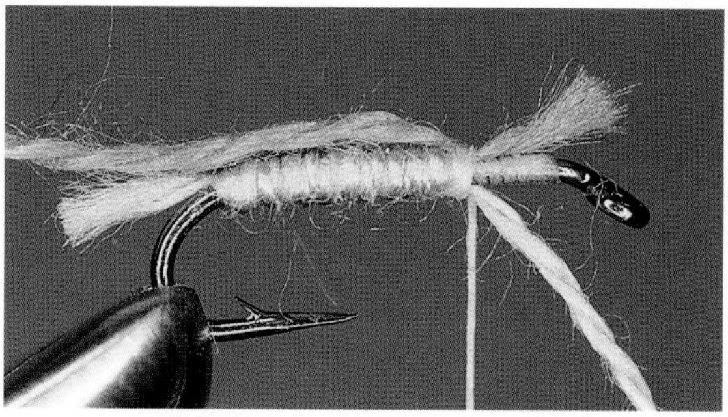

Adding the orange floss.

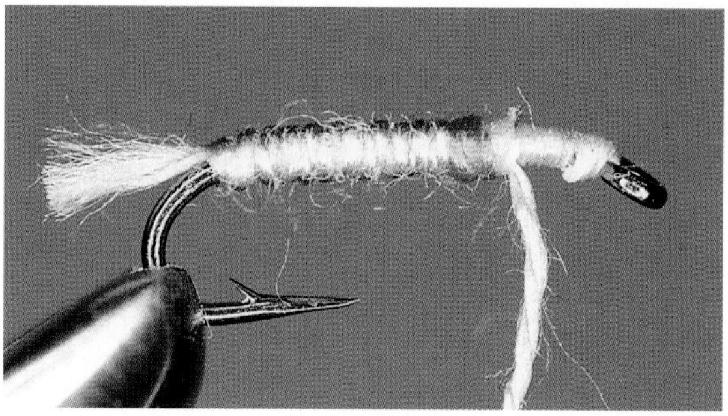

Forming the orange dot. (You could, instead, pull the orange over the top of the next khaki wrap and form what would look more like a dot.)

Step 2. Tie in one strand of DMC 740 tangerine floss at this point, with the long end to the rear. Wrap one turn of this floss around the hook, tie off, and trim the excess. This step forms the orange dot. Half-hitch the tying thread, and cut it off.

A head was formed on this pattern to represent legs.

Step 3. Using the remaining khaki floss strand, and starting just ahead of the orange wrap, wrap it to the eye and back to the orange dot. Then half-hitch it two or three times as if it were tying thread. Snug the hitches tight.

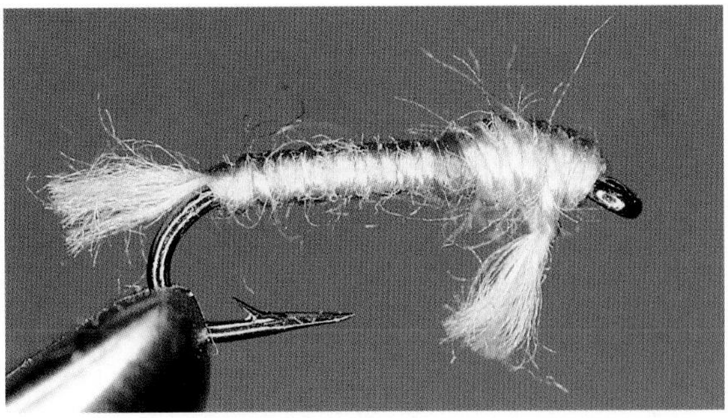

Completed Orange Dot Shrimp.

Step 4. Make sure the last hitch ends with the tag end on the bottom of the hook. Trim it off so it reaches almost to the midhook position. Cement the front wraps with thinned vinyl cement, and use your bodkin needle to flare the front and rear tag ends by pushing on the ends with the side of the needle. I've had the most luck with this one in late summer.

LIGHT TANGERINE SHRIMP

Tying in the body material and forming the tag.

Return the thread forward.

Step 1. Place a size 20 Mustad 94840 hook in the vise, and attach white 6/0 tying thread at the front. Wind it back to the bend in even wraps. Attach one strand of DMC 742 light tangerine cotton embroidery floss on top of the hook, with the tag end extending out the rear about 1/8 inch or less. Return the thread to just behind the eye.

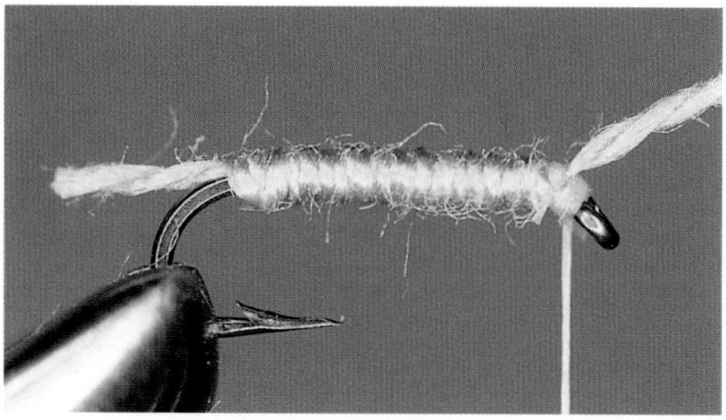

Wrap the body material forward.

Step 2. Wrap the floss strand to the front in tight turns, forming the body. Tie it off at the eye and whip-finish, making sure the floss tag end is on top.

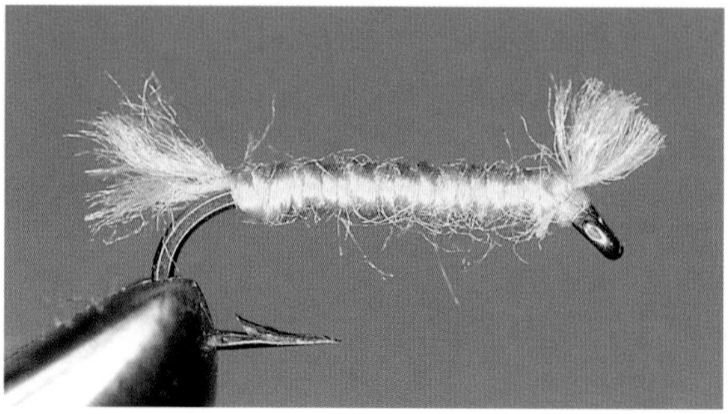

Completed Light Tangerine Shrimp.

Step 3. Cut the thread, trim the front tag the same as the rear one, and fluff the ends with a bodkin needle. This is a recent pattern and is simpler than the others. It appears to have promise.

What trout fishermen commonly identify as freshwater shrimp.

CHAPTER 10

Topwater Patterns

I never fished dry flies much, even though my first fish caught on a fly was with an Adams dry. The Cumberland Valley, where I've lived and fished the past thirty years, has heavy sulfur and white-fly hatches, among others. And I'll fish these hatches during those times. I was just never too interested in prospecting with a dry when I knew they were eating nymphs. I did like to tie them, though. Of all the categories of flies, I think my drys were my best work. And I fished the little midge dry patterns out of Ed's *Fishing the Midge* book with success. The only problem back then was finding hackle that small and at a price a young tier could afford. Good grizzly was pretty much available locally but at a premium price. Other colors were a little harder to come by. Still, we made do with what we could get. Ed Shenk's No-Name Midge pattern used grizzly hackle and muskrat fur, which I could obtain inexpensively, as I trapped muskrats, and I caught many fish on these over the years.

When poly wing material hit the market, everybody started tying spinners for all the major mayfly hatches. I began tying them in size 22 with dun hackle tails and tying thread of various colors for the body. Since I caught as many fish on these spinners as I ever did on conventional hackled drys, there seemed to be no point in bothering with the drys.

Oh, there are a couple of favorites I won't let go of, and I'm experimenting with bodies similar to those of the Rainbow Midges. And I've started floating nymphs during hatches after losing my leader weight one night and wondering why I suddenly started catching fish.

Study the shapes, colorations, and proportions of midge adults, such as this one and those in the following photos, before you start designing your own midge drys. The smaller insects tend to have stubbier bodies.

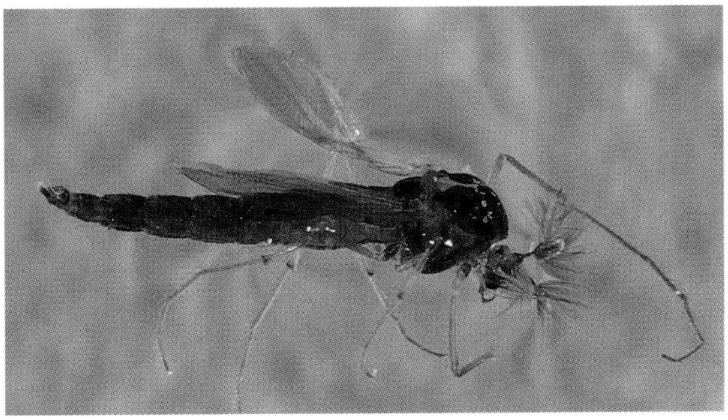

Notice the leg and wing coloration on this midge adult. A poly wing other than clear might be best to imitate it.

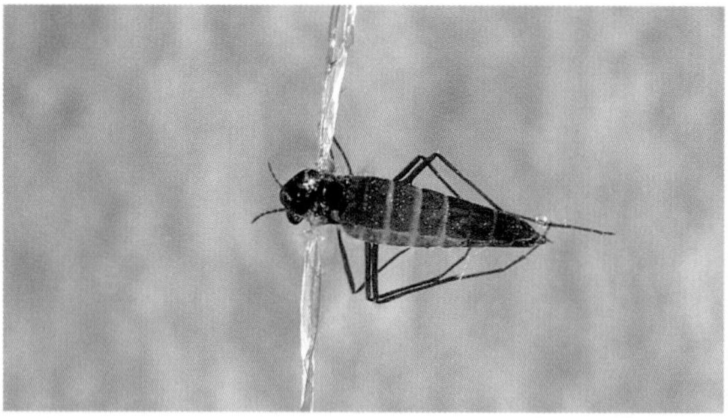

A clear poly wing with a few strands of black mixed in might work to imitate this midge adult.

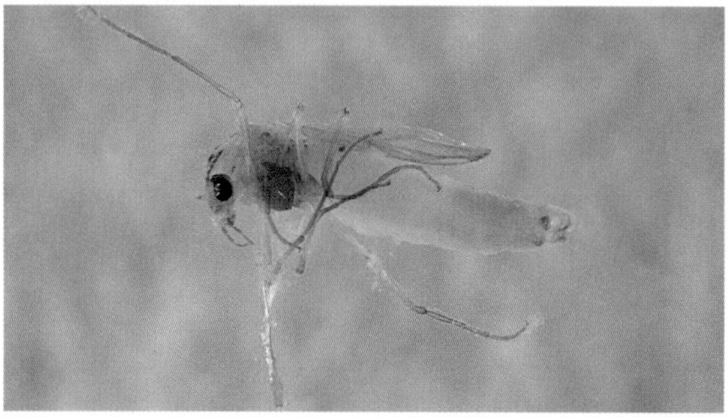

Midge adult.

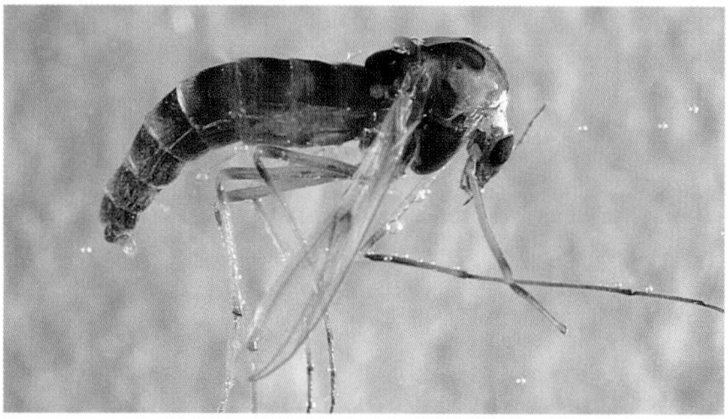

What color would you call this midge adult if it flew by you? Best to catch one and inspect it closely.

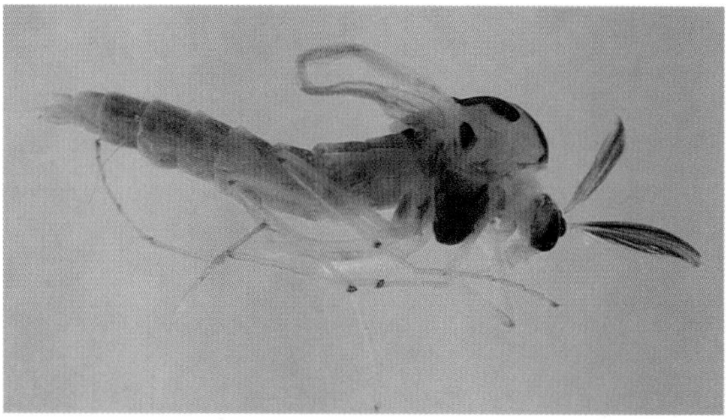

Midge adult.

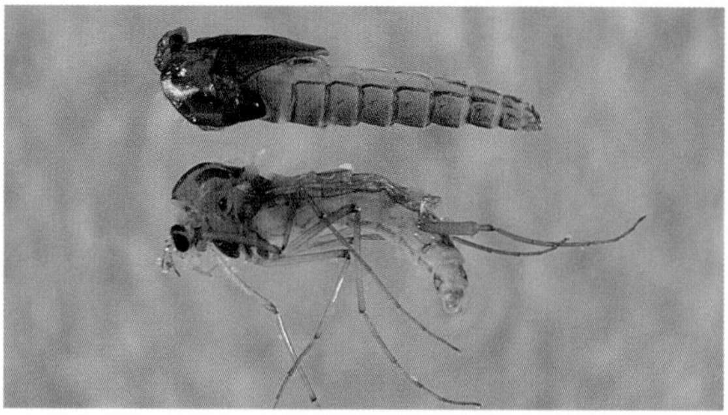

This and the accompanying photos show midge pupae and the corresponding adults. Sometimes the pupa looks like the adult, but sometimes not.

Midge pupa and adult.

Midge pupa and adult.

Midge pupa and adult.

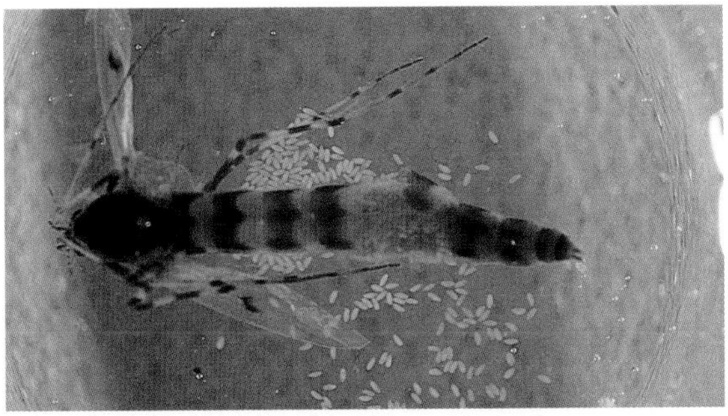

This pupa was accidentally broken while being photographed, releasing an unbelievable number of eggs.

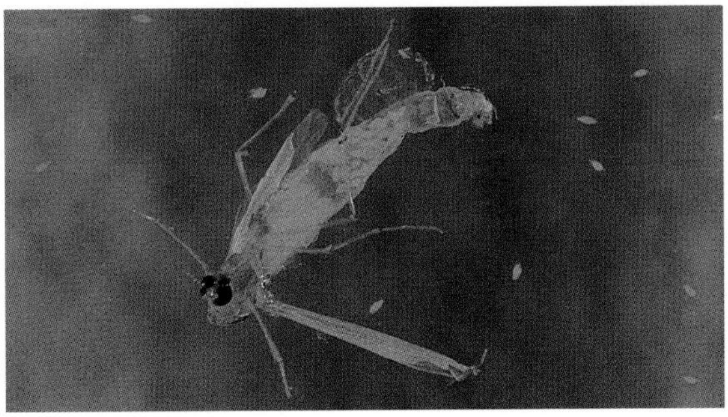

After the eggs are laid, there's not much left.

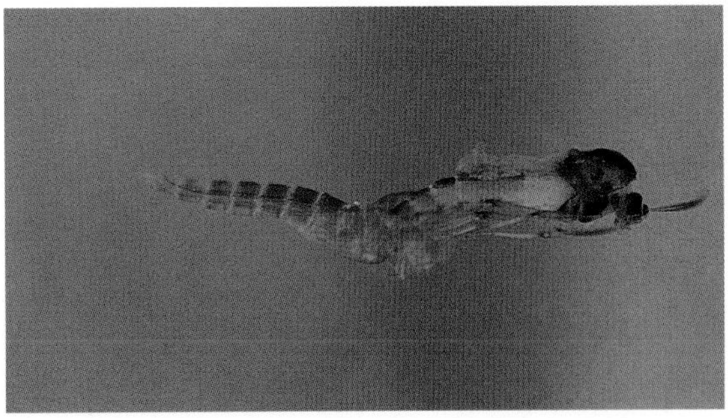

Stages of a pupa emerging from its shuck are shown in this and the following photos.

Not all escape perfectly.

Almost there.

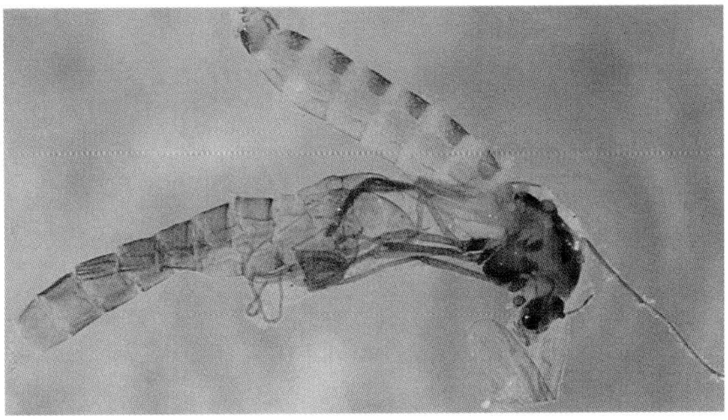

Free at last.

TOPWATER PATTERNS

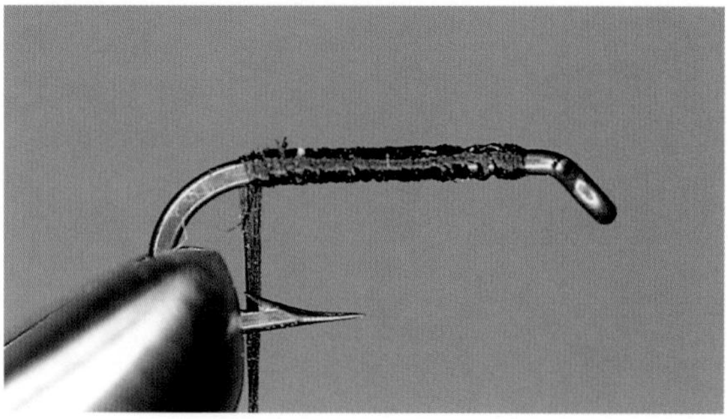

Step 1. You can tie these in any size you want, but a size 22 Mustad 94840 hook should match most midge hatches you'll run into (barring, of course, those evil ones size 40 and smaller). Insert the hook into the vise, and attach the tying thread at the front. I generally use 6/0 for 22s, but since the thread is the body color, you can use something else if the color is right.

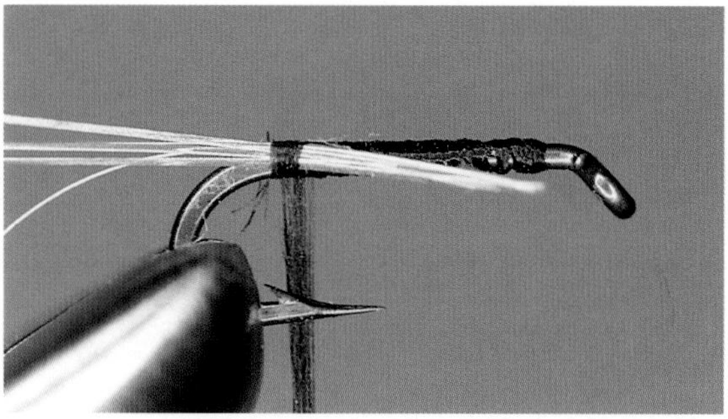

Lightly tie the tail fibers on the side of the hook.

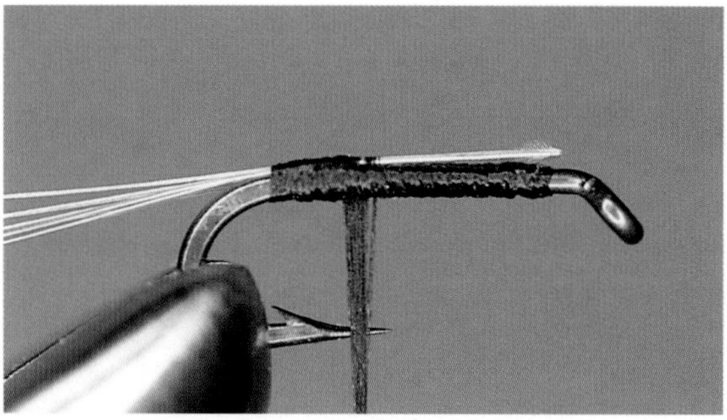

Roll the tail fibers to the top of the hook with thread pressure.

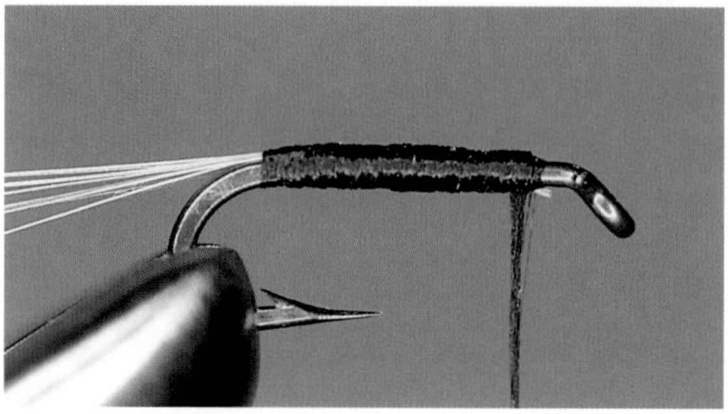

Wrap the body thread forward.

Step 2. Wrap the thread to a point just above the barb. Select your tailing material. I sometimes use the synthetic Micro Fibetts, in which case I only use three fibers. Normally, though, I use four or five fibers from the short, stubby hackles at the base of a light blue dun saddle. They are very stiff, and I feel they handle a little better than the synthetics. If you use hackle fibers, cut the webby base ends off after you pull them off the feather, and they will tie in easier.

With such a small hook, some tiers have difficulty tying the fibers on top of the hook using the normal procedure of holding them on top, looping the thread between the finger and thumb, and pulling down. Tie in the tail at the thread location by holding the fibers by the tips and positioning them on the side of the hook toward you at a slight angle from horizontal. Take one light turn of thread over them, pinning them to the side of the hook. Then, while still holding them by the tips, take one more turn right in front of the first, with a little bit more pressure. If done right, this will roll the fibers almost onto the top of the hook. Another turn, just a little tighter still, will finish the job and make as perfect a tail as you've ever tied. Practice with a few until you know exactly where to place the fibers so they'll roll on top correctly every time. I like long tails, one and a half or two times the body length, maybe even longer, because I think they look better. This won't affect hooking the fish; they eat bigger things than this. Wrap the tying thread forward in even turns, stopping about one eye width back of the eye. Trim the excess tailing.

Tie the poly wing on, parallel to the hook.

Pull the front and rear halves of the wing, one side at a time, at right angles to the hook and bind them down with cross turns.

The fly is finished, except for trimming the wings to length.

Step 3. Select a piece of poly type material for the spinner wing. Look at all the material in the fly shop, and pick the shiniest, clearest one that is suitable. Tie in a piece consisting of about ten or fifteen fibers about ¾ inch long, so you can handle it, on top of the hook at the thread location. It can be difficult to figure-eight this onto such a small hook in the normal manner, but there's an easier way. The wing will have a little kink to it when done this way, if you look at it from the top, but it doesn't bother the fish. Hold the fibers on top of the hook and parallel to the shank. Tie them on with two or three easy wraps. Pull the rear half straight toward you, and take two or three cross turns front to rear. The thread will now be hanging behind the wing location. Hold the front half straight out away from you, and take some cross turns from rear to front. A couple more each way and a little tweaking will work wonders. Touch on a little thinned vinyl cement. Whip-finish in front of the wing, and cut the thread. Cut the wing to length. Keep it shorter than the body or it will spin. Give it a touch of silicone paste, and it will float forever.

Although you can tie these spinners as small as size 28, the tying gets more difficult the smaller you go. As I mention in chapter 7, I've been experimenting with floating midge pupae patterns in the surface film by working a little silicone paste into their bodies. I've had exceptional success with size 26 midge pupae patterns fished in this manner, and I believe they will eventually replace spinners as my topwater pattern of choice. Although best suited to flat water, these patterns—in the right color—will catch every rising trout in reach.

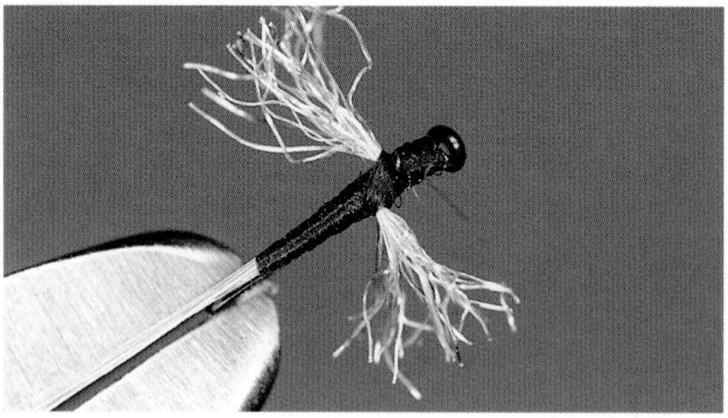

Top view of the finished fly, showing wing proportions.

Size 22 Brown Thread Spinner.

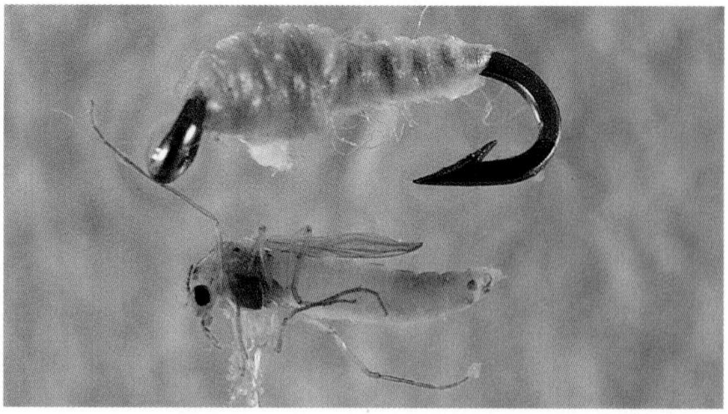

A floating pupa pattern. Very effective in the 26 to 28 range.

A size 20 floating pupa pattern. Add a very light coating of silicone paste.

CHAPTER 11

Peacock Patterns

The first midge pattern I ever fished was one Ed Koch gave me in his fly shop in Boiling Springs in the fall of 1974. I hadn't been having any luck on the Yellow Breeches, and I stopped in. He suggested I try this little size 18 gray nymph with a muskrat fur body and a couple turns of peacock herl at the front. He tied one to show me how to do it, and gave it to me. I immediately caught four fish in the Yellow Breeches, including the largest one I had ever caught to date.

I still carry herl midges with me, though I don't fish them as much. I can only fish so many patterns in a day, and I'm constantly trying something new that I've dreamed up. But they're there, and I know when to use them.

When I was first taught to tie flies at the Carlisle Fish and Game winter program, the instructors marked patterns in our books that they thought we should try. Otherwise, we probably would have tied the whole book. Quite a few of them were peacock-bodied flies, and I always did well on them. Add to this the fact that peacock feathers seem to work magic when you turn them in the light and watch the iridescent colors change before your eyes. I don't care what it is—if it has peacock in it, I like it.

Probably one of my early reasons for not fishing drys was that I was not very good at casting. I only owned heavy rods, which didn't help on these small streams, but my own ineptness was a bigger problem. Still, I was somewhat fascinated by the many rising fish when the midges hatched in the early evenings on the Big Spring Creek, near Newville, Pennsylvania. Occasionally I'd hear the splashing of a fish being caught and would look around to see a lady releasing a trout back into the stream. She had a little dog that dutifully followed her along the bank (no wading was allowed in this section) and waited while she cast to the next rising fish. She didn't miss too many, and it got to where I would step back when she got to the area I was fishing and invite her to fish through. She did, and she caught most of the risers. I didn't perceive this as a problem, as I was normally fishing nymphs, so we were after different quarry—and I wasn't having much success on the top, anyway. This went on for two or three years, with not much more than a polite hello.

Then, one very hot July evening in 1977, I had been catching fish until they started rising, but then I couldn't touch a fish. I even resorted to fishing dry flies on top, to no avail. Hearing that now familiar noise, I looked around to see her releasing another trout. She worked her way up to where I was waiting. I couldn't take it any longer. I just had to ask what she was using. To my great surprise, she showed me a little size 26 dry fly with a peacock herl body and white hackle and tails. She gave me one and made me promise not to show it to anyone, and I didn't—until now.

The lady is Peg Myers, from Newville. She doesn't tie these flies—her husband, Barry, does it. I suspect it's really his pattern, but I'm not going to ask. She may have another secret one I can weasel out of her some day. This is another pattern I wouldn't be without.

PEACOCK PATTERNS

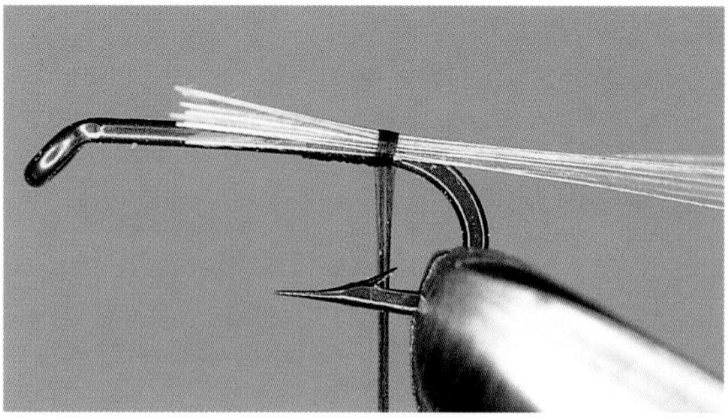

Tie the tail fibers slightly to the side of the hook at a little bit of an angle.

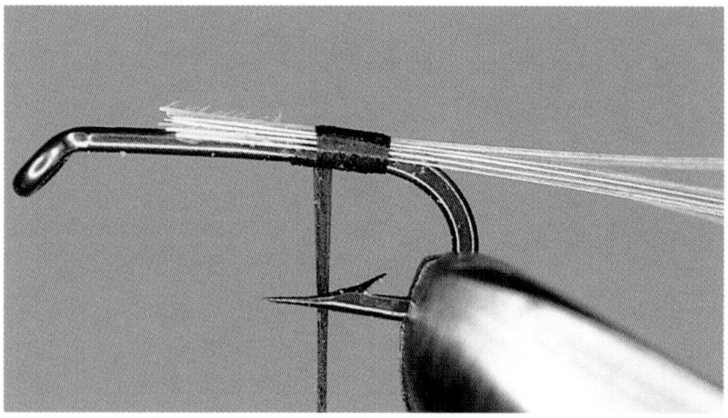

Roll the tail fibers on top with a couple of tighter turns of thread. You can also tie them on the conventional way—by pinching on top.

Step 1. Insert a size 24 Mustad 94840 hook in the vise, and attach tying thread near the hook point. Wrap the thread to the rear, just above the barb. Using three or four white or palest cream hackle fibers for the tail, tie them in at this point by holding them on the side of the hook and letting the thread roll them on top, as in the chapter on topwater patterns. Make them twice the hook length. Try to use only three turns.

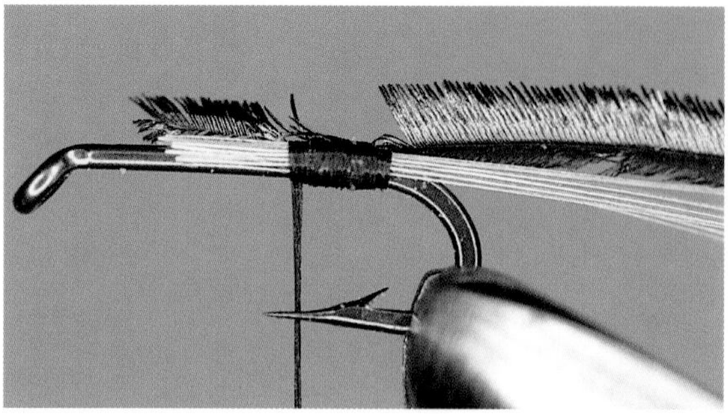

Step 2. Select the smallest peacock herl you can find, and tie it in by the tip at the point where the thread hangs. Gently stroke the fibers on the stem if you like them to stand up. Take two turns of thread to the rear, which should put you at the point where the tail was tied in. Return the thread to the front in tight turns, stopping just far enough behind the eye for three hackle wraps and a tiny head.

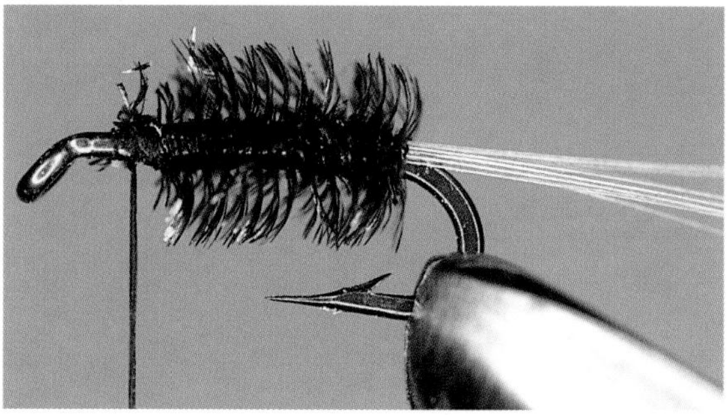

Step 3. Wrap the peacock forward, and tie off where the thread hangs.

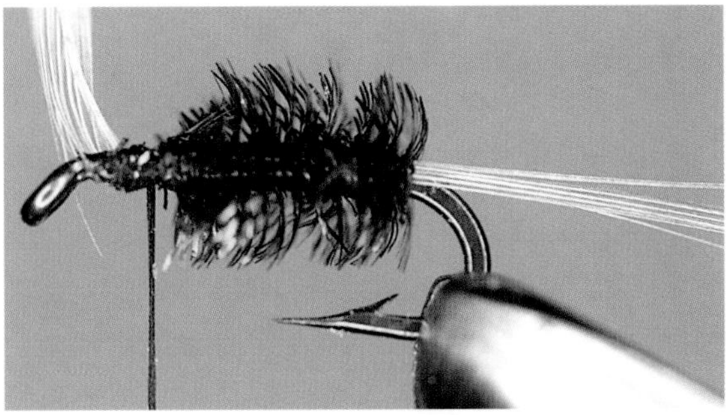

Here's an unusual way of hackling a dry fly. Whichever method you use, go easy on the turns.

Step 4. Select a white hackle of about two times the hook gap. The little ones are hard to come by, so do the best you can. Use pale cream or the lightest blue dun if you have to. Tie it in on top of the hook shank by the tip, dull side down. Let the tip lie back through the peacock body, with the rest extending out over the eye. This makes it easier to handle. Make no more than three turns of hackle, and tie off. Trim the excess feather. Always whip-finish these small drys. You won't have to use cement, which can get on the rest of the fly in these sizes.

Completed Peg's Midge Dry, size 24.

A size 26 Peg's Midge Dry, tied by Peg Myer's husband, Barry.

ED KOCH'S MIDGE CADDIS NYMPHS

Ed Koch got me started on midge flies with that little gray caddis nymph he gave me, and since I had some success using them, I eventually got around to buying a copy of his book *Fishing the Midge.* There were about a dozen patterns in the book, and I tried them all. I did the best when fishing the caddis nymph patterns, and they quickly became my favorites. They are some of the few fur-based patterns I still carry.

I carry only three of them now, in a size 18: a muskrat gray, an olive (leaning toward brown rather than green), and a tan one almost always tied with bleached mole fur. If you ever fish the Yellow Breeches during the heat of summer, make sure you run the little tan one through the riffles if you're not having much success. I'm always amazed at how many times I stop and talk to someone on the stream and see one of these flies in his or her box.

Here are Ed's original tying instructions. I never noticed before this that all the photographs in his book were printed as if tied left-handed. Maybe that's why I liked them so much, as I tied that way too. But since most of you tie right-handed, I've tied them that way for the accompanying photos.

ED KOCH'S MIDGE CADDIS NYMPHS

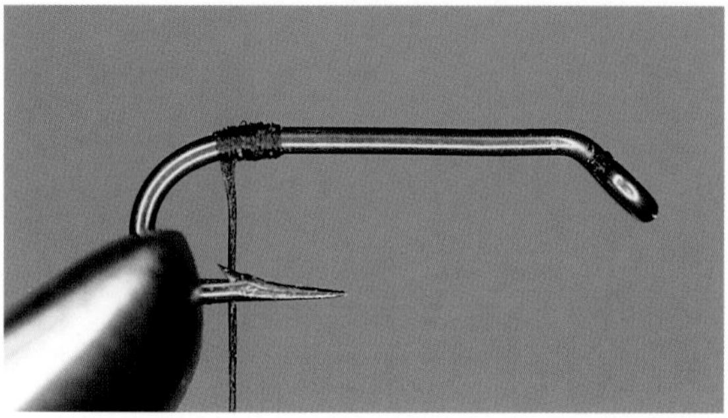

Step 1. Insert the hook in the vise, and attach the thread directly above the barb of the hook.

Step 2. Dub a small amount of fur on the thread. Wrap an evenly tapered body forward to the hook eye, and half-hitch to secure.

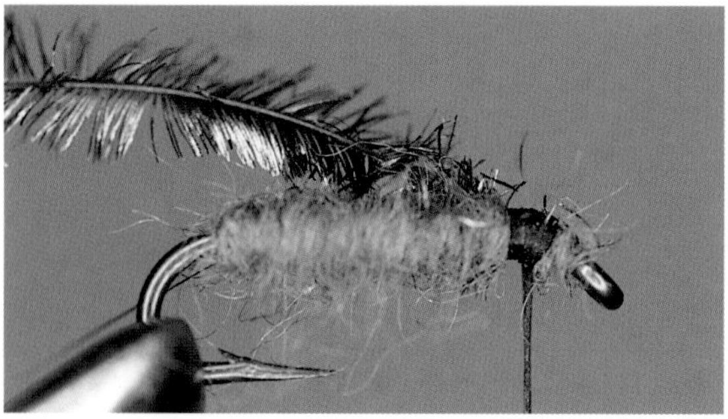

Step 3. Tie in a single strand of peacock herl.

Completed Caddis Nymph.

Step 4. Wrap two or three turns of peacock herl for the head. Tie it off and half-hitch to secure.

Step 5. Wrap the head with thread, whip-finish, and apply head cement.

This tan pattern is the author's personal favorite.

Ed Koch carries his Midge Caddis Nymphs in four sizes: 14, 16, 18, and 20. PHOTO BY NORM SHIRES

CHAPTER 12

Orphans

The flies in this chapter don't fit in anywhere else. They are one of a kind. While I'm very confident in all the patterns presented in this book, I'm realistic enough to know that nothing works all the time, even when the conditions are the same as the last time. You know what I mean. That's why you always need to carry a variety of patterns.

FAT BOYS

When I was first learning to tie, one of the patterns I was taught was the Sucker Spawn Fly, made of sheep's wool. Not long after that, I was introduced to Honeybugs, which are originally from northern Pennsylvania and are made from a certain type of chenille wrapped around a short hook. Later on, I was given flies that were simply white fur nymphs, with no tails, wing cases, or anything else. For reasons I never understood, trout would sometimes hit a plain white fly.

One day, for lack of something better to do, I took a piece of white embroidery floss, all six strands, and tied it onto a hook so the stub end stuck out as a short tail. I wrapped the rest forward to form a body, and I made a head with the six-stranded floss by half-hitching it. I cut it off, leaving a nice stub underneath. It works about as well as the aforementioned flies and is easier to tie. I've tried several colors. It's just something else to fool with in your spare time.

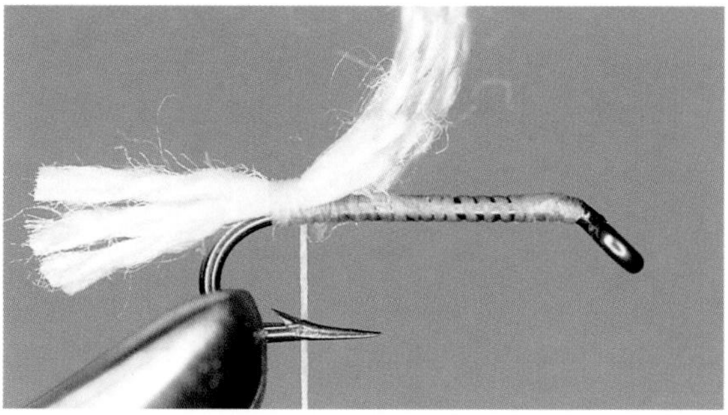

All six strands of floss are used for the body of the Fat Boy.

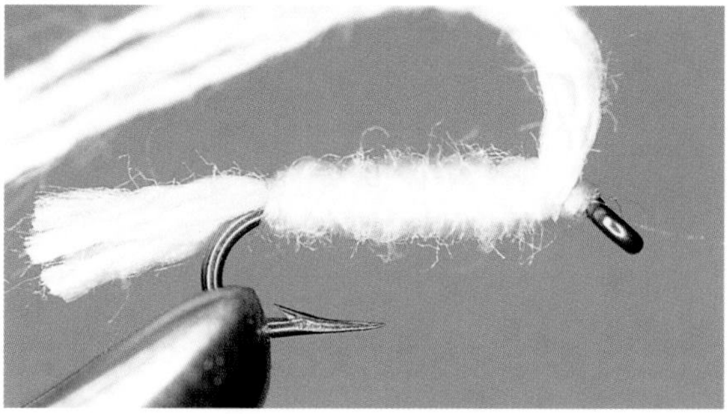

Cut the thread off after half-hitching the body.

Using a large half-hitch tool, form the head area with the remaining floss and let the tag end hang out the bottom to represent legs.

Cream Fat Boy, size 18.

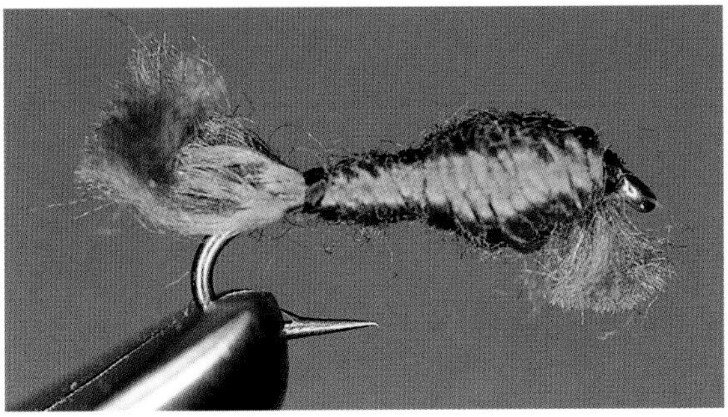

Olive Fat Boy, size 18.

WET FLIES

You don't see many people fishing wet flies anymore. I guess they're no longer stylish. Gene Utech, the retired local game warden, still fishes them religiously, three to a cast. On several occasions, I've taken a midge pupa fly that wasn't working quite like I thought it should and added a poly wet wing. Almost without fail, its effectiveness increased dramatically. It's especially effective on size 24 flies.

Tying in the wing at the front in the conventional manner didn't suit me. So, using four or five fibers of a clear poly wing material, I tied them in at the body tie-off point, just before I formed the head with half-hitches. Make it long enough to work with, and then trim it off at body length. Tie your Trico this way and try it. You might be surprised.

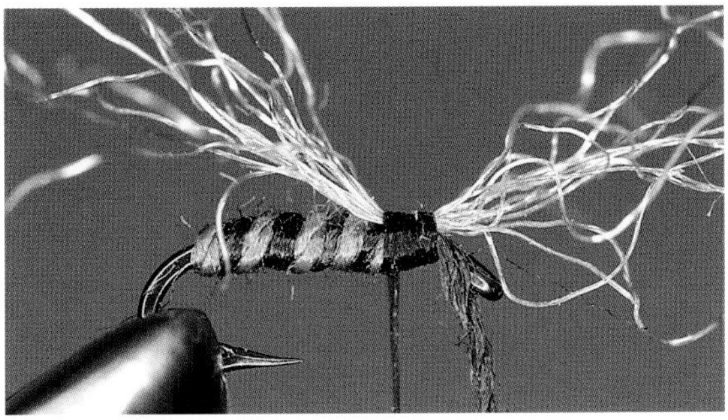

Tie in the wing before you form the head.

Forming the head.

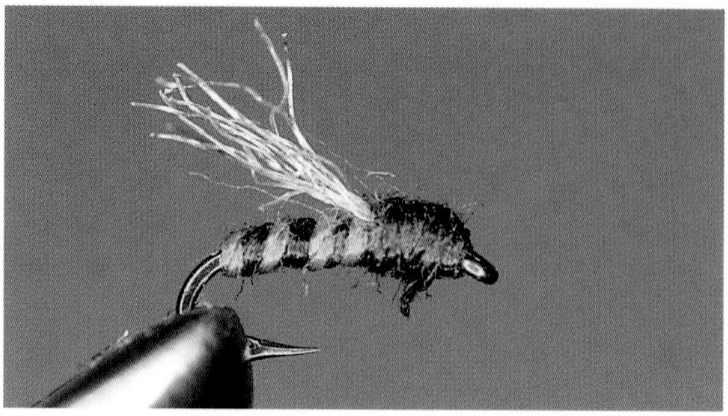

Completed Rainbow Wet.

WEIKERT MIDGE LARVAE

Years ago, I liked fishing Weikert Run, a little tributary to Penns Creek in Union County, Pennsylvania. It's since become pretty acidic and is no longer stocked in the upper stretches. But the crowds are gone, too, so you can fish undisturbed.

One spring day, I was looking under rocks in the run to see what insects might be clinging to them, when I spotted the prettiest little midge larva. After taking it home and examining it, I decided that I could imitate it using the technique of the Rainbow Midge Pattern, but leaving off the large head. I had a good color match for the body: one strand each of DMC floss 3013, light khaki green, and 712, cream. Tie them off at the front and cut the excess, then form a cylindrical head with your tying thread just a little longer than normal. In this case, a reddish brown BCS 76 tying thread was very close. This pattern in a size 18 has worked in several streams for me. If midge larvae of this color are not in your area, the style may still be of use to imitate the ones that are.

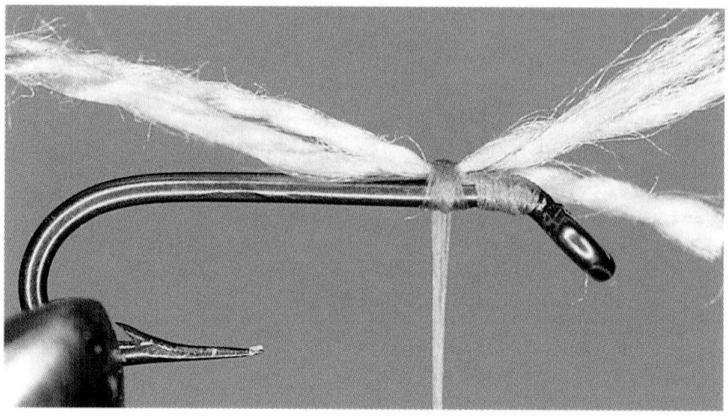

Tie this just like a Rainbow Midge, but leave off the enlarged head. Pick a thread color to match the color of the insect's head.

Wrap the tying thread to the rear and return.

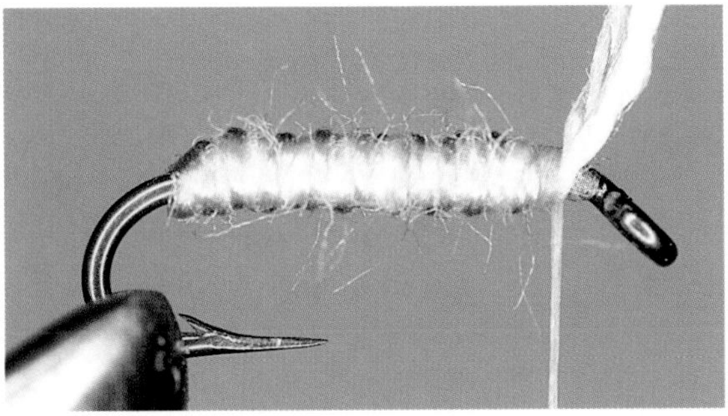

Wrap the body strands forward, tie off and trim the excess.

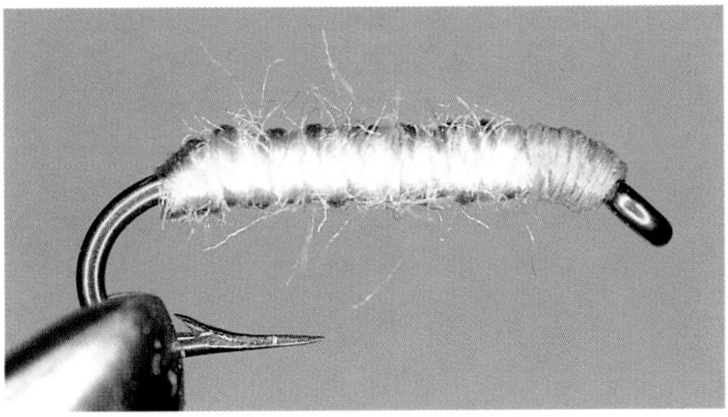

Form a thread head no bigger in diameter than the body. (For reference, see midge larva photos in chapter 5.)

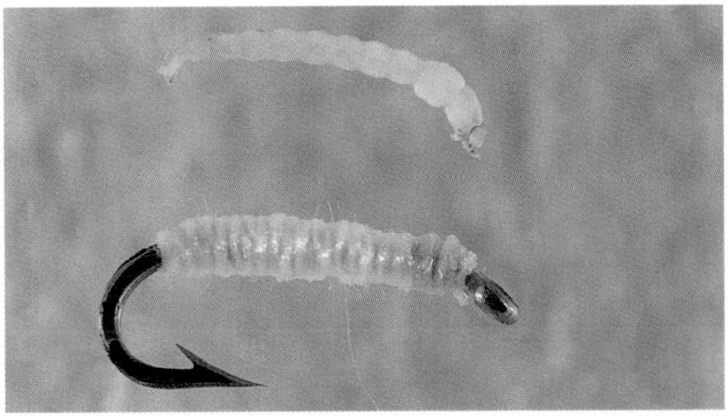

A size 24 single-color pattern: C&C 295A body with a BCS 94 thread head.

CHAPTER 13

Elk River 32s

In 1998 I had the pleasure of meeting three West Virginia die-hard fly fishermen: Sam Knotts, a guide who runs Appalachian Fly Fishing Guide Service; Dave Breitmeier, a guide for the Elk River Trout Ranch and a Pennsylvania transplant who fell in love with the Elk River some twenty years ago; and Ken Yufer, a Pennsylvania transplant by way of the navy who discovered the Elk almost thirty years ago. They turned out to be three of the most dedicated fly fishers and conservationists it has been my pleasure to call friends. The following is but a small part of what these three have been involved in over the years.—Ed Koch

A pool filled with rising trout on a beautiful stream is the perpetual dream of all fly fishermen. Add a host of little white insects, and you have the recipe for more than five years of bedevilment for Dave Breitmeier and Ken Yufer, who were two frustrated fly fishermen. The fertile limestone waters of the catch-and-release section of the Elk River near Monterville, West Virginia, have an impressive variety of invertebrate life, often producing multiple hatches. The river has all the traditional eastern hatches except Tricos. After midsummer, small insects dominate. A typical netting on late September afternoons since the fishermen first started sampling in 1994 produces size 24 to 28 *Chironomids,* size 22 black-fly larvae, a few Pseudocloeon spinners, and numerous size 32 or smaller insects, predominantly down-wing specimens. The last netting after dark usually reveals hundreds of the little unknowns that have been christened "white ghosts" by Dave and Ken.

So far, these insects remain unidentified scientifically, although Ed Koch has sent samples to entomologist Greg Hoover at Penn State. If anyone can identify them, Greg can. What we do know about them is this: They are a true size 32 with white down-wings. Most have primrose (pale yellow) bodies, although some are cream and others green. They appear in the greatest numbers from early September to mid-October. At the peak of the hatch, the numbers can be staggering, and they form dense, white clouds. Trout are quite fond of them, and they are often responsible for frantic surface feeding. When the little whites are on, they are the only thing the trout want. Find a hatch and phenomenal fishing is possible; fail to do so and a long evening ensues.

A couple years ago, Dave and Ken were growing frustrated over a recurring phenomenon. In early autumn, the late-afternoon fishing typically went well for the pair. The trout sipped black *Chironomid* pupae in the film freely and took size 32 vertical CDC emergers treated with a fly-sinking liquid on 8X tippet. As the evening wore on, a switch to a white size 28 CDC emerger usually worked briefly, but more and more trout were taking the white ghosts. By dusk, a fog of little white insects appeared, with trout rising everywhere, and Dave and Ken were having no success. Their size 28 white patterns looked like salmon flies compared with the naturals.

One night after fishing, the two men relaxed with gin and tonics at the Elk River Trout Ranch and tried to shake off their frustration. The trout's switch to a different hatch was expected—it's a major part of the river's challenge.

But they were puzzled over the size of the white insects and how exclusively the trout fed on them—even large trout. They became determined to do something about it. To start with, they needed size 32 hooks. Patterns short-tied on size 28s worked well only with the help of encroaching darkness.

Repeated punishment by the white ghosts fueled a long pursuit, but invariably Dave and Ken were met with raised eyebrows and headshakes, and even outright derision. But finally, in August 1998, they scored. They got two hundred size 32 gold-plated eyeless Mustad hooks from a small shop in Virginia. Dave spent countless hours learning to tie patterns that might work. There are several prevalent size 32 or smaller insects that the trout take; he and Ken wanted to try the others too.

It was finally time for the first test. Spentwing size 32 whites tied on 8X tippets were offered to the trout for their approval. The trout took the little fly with total confidence and satisfying regularity, but the tiny hook gap didn't provide enough grip, or the 8X mono loop cinched to the hook shank to form the eye pulled out, or the 8X and subsequently tried 9X simply weren't up to the task. Over the next two months, the fishermen were able to get only about 30 percent of the trout to hand. None were bigger than 15 inches, with most only 8 to 11 inches, although trout in the 18- to 22-inch class were being hooked. Dave and Ken were grudgingly beginning to accept that their reward might have been the fact that they had developed a pattern close enough to the white ghosts to get strikes.

Then, in September 1998, Ed and his wife, Betty Ann, visited the small Swiss settlement of Helvetia, West Virginia. During the trip, Ed dropped in at the Appalachian Adventures Shop in Millcreek and left his card for Sam Knotts, a popular trout guide whom he had met at a previous fly-fishing show. Being a good friend of Dave and Ken's, Sam knew about the white ghost problem and called Dave to give him Ed's telephone number. After all, it was Koch's book *Fishing the Midge* that had introduced Dave and Ken to the world of small flies.

When Dave telephoned, Ed responded quickly and enthusiastically. He wound up sending the two men 9X and 10X tippet material and stomach pumps to use on the trout. Eventually, Ed visited the Elk River twice. On the first visit, the men collected the two most prominent white ghost specimens. After a session of fishing, Dave, Ken, and Sam watched as Ed tied several freshwater shrimp patterns. He showed them the most beautiful and useful size 28, 30, and 32 hooks they had ever seen. The most fascinating were the size 32 Tiemco hooks with eyes and usable gaps. Ed had gotten them from Bob Miller (author of *Tricos*) of Allentown, Pennsylvania, and he promised to send some to Dave as soon as possible. Dave and Ken tried the hooks, and they worked well. The size of the trout and percentage brought to hand increased dramatically.

Dave and Ken know that they still have a lot to learn but believe they are a giant step closer to meeting the challenge of the white ghost and other unidentified small insects in the upper Elk River. They are very grateful to Ed for his encouragement, supplies, advice, and wonderful company. He is truly one of the finest gentlemen in the sport of fly fishing.

The following are tying instructions for some of Dave and Ken's patterns. These patterns work well on the catch-and-release stretch of the Elk River.

LITTLE PRIMROSE
Hook #32 TMC 518
Body 8/0 Orvis primrose (pale yellow)
Wing White CDC

1. Cinch down CDC barb ends forward halfway to eye of hook.
2. Build up back half of the body up to a point slightly more than half the shank length.
3. Jump in front of the wing and build the front half, causing the wing to slope slightly rearward.
4. Whip-finish.

WHITE FEATHER FLY
Hook #32 TMC 518
Thread 8/0 cream
Body White duck feather fibers from wing feathers

1. Lay down a good thread foundation.
2. Select five or six 1½-inch or longer feather fibers and tie them in at the hook bend.
3. Wrap the fibers forward, building the body to the desired contour.
4. Tie off and whip-finish.

LITTLE BLACK FLY
Hook #32 TMC 518
Body 8/0 or 10/0 black thread
Wing Dark dun CDC

1. Cinch down the barb ends of the CDC wing forward halfway to the eye of the hook.
2. Build up the back half of the body to a point slightly more than half the shank length.
3. Jump in front of the wing and build up the front half of the body, causing the wing to slope slightly rearward.
4. Whip-finish.

The Little Primrose and White Feather flies fish well dead-drifted on the surface film. The men's usual rig when the white ghosts are on is to put the Little Primrose on the end of a long 10X tippet and run the feather fly on about 14 inches of 10X tippet tied to the bend of the Primrose hook. They treat the top fly's CDC wing with Frog Fanny, encasing it in a bubble shield, then apply Xink (fly sink) to the feather fly, which causes it to ride a couple inches under the surface.

Both flies fished this way elicit about equal number of takes. At times, it pays to fish downstream, casting at about 3 o'clock, with the fish at the 12 o'clock position and the fisherman at the 7 o'clock position, leaving just enough slack in the tippet so that as it nears the fish, the point fly (White Feather) swings up to the surface just in front of the fish. This often leads to aggressive takes. It likely simulates emergence.

It usually helps to pick out one fish at a time. Lead him short, 12 to 14 inches, and stick with him. There are often tens of thousands of naturals on the water, so accuracy and patience pay dividends. In other words, don't try to catch all the fish at once!

After using Dave Breitmeier's patterns with success on Pennsylvania limestone streams, Ed Koch began collecting specimens and developed the following patterns. Try tying these patterns in size 28 until you become comfortable with small hooks, then move down to 30 and 32. Use 8X to 10X tippets (though tippets down to 12X and 14X may soon be available) and 1- to 4-weight line. Rods can range from 5 1/2 to 8 1/2 feet.

FOR ALL PATTERNS:
Hook #28, 30, or 32 TMC 518
Body 8/0 Gudebrod white (BCS 107) or black (BCS 118) thread
Wing White fluff or down from the bottom of a grizzly or white hackle, or a white CDC

WHITE FEATHER FLY SPINNER

1. Wrap hook shank with white thread, starting at the rear of the shank, just before the bend, and moving forward to the eye.
2. Wrap thread back to the middle of the shank and tie off with a half hitch.
3. Tie in 3 or 4 fibers of the white fluff, hold it upright and divide into wings; then wrap thread behind and in front of fibers and half-hitch. Wrap thread forward to hook eye and whip-finish.
4. Moisten thumb and forefinger, hold wings upright and clip to 1/32 inch.

WHITE FEATHER FLY EMERGER

Follow instructions for the Spinner, above, but tie wing in an upright clump and slant forward toward the eye.

BLACK FEATHER FLY EMERGER

Same as White Feather Fly Emerger, but with black thread and wing.

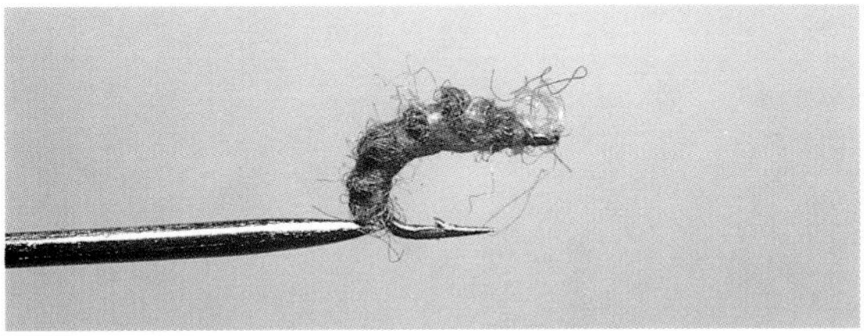

BLACK LARVA

1. Wrap hook shank with black thread, starting at the eye and moving back to where the hook bend begins.
2. Wrap thread forward to the eye.
3. Make two or three wraps just behind the eye and whip-finish.

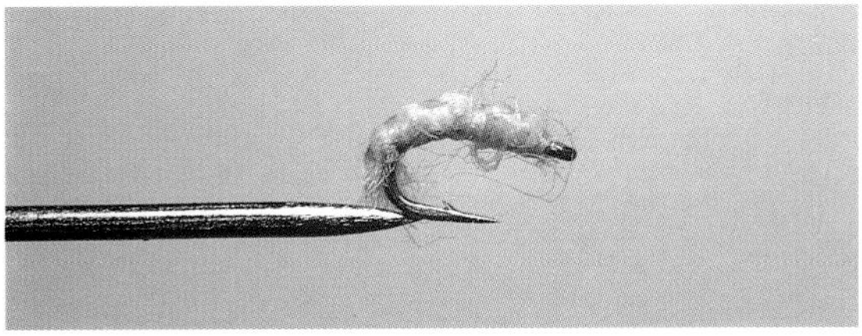

WHITE LARVA

Same as Black Larva, but with white thread.

HATCH CHART

OF CENTRAL PENNSYLVANIA MIDGES

This chart, created from years of fishing notes, lists those patterns that were particularly effective on a specific week of the year. Each pattern is either an attractor or as close a match to an actual insect as I could make at the time. Most of the data was collected in south-central Pennsylvania, although I would not hesitate to use the patterns elsewhere, making some allowance for different temperature zones. Not all midges exist everywhere, but so little data is available for fishermen that this will at least get you started.

This chart uses a system to help you match the colors accurately. The main fly ingredients are DMC six-strand cotton embroidery floss and Coats & Clark Dual Duty Plus sewing thread (C&C). The numbers following these abbreviations refer to colors. For tying threads, I used the Borger Color System (BCS) chart. Thus, in the pattern descriptions below, the first number is the hook size, followed by the material (DMC or C&C) and color number, and then thread colors and numbers where appropriate.

JANUARY

1st Week
18 - DMC 762/white
24 - C&C 293A/126
26 - C&C 102/iron gray Unithread head (BCS 114)

2nd Week
20 - DMC 831/silver

3rd Week
22 - DMC 762/white
26 - C&C 102/iron gray Unithread head (BCS 114)

4th Week
18 - DMC 918/silver
18 - DMC 938/silver
18 - DMC 543/712

FEBRUARY

1st Week
22 - C&C 295A/iron gray Unithread head (BCS 114)

2nd Week
18 - DMC 762/white
24 - C&C 54/47

3rd Week
No Data (Did Not Fish)

4th Week
22 - C&C 295A/iron gray Unithread head (BCS 114)

MARCH

1st Week
No Data (Did Not Fish)

2nd Week
18 - DMC 543/712
18 - DMC white/brown mono rib

3rd Week
20 - DMC 762/white
22 - DMC 762/white
24 - C&C 54/47

4th Week
18 - DMC 840/yellow thread underbody (BCS 50)
18 - DMC 762/white
20 - DMC 762/white
24 - C&C 47/silver
24 - DMC 3032/C&C 293A

APRIL

1st Week
18 - DMC 950/off-white fur (Original Shrimp)
18 - DMC 742/white
18 - silver/mono
24 - C&C 54/47

2nd Week
24 - C&C 325A/27
24 - C&C 102/27
24 - C&C 293A/347
24 - C&C 475/126
24 - red thread

3rd Week
18 - DMC 950/off-white fur (Original Shrimp)
18 - silver/mono
18 - copper/mono
18 - DMC 762/white
20 - DMC 3047/3790
24 - C&C 54/47
24 - C&C 54/silver
24 - C&C 280/rainbow tinsel
24 - C&C 128

4th Week
20 - DMC 3047/3790
24 - C&C 54/47

MAY

1st Week
18 - DMC 950/off-white fur (Original Shrimp)
18 - copper/mono
18 - DMC 898/silver

2nd Week
18 - DMC white/brown mono rib
18 - copper/mono
18 - DMC 898/silver
20 - DMC 762/white

3rd Week
18 - DMC white/brown mono rib
18 - DMC 950/off-white fur (Original Shrimp)
18 - DMC 898/silver
18 - DMC 842/white
20 - DMC 762/white

4th Week
18 - DMC 742/white
18 - DMC 950/off-white fur (Original Shrimp)
18 - DMC 898/silver
20 - DMC 762/white

JUNE

1st Week
18 - DMC 950/off-white fur (original shrimp)
18 - DMC 842/white
22 - DMC 543/712
24 - DMC 745/rust brown thread rib and head (BCS 71)

2nd Week
18 - DMC 830/silver
18 - DMC 762/white
18 - DMC 839/white
18 - DMC 742/white
18 - DMC 842/white
18 - DMC 415/silver
20 - DMC 666
24 - C&C 54/silver
24 - C&C 47/silver

3rd Week
18 - DMC 3021/3032
18 - DMC 676
18 - DMC 841
18 - DMC 762/white
18 - DMC 950/off-white fur (Original Shrimp)
24 - C&C 347/27
24 - C&C 47/silver
24 - C&C 54/47
26 - C&C 293A/361
26 - C&C 309A/dark brown Unithread head (BCS 98)

4th Week
18 - DMC 310/silver
18 - DMC white/brown mono rib
18 - DMC 830/silver
18 - DMC 762/white
20 - DMC 762/white
22 - DMC 762/white
24 - DMC 745/rust brown thread rib and head (BCS 71)
24 - green beadhead/C&C 361
24 - C&C 293A/361
24 - C&C 280/rainbow tinsel

JULY

1st Week
18 - DMC 415/silver
18 - DMC 950/off-white fur (Original Shrimp)
18 - DMC 310/silver
18 - DMC 762/white
20 - DMC 762/white
24 - DMC 918/silver
26 - C&C 280/rainbow tinsel
26 - C&C 361/light gray thread head (BCS 110)
26 - C&C 102/dark brown Unithread head (BCS 98)

2nd Week
18 - Orange Dot Shrimp
18 - DMC 415/silver
18 - DMC 310/silver
20 - DMC 762/white
24 - red beadhead/C&C 128
24 - C&C 54/47
24 - C&C 47/silver/poly wet wing
26 - C&C 293A/361/poly wet wing

3rd Week
18 - silver/mono
18 - DMC 762/white
18 - DMC 310/silver
18 - DMC 712/off-white fur (Original Shrimp)
20 - DMC 762/white
20 - DMC 666
22 - DMC 310/silver
24 - C&C 361/light gray thread head (BCS 110)
24 - red beadhead/C&C 128
26 - C&C 475
26 - C&C 102/dark brown Unithread head (BCS 98)
26 - iridescent beadhead/C&C 126
26 - iridescent beadhead/C&C 361

4th Week
18 - DMC 676/712
18 - DMC 712/off-white fur (Original Shrimp)
18 - DMC 310/silver
18 - DMC 415/silver
18 - DMC 762/white
20 - DMC 833/silver
20 - DMC 831/silver
20 - DMC 666
26 - C&C 102/dark brown Unithread head (BCS 98)

AUGUST

1st Week
18 - DMC 950/off-white fur (Original Shrimp)
18 - DMC 762/white
20 - DMC 831/silver
20 - red thread underbody/olive mono/olive brown thread head (BCS 32)

2nd Week
18 - Orange Dot Shrimp
18 - DMC 950/off-white fur (Original Shrimp)
18 - DMC 762/white
18 - DMC 831/silver
20 - red thread underbody/olive mono/olive brown thread head (BCS 32)

3rd Week
18 - copper/mono
18 - DMC 950/off-white fur (Original Shrimp)
20 - DMC 831/silver
20 - red thread underbody/olive mono/olive brown thread head (BCS 32)
26 - C&C 475

4th Week
18 - DMC 950/off-white fur (Original Shrimp)
18 - DMC 762/white
18 - DMC 666
20 - red thread underbody/olive mono/olive brown thread head (BCS 32)
20 - DMC 831/silver
26 - peacock/white hackle dry

SEPTEMBER

1st Week
18 - red beads
20 -red thread underbody/olive mono/olive brown thread head (BCS 32)
22 - DMC 3078 w/ C&C 319A overwrapped head only
28 - red thread or C&C 128

2nd Week
18 - DMC 950/off-white fur (Original Shrimp)
20 - red thread underbody/olive mono/olive brown thread head (BCS 32)
24 - red beadhead/C&C 128 red
26 - C&C 47/dark brown Unithread head (BCS 98)

3rd Week
18 - DMC 3777/3371
18 - DMC 831/silver
18 - DMC 950/off-white fur shrimp
26 - C&C 47/dark brown Unithread head (BCS 98)
26 - C&C 361

4th Week
18 - DMC 841/white

OCTOBER

1st Week
24 - C&C 475/361
26 - C&C 47/dark brown Unithread head (BCS 98)

2nd Week
18 - DMC 762/white
24 - C&C 475/361

3rd Week
18 - DMC 831/silver
24 - C&C 126

4th Week
18 - DMC 762/white
18 - DMC 950/off-white fur (Original Shrimp)
24 - red beadhead/C&C 128

NOVEMBER

1st Week
(deer season)

2nd Week
(deer season)

3rd Week
18 - DMC 831/silver
18 - DMC 950/off-white fur (Original Shrimp)

4th Week
18 - DMC 950/off-white fur (Original Shrimp)
22 - DMC 840/ecru
24 - red beadhead/C&C 128

DECEMBER

1st Week
18 - DMC 3777/3371
18 - DMC 762/white

2nd Week
18 - DMC 762/white

3rd Week
18 - DMC 543/712
18 - DMC 950/off-white fur (Original Shrimp)
22 - DMC 840/ecru
26 - C&C 102/dark brown Unithread head (BCS 98)
26 - C&C 102/iron gray Unithread head (BCS 114)

4th Week
26 - C&C 102/iron gray Unithread head (BCS 114)

Size 18

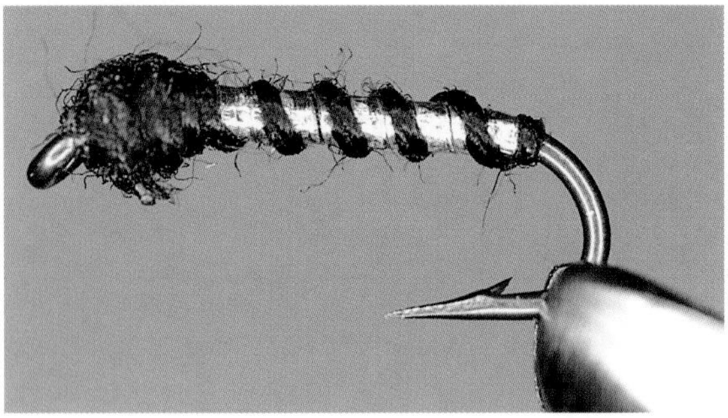

DMC 310/silver

DMC 415/silver

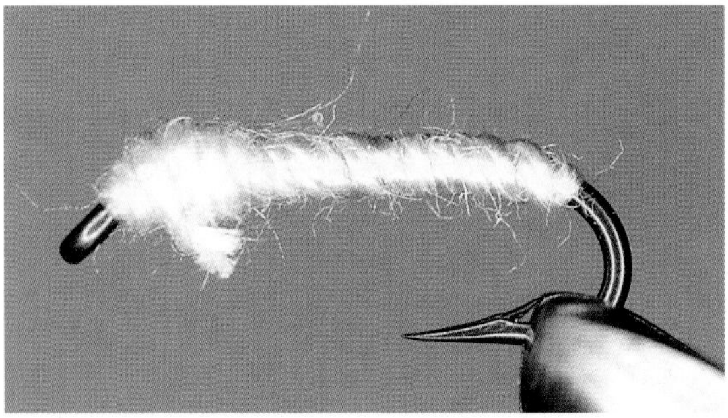

DMC 543/712

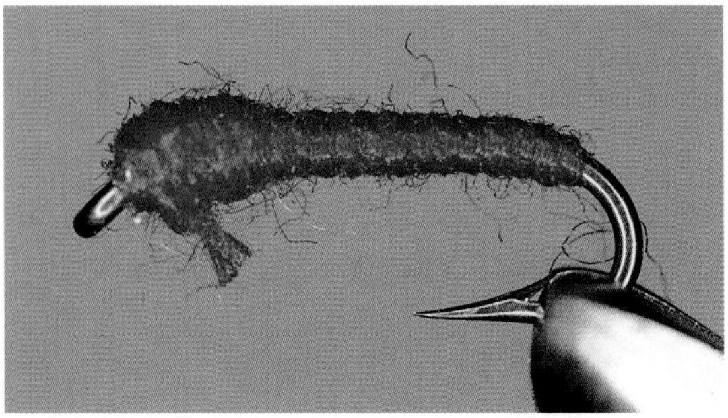

DMC 666

Size 18

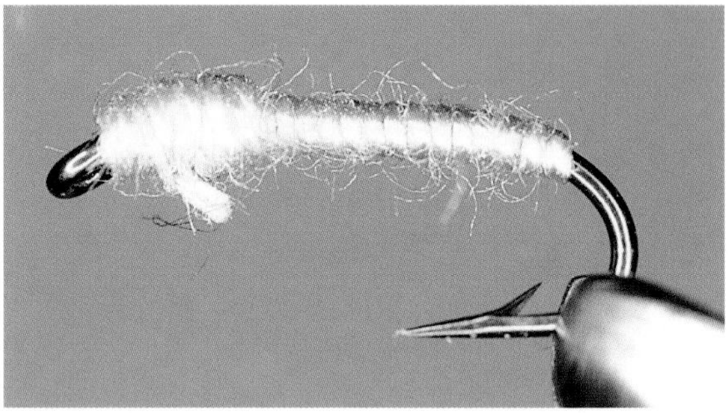

DMC 676

DMC 676/712

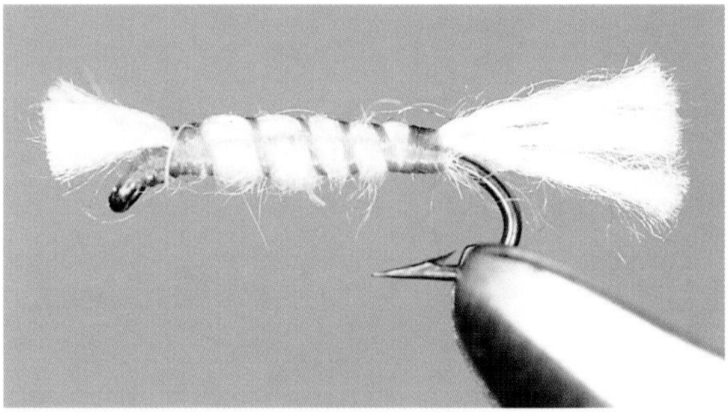

DMC 712/off-white fur (Original Shrimp)

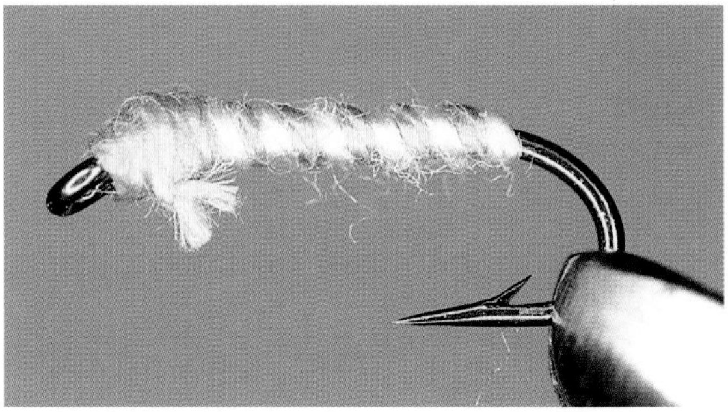

DMC 742/white

Size 18

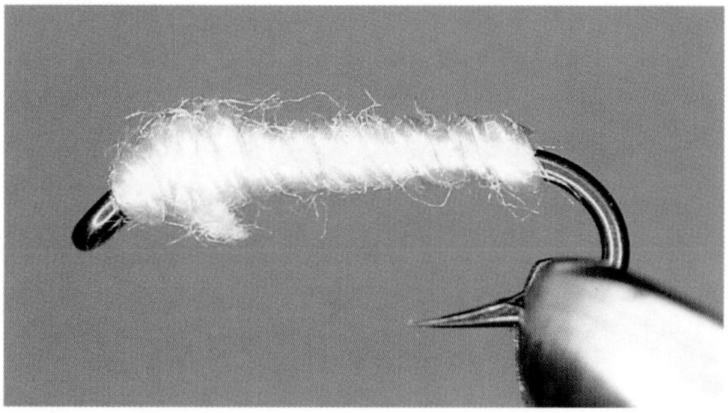

DMC 762/white

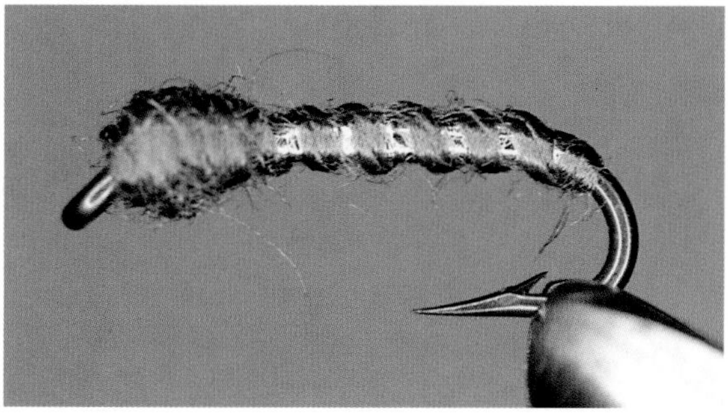

DMC 830/silver

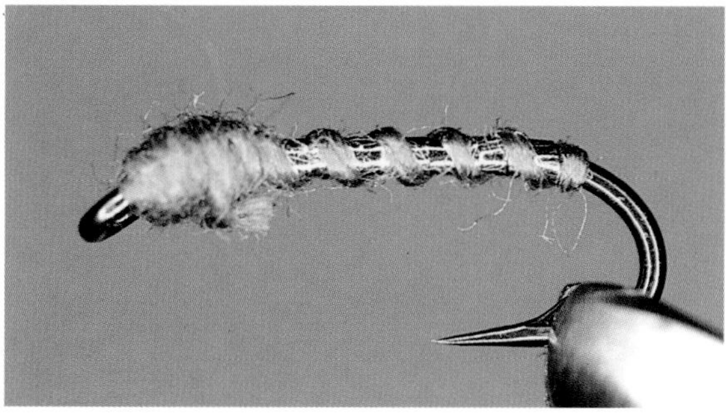

DMC 831/silver

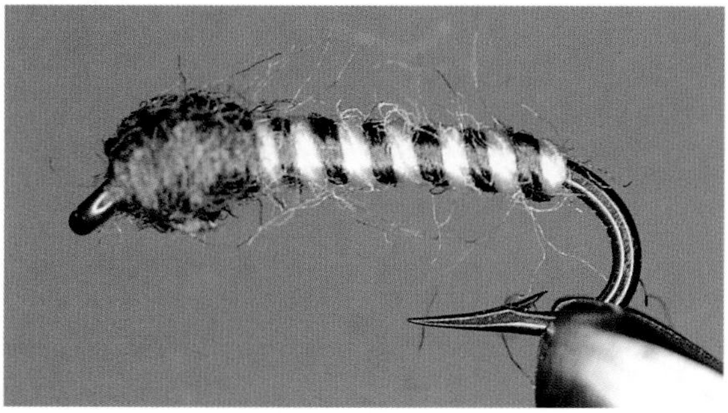

DMC 839/white

Size 18

DMC 840/yellow thread underbody (BCS 50)

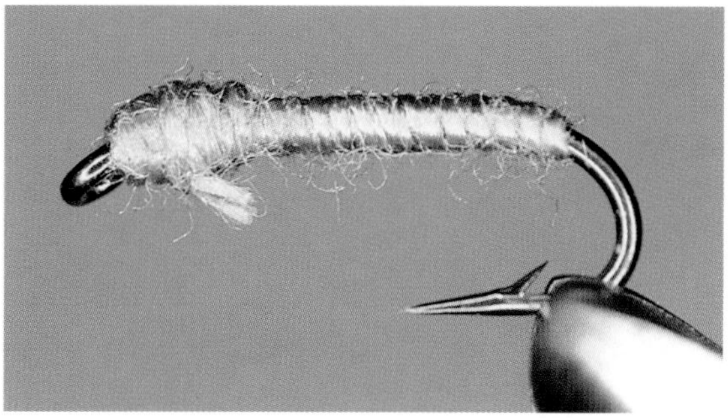

DMC 841

DMC 841/white

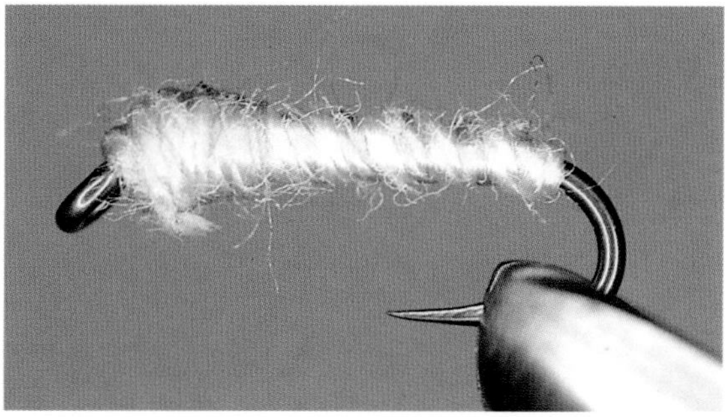

DMC 842/white

Size 18

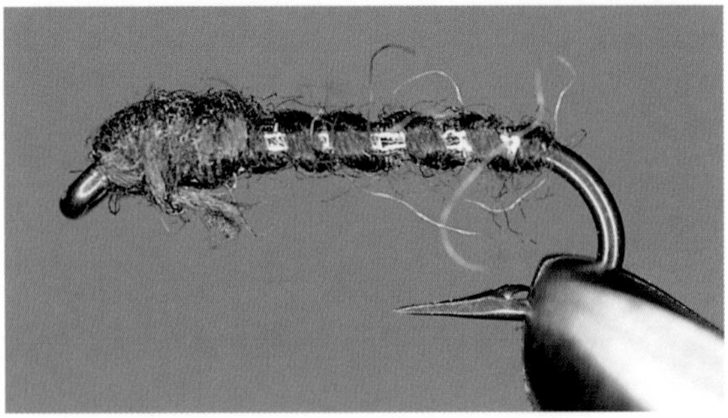

DMC 898/silver

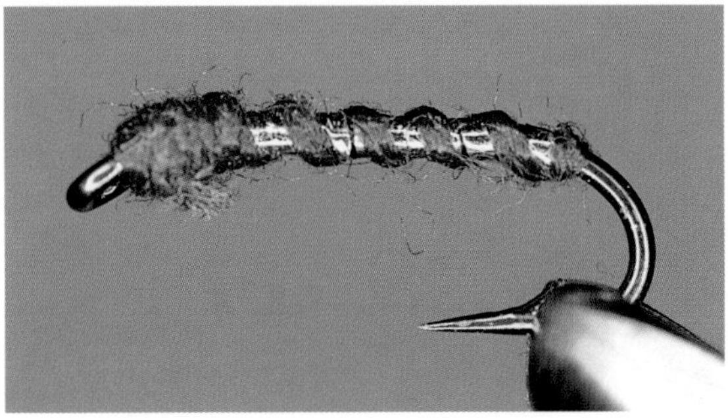

DMC 918/silver

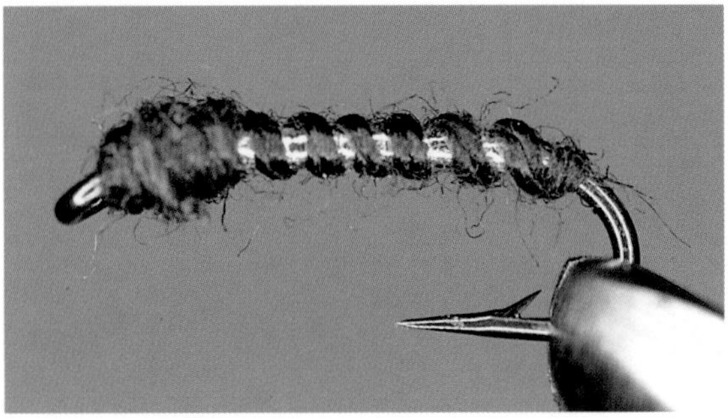

DMC 938/silver

DMC 950/off-white fur (Original Shrimp)

Size 18

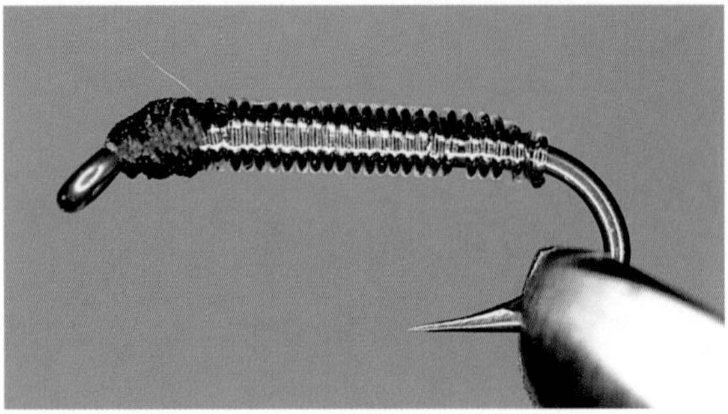

Copper/mono

Orange Dot Shrimp

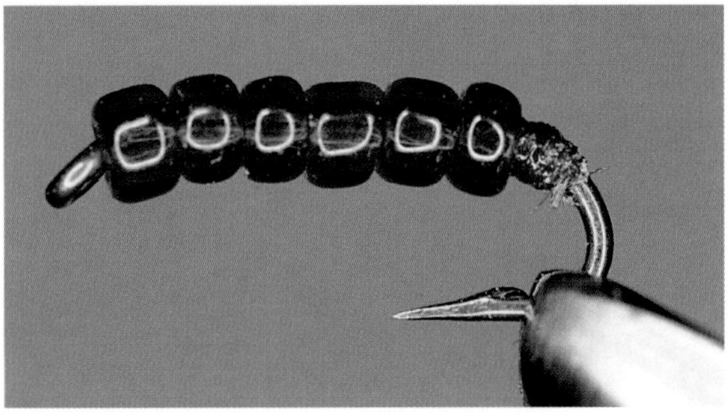

Red beads

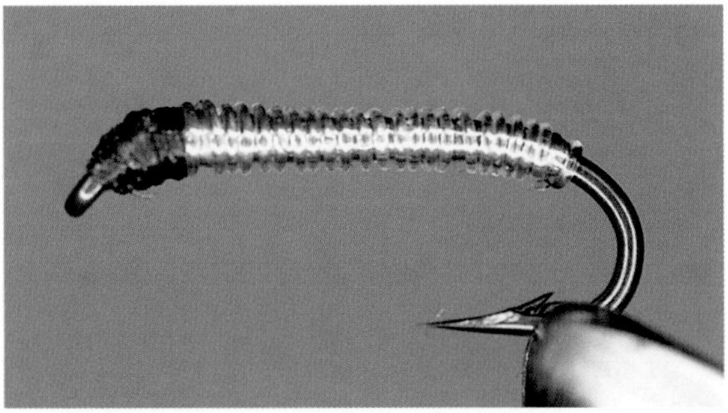

Silver/mono

Size 18

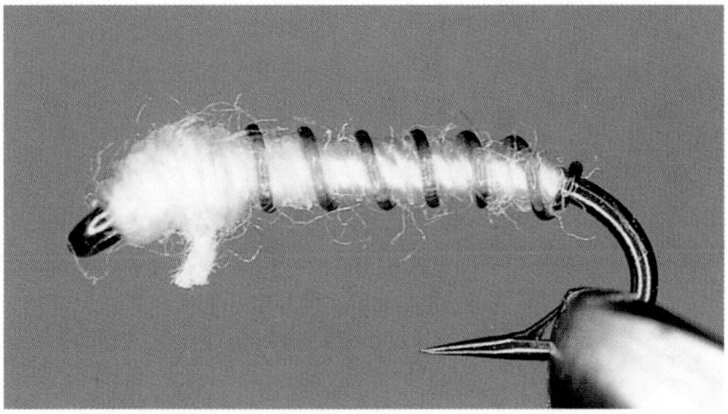

DMC white/brown mono rib

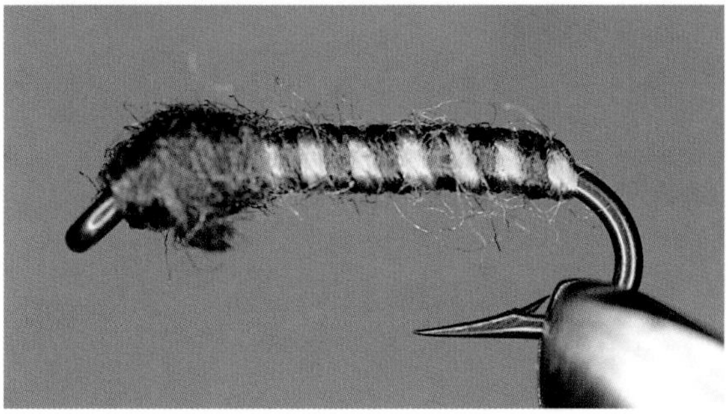

DMC 3021/3032

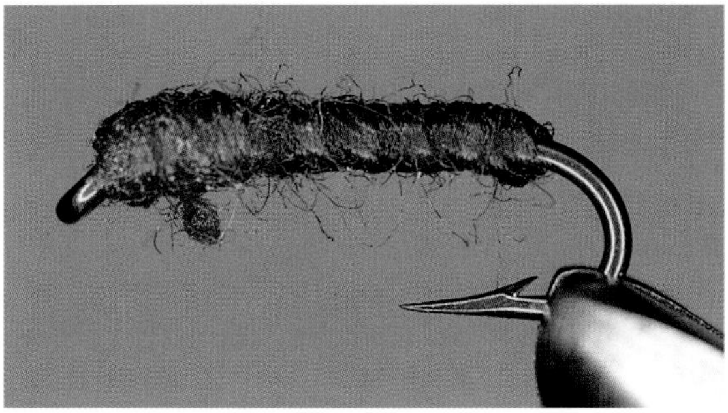

DMC 3777/3371

Size 20

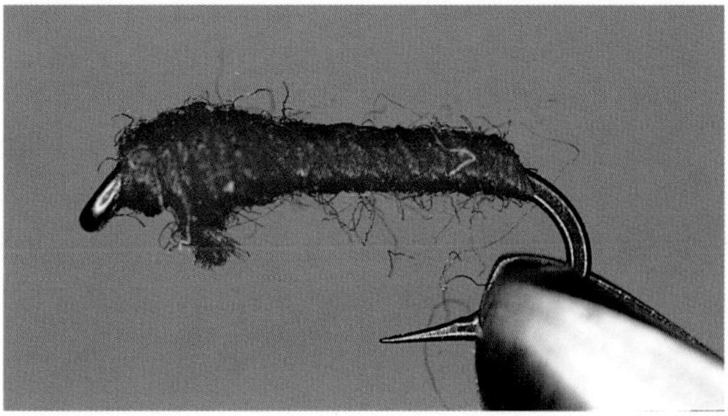

DMC 666

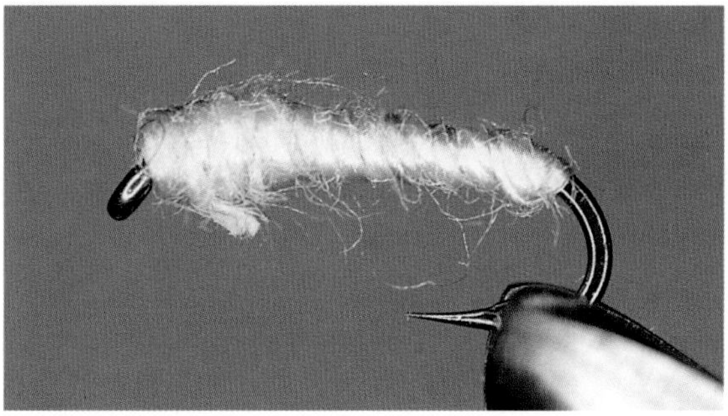

DMC 762/white

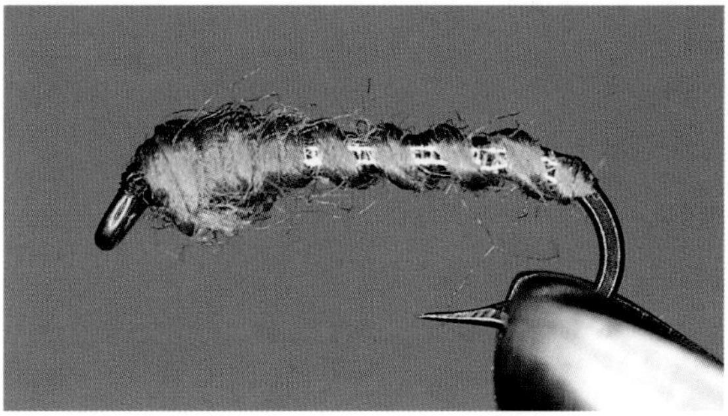

DMC 831/silver

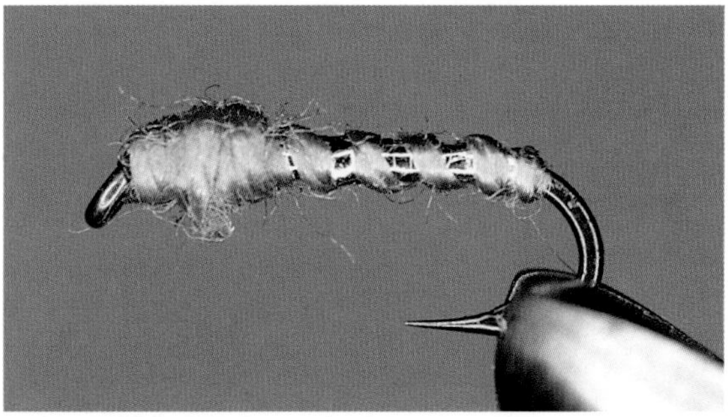

DMC 833/silver

Size 20

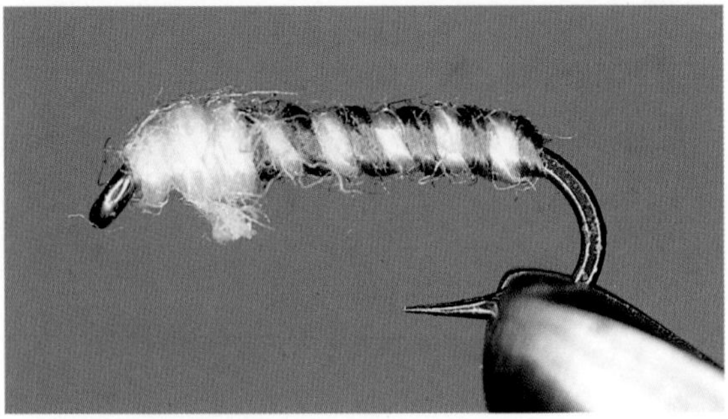

DMC 3047/3790

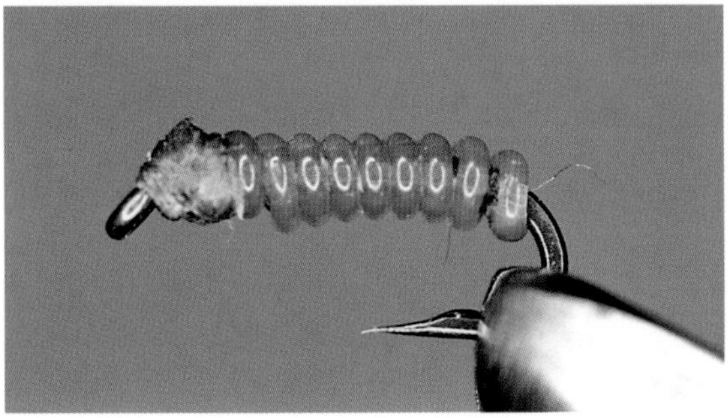

Red thread underbody/olive mono/olive brown thread head (BCS 32)

Size 22

C&C 295A/iron gray Unithread head (BCS 114)

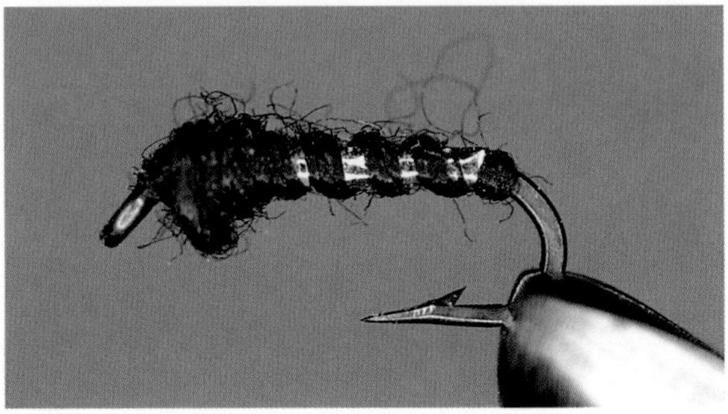

DMC 310/silver

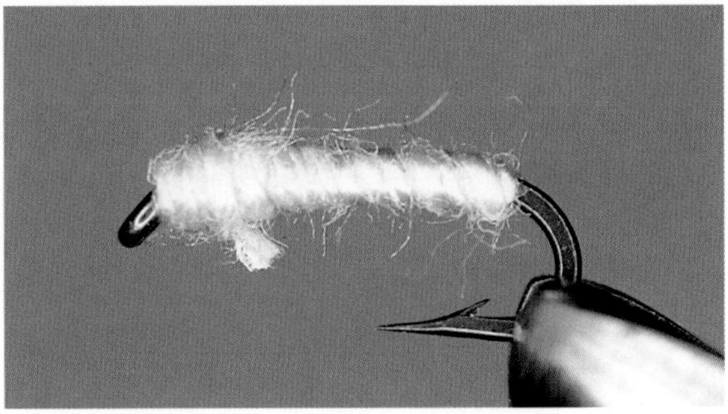

DMC 543/712

DMC 762/white

Size 22

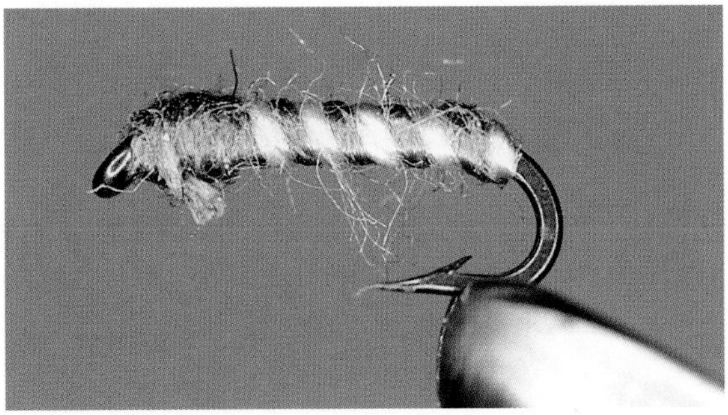

DMC 840/ecru

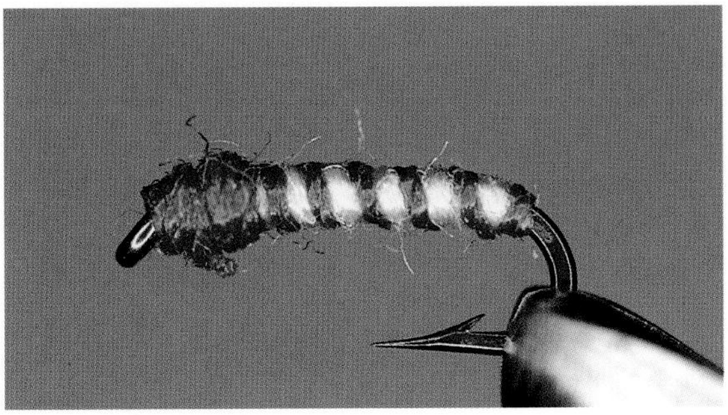

DMC 3078/C&C 319A

Size 24

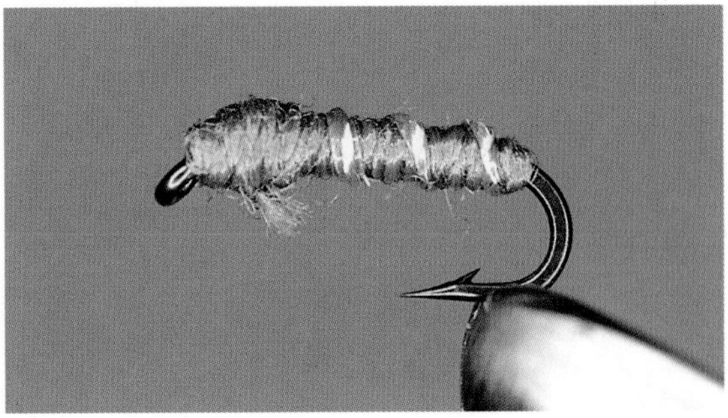

24 - C&C 47/silver

When I began tying this pattern many years ago, I was ribbing flies with silver metallic thread. Until I began photographing flies, I didn't realize that wrapping this thread tightly around a hook exposes its core, making the rib look white. It works so well I can't stop using it. I now also tie this pattern using the Diamond Midge technique. I wouldn't be without either one.

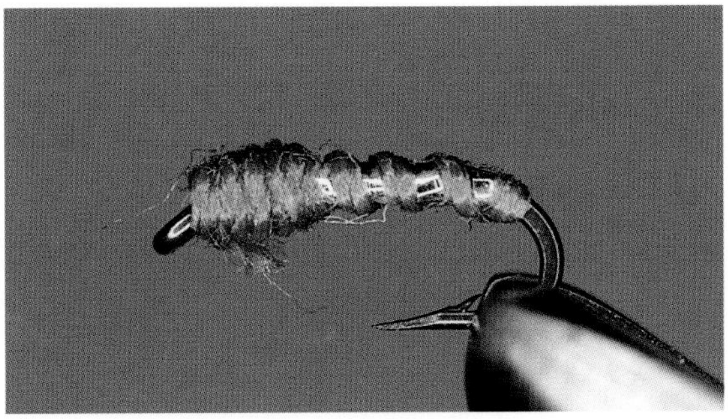

C&C 47/silver (Diamond Midge style)

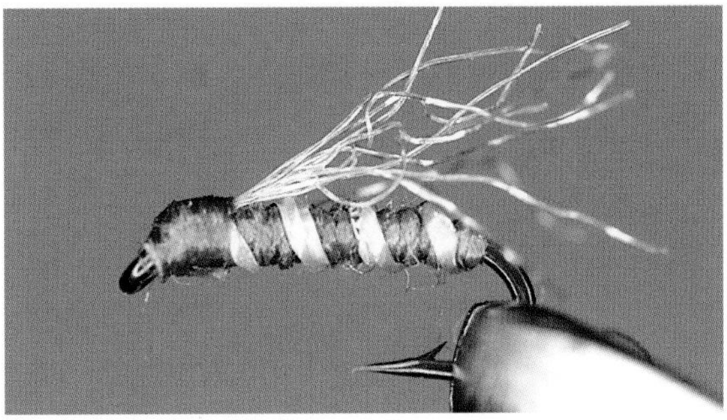

C&C 47/silver wet (old style, with metallic thread)

Size 24

C&C 54/silver (old style with metallic thread)

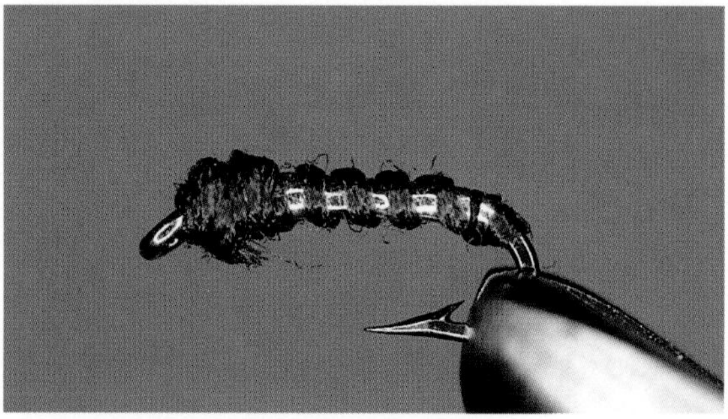

C&C 54/silver (Diamond Midge style)

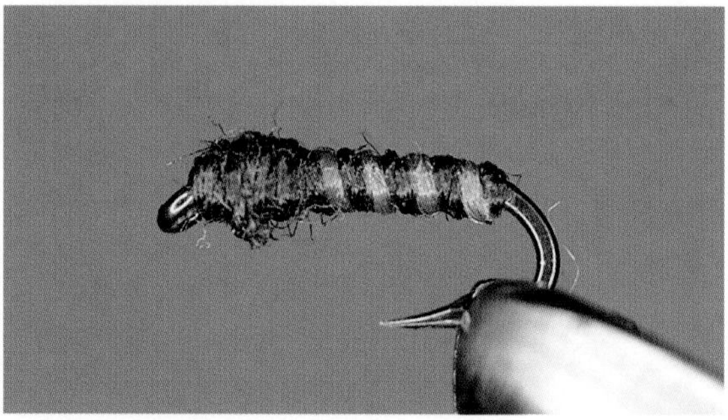

C&C 54/47

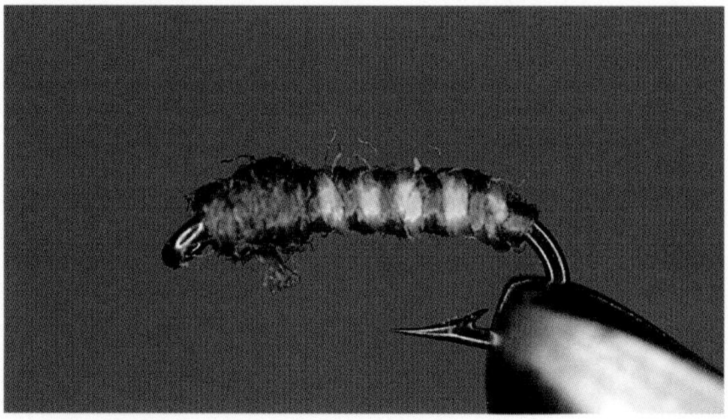

C&C 102/27

Size 24

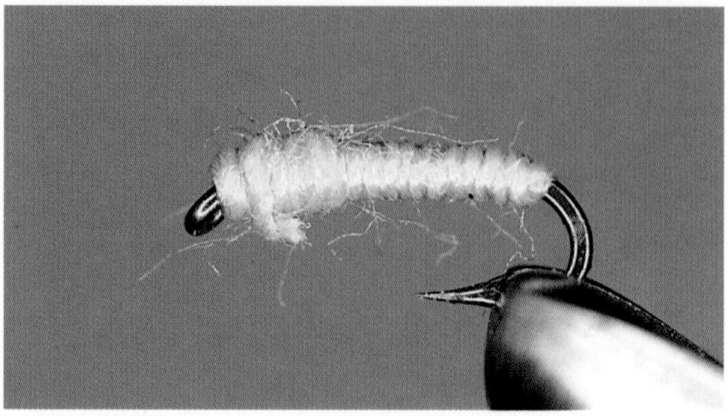

C&C 126

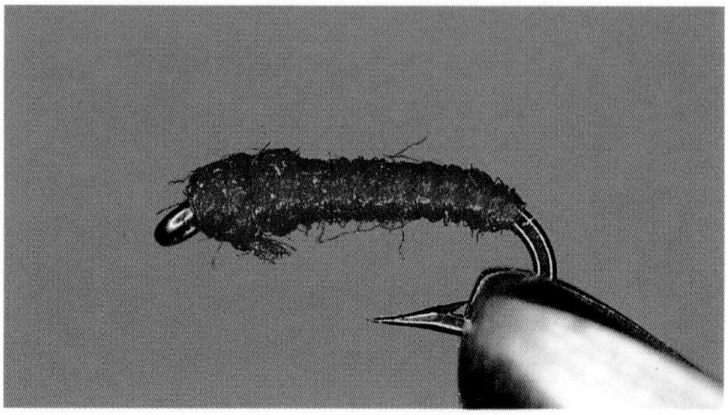

C&C 128

C&C 128/red beadhead

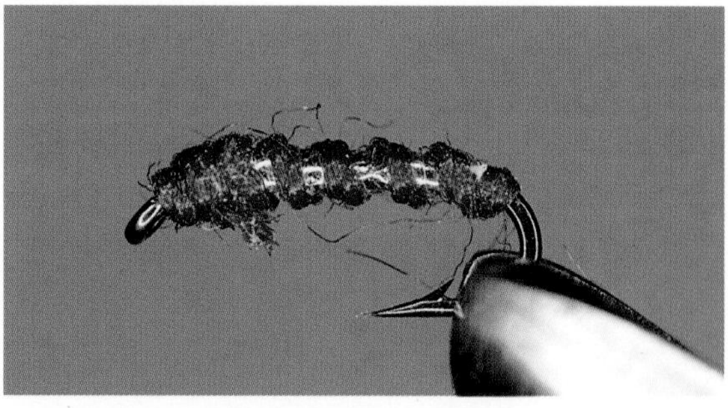

C&C 280/rainbow tinsel

Size 24

C&C 293A/126

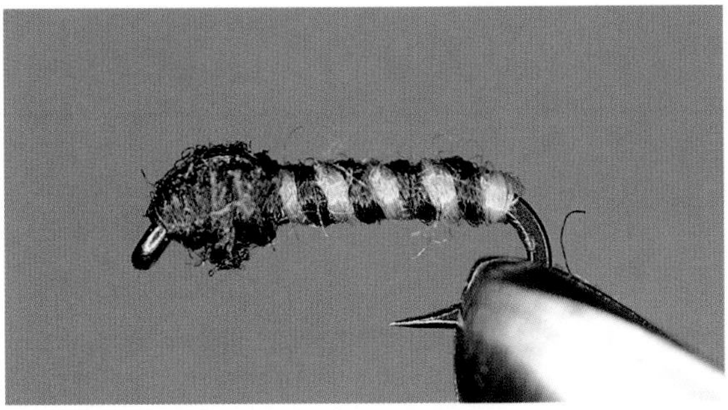

C&C 293A/347

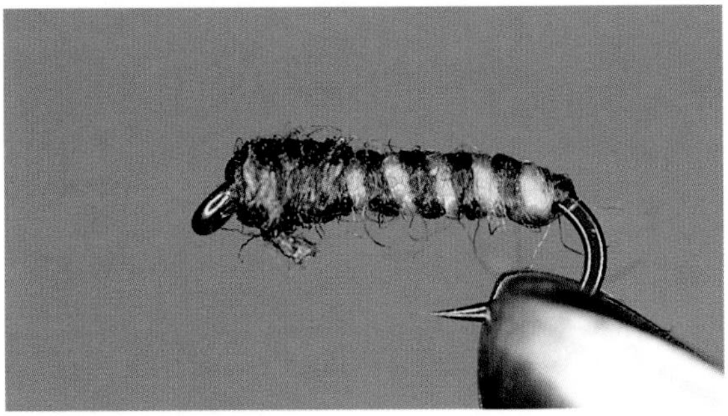

C&C 295A/361

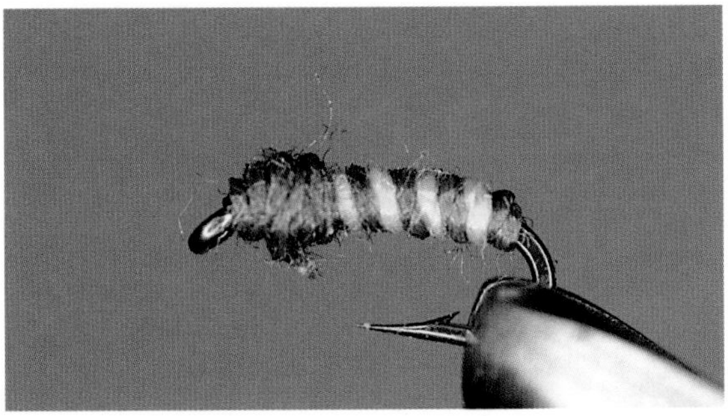

C&C 325A/27

Size 24

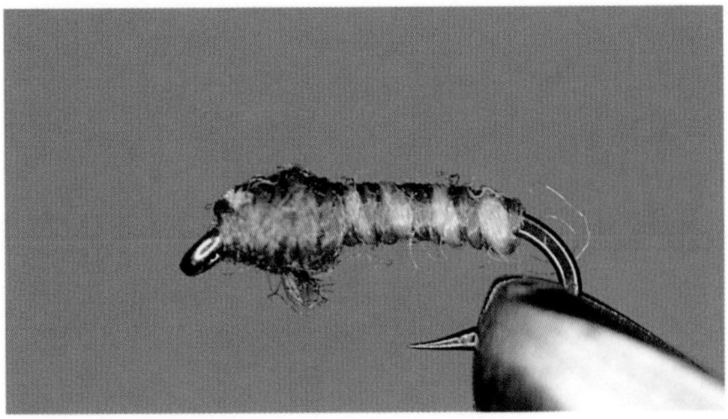

C&C 347/27

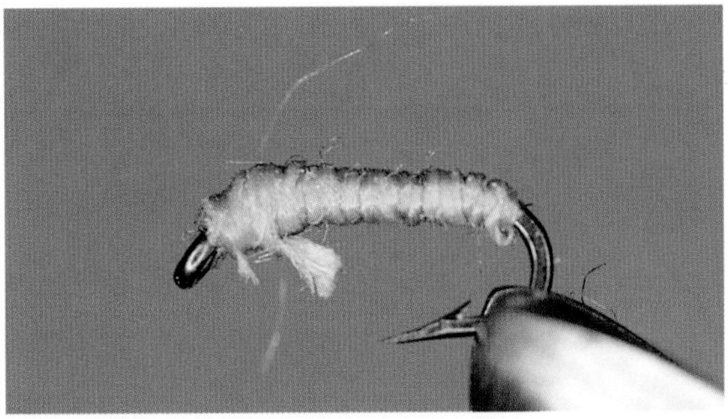

C&C 361/light gray thread head (BCS 110)

C&C 361/iridescent beadhead

Size 24

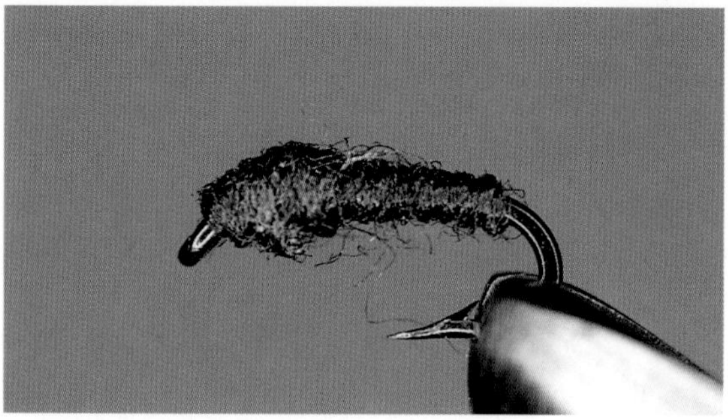

C&C 475
This color, raisin, has been discontinued. If something works, buy a lifetime supply.

C&C 475/126

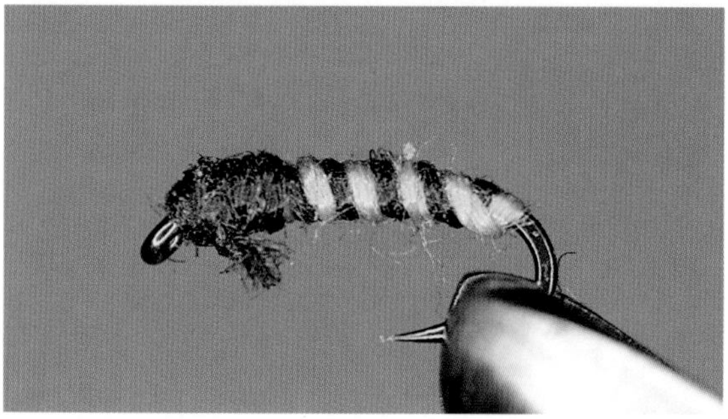

C&C 475/361

Size 24

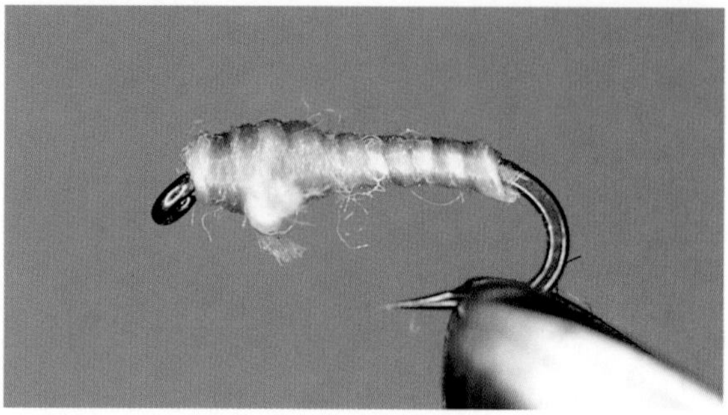

C&C 745/rust brown thread, ribbing and head. (Another older pattern that works too well to discard. Pick a light rust-colored tying thread. When you tie the body strand down along the hook, leave the thread at the rear, wind the body forward, and half-hitch a head with it, as in a Rainbow Midge. Then spiral the tying thread forward as a ribbing and overwrap the head with it.)

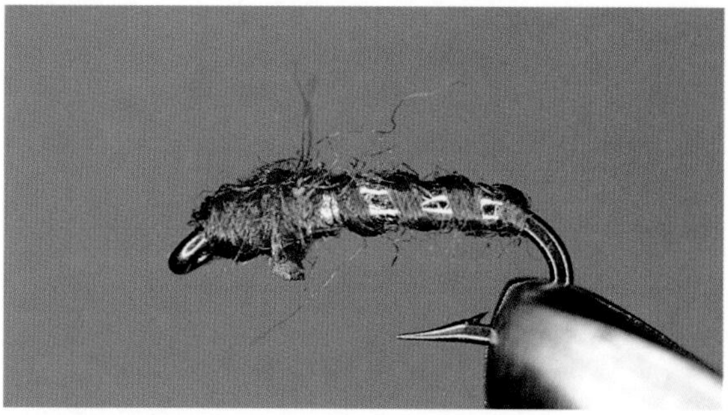

DMC 918/silver

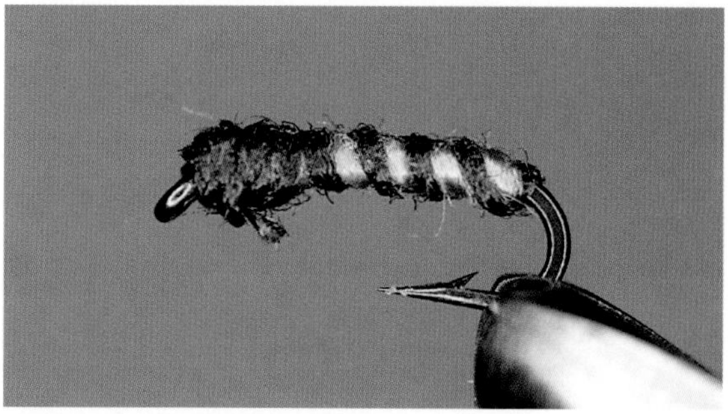

DMC 3032/C&C 293A

Size 24

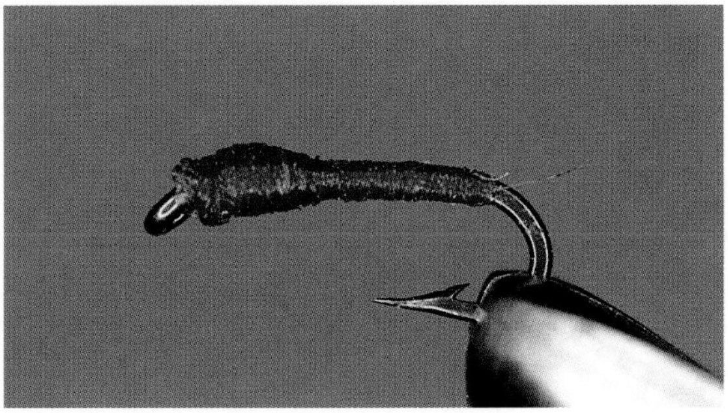

Red thread

Size 26

C&C 47/dark brown Unithread head (BCS 98)

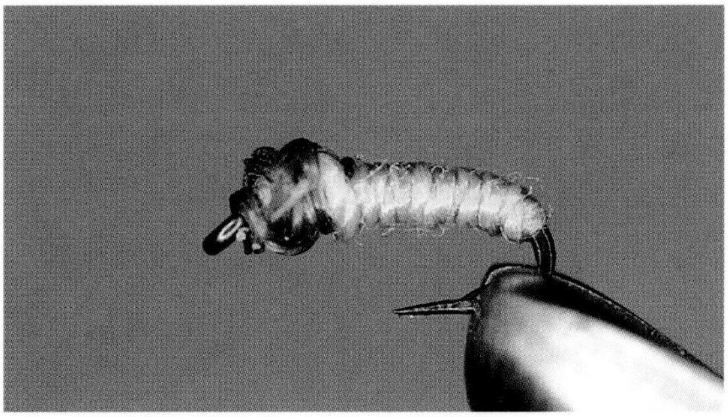

C&C 102/dark brown Unithread head (BCS 98)

C&C 102/iron gray Unithread head (BCS 114)

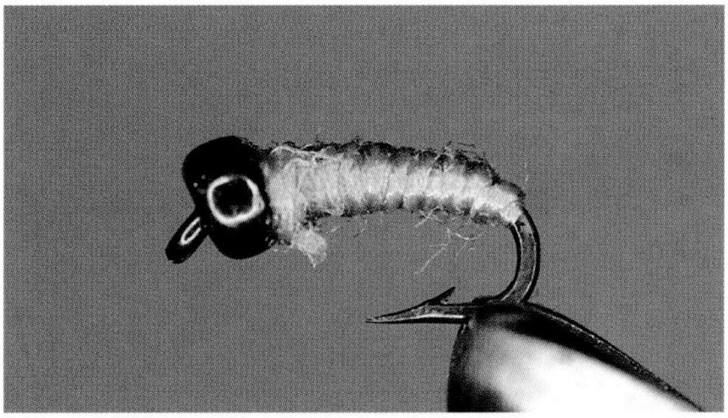

C&C 126/iridescent beadhead

Size 26

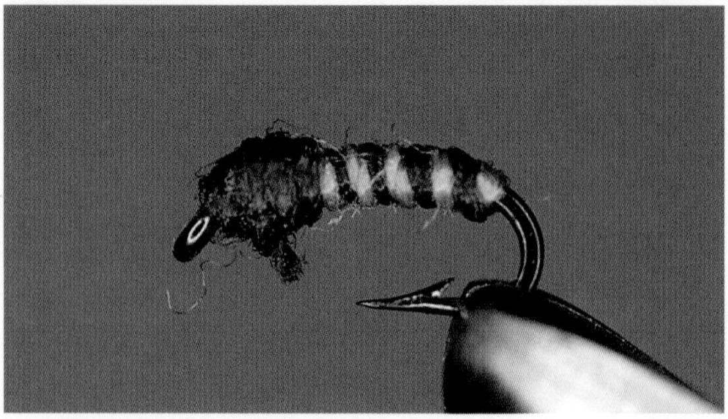

C&C 293A/361

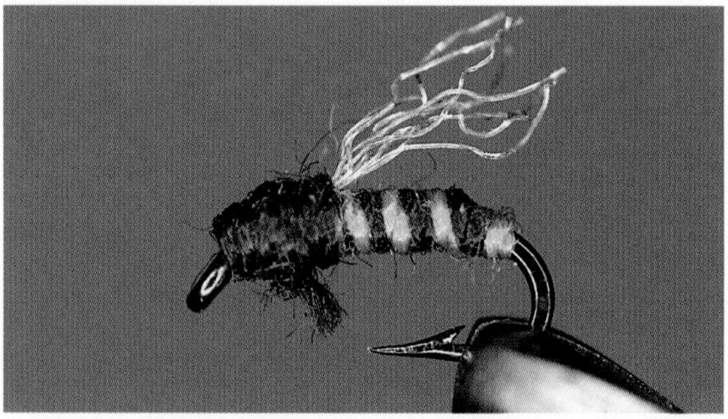

C&C 293A/361 wet

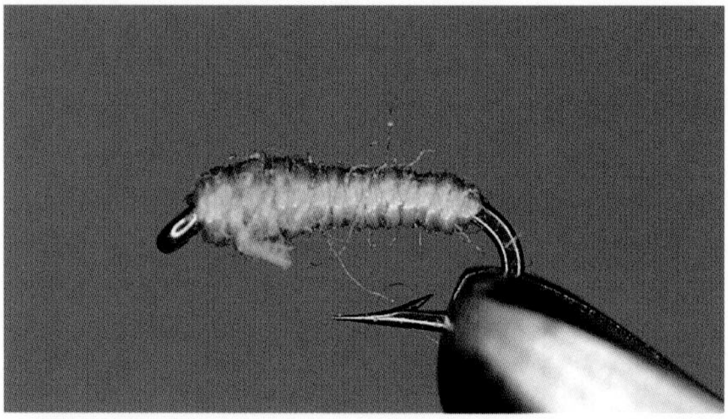

C&C 361

C&C 361/light gray thread head (BCS 110)

Size 26

C&C 361/iridescent beadhead

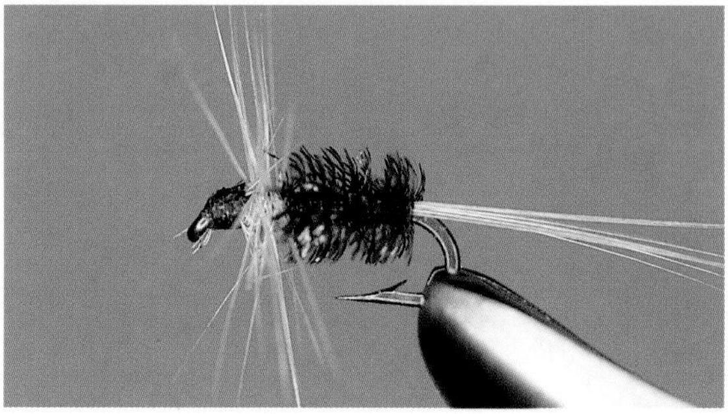

Peacock/white hackle dry

Size 28

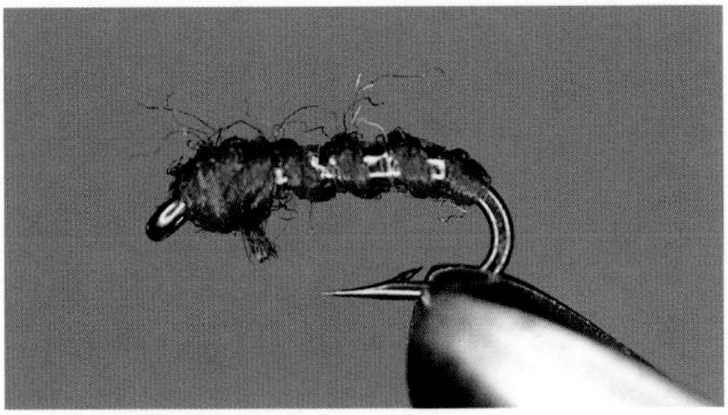

C&C 280/rainbow tinsel

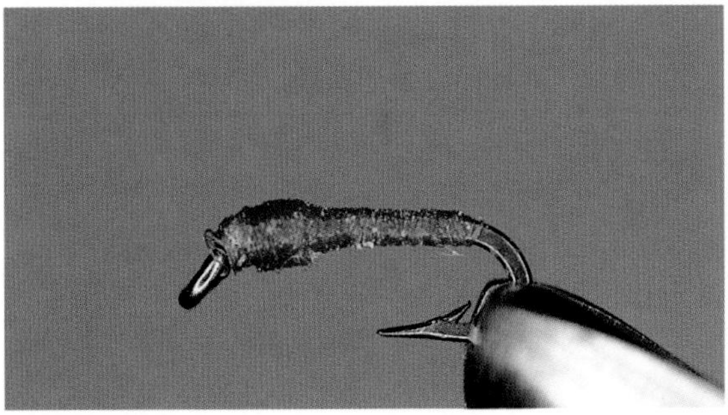

Red thread

Coats & Clark Dual Duty Plus #200 Thread Color Numbers

These are the colors I normally keep on hand. For convenience, I rewind them on small bobbins available at sewing stores. Not all colors are available everywhere, and occasionally a color is added or deleted. A color chart is available on the Coats & Clark website, www.coatsandclark.com.

1	White	135a	Tomato Bisque	452	Spanish Gold
2	Black	135b	Coral Rust	454	Yellowstone
15a	Pongee	155	Dogwood	460	Pale Apricot
16	Ecru	157a	Yellow	470	Winter White
17	Buff	164b	Bronze Green	471	Granite
18	Beige	184	Brick Rust	472	Sand
18a	Taupe Clair	207	Apricot	473	Mushroom
21b	Cocoon	222	Lime	474	Taupe
23a	Nugrey	256	Natural	475	Raisin
24	Nickel	280	Rustana Red	480	Silver
25	Steel	281a	Grey	524	Chartreuse
26	Slate	292a	Olive Nite	525	Okra
27	Smoke	293a	Taupe Green	530	Chamois
28	Oxford Grey	294a	Celery	531	Saffron
47	Cafe Beige	295a	Lemon Yellow	540	Pearl
48a	London Tan	299a	Nutmeg	541	Fawn
50	Dark Brown	300a	Bright Rust	542	Tan
51	Chona Brown	309a	Camel	543	Hemp
54	Seal Brown	311a	Henna Brown	544	Praline
54a	Summer Brown	312a	Copper Mist	545	Cheery Mahogany
56b	Cloister Brown	319a	Spanish Tile	550	Dark Silver
72a	Primrose	324a	Kumquat	551	Pewter
73c	Maize	325a	Pale Grey	573	Straw Green
77a	Rust	336	Dark Primrose	574	Bright Chartreuse
83a	Jungle Gold	337	Pebble	580	Lemonade
83b	Temple Gold	345	Flannel	581	Cinnamon
83f	Mine Gold	347	Green Linen	585	L L'orange
102	Dark Linen	357	Brown Chestnut	586	Terracota
102a	Maple Sugar	361	Safari	590	Creme Decacao
102g	Dark Dogwood	370	Stone	591	Coffee
116	Cream	371	Light Slate	592	Brown Sugar
126	Khaki	372	Gunmetal	593	Expresso
127a	Army Drab	373	Charcoal	594	French Roast
128	Red	444	Olive		

DMC 6-Strand Cotton Embroidery Floss (by color number)

—	Ecru
—	Blanc Neige (White)
B5200	Snow White
300	Mahogany, Very Dark
301	Mahogany, Medium
307	Lemon
310	Black
317	Pewter Grey
318	Steel Grey, Light
355	Terra Cotta, Dark
356	Terra Cotta, Medium
370	Mustard, Medium
371	Mustard
372	Mustard, Light
400	Mahogany, Dark
402	Mahogany, Very Light
407	Sportsman Flesh, Dark
413	Pewter Grey, Dark
414	Steel Grey, Dark
415	Pearl Grey
420	Hazel Nut Brown, Dark
422	Hazel Nut Brown, Light
433	Brown, Medium
434	Brown, Light
435	Brown, Very Light
436	Tan
437	Tan, Light
444	Lemon, Dark
445	Lemon, Light
451	Shell Grey, Dark
452	Shell Grey, Medium
453	Shell Grey, Light
522	Seafoam Green, Medium
523	Forest Green, Light
524	Seafoam Green, Very Light
535	Ash Grey, Very Light
543	Beige Brown, Ultra Very Light
610	Drab Brown, Very Dark
611	Drab Brown, Dark
612	Drab Brown, Medium
613	Drab Brown, Light
632	Flesh, Very Dark
640	Beige Grey, Very Dark
642	Beige Grey, Dark
644	Beige Grey, Medium
645	Beaver Grey, Very Dark
646	Beaver Grey, Dark
647	Beaver Grey, Medium
648	Beaver Grey, Light
666	Christmas Red, Bright
676	Old Gold, Light
677	Old Gold, Very Light
680	Old Gold, Dark
712	Cream
726	Topaz, Light
727	Topaz, Very Light
729	Old Gold, Medium
730	Olive Green, Very Dark
731	Olive Green, Dark
732	Olive Green
733	Olive Green, Medium
734	Olive Green, Light
738	Tan, Very Light
739	Tan, Ultra Very Light
740	Tangerine
741	Tangerine, Medium
742	Tangerine, Light
744	Yellow, Light
745	Yellow, Light Pale
746	Off-White
754	Peach Flesh, Light
762	Pearl Grey, Very Light
775	Baby Blue, Light
780	Topaz, Ultra Very Dark
781	Topaz, Very Dark
782	Topaz, Dark
783	Topaz, Medium (Christmas Gold)
801	Coffee Brown, Dark
818	Baby Pink
819	Baby Pink, Light
822	Beige Grey, Light
829	Olive Gold, Very Dark
830	Olive Gold, Dark
831	Olive Gold, Medium
832	Olive Gold
833	Olive Gold, Light
834	Olive Gold, Very Light
838	Beige Brown, Very Dark
839	Beige Brown, Dark
840	Beige Brown, Medium
841	Beige Brown, Light
842	Beige Brown, Very Light
844	Beaver Grey, Ultra Dark
869	Hazel Nut Brown, Very Dark
898	Coffee Brown, Very Dark
907	Parrot Green, Light
918	Red Copper, Dark
919	Red Copper
920	Copper, Medium
921	Copper

922	Copper, Light
935	Green Avocado, Dark
938	Coffee Brown, Ultra Dark
945	Flesh, Medium
948	Peach Flesh, Very Light
950	Sportsman Flesh
951	Flesh
975	Golden Brown, Dark
976	Golden Brown, Medium
977	Golden Brown, Light
988	Forest Green, Medium
3011	Khaki Green, Dark
3012	Khaki Green, Medium
3013	Khaki Green, Light
3021	Brown Grey, Very Dark
3022	Brown Grey, Medium
3023	Brown Grey, Light
3024	Brown Grey, Very Light
3031	Mocha Brown, Very Dark
3032	Mocha Brown, Medium
3033	Mocha Brown, Very Light
3045	Yellow Beige, Dark
3046	Yellow Beige, Medium
3047	Yellow Beige, Light
3052	Green Grey, Medium
3053	Green Grey
3064	Sportsman Flesh, Very Dark
3072	Beaver Grey, Very Light
3078	Golden Yellow, Very Light
3371	Black Brown
3770	Flesh, Very Light
3772	Flesh, Dark
3773	Sportsman Flesh, Medium
3774	Sportsman Flesh, Very Light
3776	Mahogany, Light
3777	Terra Cotta, Very Dark
3778	Terra Cotta, Light
3779	Terra Cotta, Ultra Very Light
3781	Mocha Brown, Dark
3782	Mocha Brown, Light
3787	Brown Grey, Dark
3790	Beige Grey, Ultra Dark
3799	Pewter Grey, Very Dark
3801	Christmas Red, Light
3819	Moss Green, Light
3821	Straw
3822	Straw, Light
3823	Yellow, Very Light Pale
3824	Apricot, Light
3825	Orange Spice, Very Light
3826	Golden Brown
3827	Golden Brown, Pale
3828	Hazel Nut Brown
3829	Old Gold, Very Dark
3830	Terra Cotta

APPENDIX

DMC 6-Strand Cotton Embroidery Floss (alphabetical by color name)

3824	Apricot, Light
535	Ash Grey, Very Light
819	Baby Pink, Light
818	Baby Pink
775	Baby Blue, Light
3072	Beaver Grey, Very Light
648	Beaver Grey, Light
647	Beaver Grey, Medium
646	Beaver Grey, Dark
645	Beaver Grey, Very Dark
844	Beaver Grey, Ultra Dark
543	Beige Brown, Ultra Very Light
842	Beige Brown, Very Light
841	Beige Brown, Light
840	Beige Brown, Medium
839	Beige Brown, Dark
838	Beige Brown, Very Dark
822	Beige Grey, Light
644	Beige Grey, Medium
642	Beige Grey, Dark
640	Beige Grey, Very Dark
3790	Beige Grey, Ultra Dark
310	Black
3371	Black Brown
435	Brown, Very Light
434	Brown, Light
433	Brown, Medium
3024	Brown Grey, Very Light
3023	Brown Grey, Light
3022	Brown Grey, Medium
3787	Brown Grey, Dark
3021	Brown Grey, Very Dark
3801	Christmas Red, Light
666	Christmas Red, Bright
801	Coffee Brown, Dark
898	Coffee Brown, Very Dark
938	Coffee Brown, Ultra Dark
922	Copper, Light
920	Copper, Medium
921	Copper
712	Cream
613	Drab Brown, Light
612	Drab Brown, Medium
611	Drab Brown, Dark
610	Drab Brown, Very Dark
—	Ecru
3770	Flesh, Very Light
945	Flesh, Medium
951	Flesh
3772	Flesh, Dark
632	Flesh, Very Dark
523	Forest Green, Light
988	Forest Green, Medium
3827	Golden Brown, Pale
977	Golden Brown, Light
976	Golden Brown, Medium
3826	Golden Brown
975	Golden Brown, Dark
3078	Golden Yellow, Very Light
935	Green Avocado, Dark
3052	Green Grey, Medium
3053	Green Grey
422	Hazel Nut Brown, Light
3828	Hazel Nut Brown
420	Hazel Nut Brown, Dark
869	Hazel Nut Brown, Very Dark
3013	Khaki Green, Light
3012	Khaki Green, Medium
3011	Khaki Green, Dark
445	Lemon, Light
307	Lemon
444	Lemon, Dark
402	Mahogany, Very Light
3776	Mahogany, Light
301	Mahogany, Medium
400	Mahogany, Dark
300	Mahogany, Very Dark
3033	Mocha Brown, Very Light
3782	Mocha Brown, Light
3032	Mocha Brown, Medium
3781	Mocha Brown, Dark
3031	Mocha Brown, Very Dark
3819	Moss Green, Light
372	Mustard, Light
370	Mustard, Medium
371	Mustard
746	Off-White
677	Old Gold, Very Light
676	Old Gold, Light
729	Old Gold, Medium
680	Old Gold, Dark
3829	Old Gold, Very Dark
834	Olive Gold, Very Light
833	Olive Gold, Light
831	Olive Gold, Medium
832	Olive Gold

830	Olive Gold, Dark
829	Olive Gold, Very Dark
734	Olive Green, Light
733	Olive Green, Medium
732	Olive Green
731	Olive Green, Dark
730	Olive Green, Very Dark
3825	Orange Spice, Very Light
907	Parrot Green, Light
948	Peach Flesh, Very Light
754	Peach Flesh, Light
762	Pearl Grey, Very Light
415	Pearl Grey
317	Pewter Grey
413	Pewter Grey, Dark
3799	Pewter Grey, Very Dark
919	Red Copper
918	Red Copper, Dark
524	Seafoam Green, Very Light
522	Seafoam Green, Medium
453	Shell Grey, Light
452	Shell Grey, Medium
451	Shell Grey, Dark
B5200	Snow White
3774	Sportsman Flesh, Very Light
3773	Sportsman Flesh, Medium
950	Sportsman Flesh
407	Sportsman Flesh, Dark
3064	Sportsman Flesh, Very Dark
318	Steel Grey, Light
414	Steel Grey, Dark
3822	Straw, Light
3821	Straw
739	Tan, Ultra Very Light
738	Tan, Very Light
437	Tan, Light
436	Tan
742	Tangerine, Light
741	Tangerine, Medium
740	Tangerine
3779	Terra Cotta, Ultra Very Light
3778	Terra Cotta, Light
356	Terra Cotta, Medium
3830	Terra Cotta
355	Terra Cotta, Dark
3777	Terra Cotta, Very Dark
727	Topaz, Very Light
726	Topaz, Light
783	Topaz, Medium (Christmas Gold)
782	Topaz, Dark
781	Topaz, Very Dark
780	Topaz, Ultra Very Dark
—	Blanc Neige (White)
3823	Yellow, Very Light Pale
745	Yellow, Light Pale
744	Yellow, Light
3047	Yellow Beige, Light
3046	Yellow Beige, Medium
3045	Yellow Beige, Dark

JOURNAL

A transcription of Don Holbrook's streamside fishing notes, 1996-2000.

1996

April - Saw march brown and gray fox at camp, cold and wet spring, not much fishing.

May 18 - Penns Creek, #14 gray fox found while sitting on top of Little Mountain while turkey hunting. Changed to spinner, body looked olive, is 54A (2 wide) and 309A (1 wide) hackle, bronze dun and dark cream or light ginger.

May 25 - Penns Creek, #10 march brown, wings dark mottled w/lemon leading edge, 2 tails, spinner tan very light #738, top ribbed beige-brown dark #839, 7 bands, wing 45 degrees back, legs heavily mottled, hackle med. brown or ginger and Plymouth Rock.

June 14 - Big Spring, weather fair. Caught about 20, missed 10, mostly at outlet on #22 olive/silver, #22 brown/olive, #18 gray/white, #18 brown/white.

June 15 - Big Spring, caught only 3 at outlet, hitting midge drys on top.

June 22 - Big Spring, hot, 92°, Caught 1 on Hare's Ear #14, and 3–5 on peacock/white dry. Did not fish outlet, most not feeding.

June 23 - Big Spring, caught few at outlet, pumped one, took pictures, 18-3021/3032, and 24-347/27.

June 29 - Big Spring, arrive late, 6pm, lots of fishermen, most spots taken, fish not interested in new colors. Caught only 1 or 2. Met Barry and Peg Myers, got permission to publish peacock and white.

June 30 - Big Spring, 80s, sprinkling rain only. Caught none till outlet, then 20, most 1 or 2 on each color, #24s, new flies plus some one shade lighter, olives, black/silver #18, 5 or 6 big fish plus several more, none on whites, silver, shrimp, brown/white. Shut off at dusk.

July 4 - Big Spring, cold, 6–7pm. Caught none below outlet area, tried black/silver, gray/white. At outlet, caught 10–15, several big, on #18 black/silver, a couple on #22 black/silver, 2 on red-brown/silver #24, 1 on beadhead pheasant, 1 on dry #22 peacock/white, none on #54/silver, rust/silver.

July 6 - Big Spring, hot, 90°, 6pm. Caught 2 on old favorite #18 olive with wood duck tails, caught 1 at lower end, black/silver still works at outlet in #18 and #22, caught 6 fish in 15 min. Others were catching on #28 nymph Krystal Flash(?) rear half, reddish hackle front half. Caught 1 on reddish brown/rainbow #24. Found flies, #28 nymphs, palest yellow, touch green, no apparent rib. Caught 1 on peacock/white, several refusals, none on white spinner.

July 7 - Big Spring, 90s, 5–9pm. Caught 5 at lower end, 1 each on copper, #24 brown/olive, cream shrimp, #18 mink, #28 yellow. None on silver, gold, gray/white, orange brown/white floss (all #28s), cream, tan, brown, red-brown, yellow-brown rib, gold, brown/silver, #24 olive/silver. At 9pm at outlet, several on #18 black/silver—dropping off. Flies (took pictures) pupae #24 pale olive-yellow-green, perhaps faint brown rib and head, #22 thin white, #18–20 whitish w/ red tinge at rib and ends.

July 14 - Big Spring, 90s, humid, 2pm. At outlet, 3 on silver, 1 on #18 black/silver, 1 on #24 pale yellow/silver, 2 on #24 red, none on #22 black/silver, #24 brown/yellow, gray/white, copper, 1 on #24 reddish brown/rainbow just before storm. Big thunderstorm at 5–5:30pm, then water cloudy. Caught 2 on black/silver, 3 on olive tan fur/wood duck, none on cream/brown mono. A fair number rising. Tried all spinners and peacock/white—nothing. Got flies, took slides and pictures, lots of red worms, some red/clear larvae, lots of reddish brown/dark brown #20s, green and cream pupae, a fair number of black fly larvae but caught none on black-fly pattern? These appear a little darker or browner, red, either #18 or #24, some reddish brown are quite red.

July 20 - Potter County, dry, few fish. Caught 3 on gray/white.

July 30 - Fisherman's Paradise, cloudy from storm, banks too wet to walk.

Caught 17 at outlet, mostly on #24 olive/brown,

August 10 - Big Spring, nice day, 5–8pm fished at outlet only. Caught few on gray/white, red brown rainbow, beige, #18 tan fur, silver. None on #24 red, copper, gold, brown/white, red brown/white, steel, olive/silver, black/silver, cress, Tricolor, #28 yellow/silver, #24 olive/brown.

August 11 - Big Spring, nice, 5–8:30pm. Caught 1 on light olive mono, 2 on light olive gray shrimp w/dot, all in regular water, 2 at outlet on pink Honeybug, 1 big fish broke off whitefly nymph, didn't act snagged, but. . . . None on brown mono, red, black sculpin, olive/silver #18 and #24, dark tan fur, cress, olive shrimp, black/silver, beige/silver, yellow/silver #24, lots of tan drys and rises at 8pm, to #26 and #28s.

August 18 - Allenberry, 6:30–8:45pm, nice, water up 8–12", cloudy, very few flies at pavilion. Caught 1 on emerger, 1 on #14 spinner, none on nymph, 2 hits on pink shrimp. Nothing from dam down. Heard more flies above dam.

August 20 - Allenberry, just watched at pavilion, 10 fish rising sporadically from 8:05–8:15, dead at 8:20. Few flies seen, Gene Utech said no flies for 9 days.

August 24 - Big Spring, 10am–1pm, fairly hot, not early enough, lots of people. Caught 3 on copper, none on 15 patterns at least, gray/white, silver, gold, brown/yellow, brass, black/silver, gray and tan fur, olive-orange shrimp, olive/silver, #28 red, red/silver, pink shrimp, several others. Not a good day!

August 25 - Allenberry, first good hatch, flies from 7:45–8:15pm, not too many fish. Caught 5 on spinner at pavilion dam, brown drakes early and #20 BWO (beige gray dark closest, mocha brown medium next).

August 26 - Allenberry, best flies yet, 7:30–8:15pm, caught 1, broke 3 fish off at pavilion below dam, more fish rising, a lot of refusals, need better spinner.

August 31 - Big Spring, 9am–1pm, 80s, sun, TU putting rocks in. Caught 2 below outlet, on #24 brown/yellow and #18 double gray. Lots of people, not worth going in morning. Pumped 1 fish—empty. None on copper, red-brown/rainbow, red-brown #28, black/silver, brown/silver, dark gray/silver, Weikert Larva, black spinner. Hatch of black #22, dark ginger legs. Must try floss body, a little thicker. Also fished at Allenberry, 6–8:30pm, start below dam. None on pink shrimp, tan caddis. New #20 BWO wet at 7:15pm, 6–7 flies, look like cahills, #14. No rises, small stuff, brown drake spinners. At 7:40pm, white-flies pretty good just below island. None on dry, none on spinner till 8pm, then 5 on #16 w/ chartreuse egg sac—should have caught 12. Over at 8:40pm, nice evening.

September 1 - Big Spring, 5–8:15pm, nice day. Hooked 2 at first corner, on #28 red and otter cress, none on copper, silver, olive silver, brick/white, red brown/silver, mink, purple worm. At outlet, caught big rainbow, about 20–22", on black fly larva, 1 on black/silver.

September 2 - Big Spring. Very heavy rain recently.

September 7 - Big Spring, water still running down road clear to hatchery, debris line 2' above blacktop, bushes at bend torn out, water high and cloudy. From 5–7:30pm, caught 1 or 2.

September 15 - Big Spring, water still down road, not quite as far, still high and cloudy, 5–7:30pm, almost nothing works.

September 22 - Big Spring, 4:30–6pm, water in road at houses, still high and cloudy. Now the cress bug works, caught 4–6, pumped fish but were empty, 1 on red, then thunderstorm.

September 25 - Big Spring, 4:30–7:15pm, dark, stillwater at first houses—unbelievable, water down some but still cloudy. Caught 1 on cress, 1 on red, 1 on Tricolor, flesh and purple worm fly—many picked up. Needed 2 hooks and maybe thinner. Big midge hatch at 6pm, reddish—no, brown?, grayish?, few rising. Pumped 2 fish, took pictures, lots of #18 terra cotta very dark and black-brown rib—head maybe grayer, white head tuft. #22 black fly—slightly greenish. #20–#22 hazelnut brown—no rib. #22–#24 drab brown light body, faint thin rib, brown gray dark head. #26 stubby gray abdomen, darker thorax, short antenna, long legs, mosquito? Few small #22–#24 gray-green, 1 white larva, 2 cress.

October - Only caught a few.

November - Didn't fish.

December 5 - Big Spring, 40°, 1–2pm. Hooked 20, most on #18 gray/white, some black/silver, took pictures. Lots of larvae almost identical to those on Sept. 25. Few black-fly larvae, several terra cotta w/ white tuft, lots of gray-green #20-#24, lots of red worms and red/white larvae.

1997

Early spring, warm winter, no snow.

January - Big Spring, few warm days, few on #18 gray/white.

March 15 - Big Spring, 3 (1,2,3) on #24-54/47 nymph, then nothing for 2-3 hrs.

March 20 - Yellow Breeches plant, black midges.

March 29 - Big Spring, 3 hrs., nothing, water running down road has finally almost stopped, holding pond just dry.

March 30 - Big Spring. From 4:30–5pm, none. From 5:30–6pm, 5 on #24-47/silver, 1 on #24 black/silver, 1 on #24 olive brown/silver. Fish feeding on top 6–6:30pm, when I left. Pumped one fish, got 100 insects: #20 red worm (pale and mottled), 40 white larva, long #18, thin, camel w/ brown head, heavily segmented, 11 segments plus head (alcohol bleaches red larvae immediately—in fish too?), 40 #24 and #22 mocha brown medium 3032 and #293A, amazing that 47/silver works so good—must try new ones.

April 12 - Penns Creek, cold, found 2 adult stoneflies on tree, 11/2 to 2" long, darkish brown w/ yellow and orange blotches on head. Brown runs down side of body like stripes.

April 17 - Yellow Breeches water plant, on unit #1, 34°–55°. Midges, most are #20 winged, bodies 3047 light yellow beige, 3790 beige gray ultra dark best for rib, 3021 brown gray very dark best for head, wings and legs long, 3047, took pictures.

April 20 - Boiling Springs, cold dry spring, 55°, night 35°, 3–5pm. Caught 1 on #24 olive/silver, 8 on new 3047/3790, 2 on darker version, then quit and went home.

April 24 -Fisherman's Paradise, 3-5:30pm, coolish, cloudy, slightly cloudy water, no grass in outlet. Caught 10–12 on new 3047/3790, 2 at start on darker one, 2 at end on #24-54/47, then quit and went home. Hatch of craneflies, #18 best match?, yellow beige dark 3045 (half width dark brown rib)—must try, and #18 caddis medium brown and mottled turkey to the eye, but in scope appears moss green light 3819—underside of wings appears dun or clearish, not mottled as on top.

April 26 - Boiling Springs, 6-8pm, nice weather, coolish, clear water. Caught 3 on new 3047/3790, 1 on 54/47, 1 on black fly, feeding on caddis and craneflies.

May 5-10 - Penns Creek, Bill Bowman stopped at camp, Johnson and Blue rock hole, best in years, sulfur, march brown.

May 15 - Big Spring, 2 on #20 gray white, 5 on unrecorded fly.

May 25 - Penns Creek, saw yellow-winged, rosy-bodied Eporus Vitrea spinner?

June 5 - Penns Creek, still cool, heard that green drakes peaked at camp.

June 7 - Penns Creek, 7:30–8:30pm, at swinging bridge, fair number of green drake spinners, lg. number of spinners over rapids, #14 olive, 2 tails, heavily mottled wings, mottled legs, overall reddish cast on top, march brown or gray fox?, saw no rises, green drake duns at 8:30pm, fished nymph—nothing.

June 8 - Boiling Springs. Caught 7 on #24-54/silver, 1 on #18 brown spinner, lots of rises at dark, #16 BWO?, 2 tails.

June 14 - Boiling Springs, nice. Caught 3 on #24 47/silver, 1 on brown spinner, 1 on yellow spinner, lots of rises at dusk, couldn't fish in spot I wanted to.

June 15 - Big Spring, nice, 70s, clear, cool evening, 6pm. Caught 7 on #24-47/silver, 1 on gray/white, none on red, 1 on brick/silver, 1 on double gray, 4 on 54/47, 5 on 47/silver wet, 1 on tan caddis nymph, none on brown/silver, 4 on mink at dark 8:45–9pm, fair number of rises dark, didn't try, took pictures. In scope, most looked gray-green #22, one #14 cahill spinner, a couple of small cress, 1 black fly, 1 #20 dark tannish body, reddish head, and #24-#26 gray-green nymph and dry.

June 16 - Boiling Springs, 7:30–8:30pm, 70s, nice, a little humid. None on #24 47/silver, 2 on tan caddis nymph, 2 on yellow wet, #16 yellow-winged sulfur duns, 2 tails, pale yellow body and legs, ruddy thorax, lg. black eyes. Spinners in air, could not tell what, also then #16 BWO olive dun, 3 tails, light yellow body w/ olive cast, light yellow legs, thorax same as body, dark dun wings.

June 21 - Big Spring, 88°–90°, nice, water clear, 6:30–9pm, at outlet. Caught on mink nymphs: 5 fish on #12 short hook, 2 on #24, 6 on #22 near dark, 2 on #24-47/silver, none on black/silver, 6 on gray/olive cream 27/17. Caught flies, took no pictures, most are gray-green type, matched in microscope is #26-293A/361, #24-361—should have slightly smoke head, some very light, almost yellow, some w/ light brownish band and head, some drys same as nymphs, med. light ones not really ribbed, almost as though segments are outlined, others have fairly dark segments, fading in fish?, few black flies, one ant, try drys w/ 361 color body, same legs.

June 23 - Boiling Springs, outlet, no one here, hot, few flies, no spinners, too hot? None on new midge or #24-54/silver or yellow Cahill wet, 2 on brown spinner at dusk, a lot of rises to something small or emerging.

June 29 - Big Spring, hot, 88°–90°, 6:30–9:15pm, tried new #24-293A/361 on 10-15 fish—no looks. Moved to outlet, 6–10 fish first half hour, then took 10 casts/fish or more, (best new one was thin ribbed), regular rib was only fair, did not try 361 only, #18 red worm—3 quick hookups, then none, none on silver, 1 hit on gray/white, none on #22 mink, few off/on on 293/361, then at 8:30pm, caught 12 or so on #24-280/rainbow, some big—no idea why. From 9-9:15pm, none on #12 mink. Caught flies, took no pictures. In scope, 90% are 293A/361, a lot tend to the light side, many are #26 or even #28, may explain no looks earlier on #24, few red but #16 long and thin, a couple black flies, a couple white larvae, a few drys of the above nymphs. Tried black-winged wet—none, next time try 361 w /gray thread head, #26? maybe gray rib? thin, none on Weikert Larva, 280/rainbow pattern must use clear narrow loose strands Firefly tinsel w/ black thread base, do not use holographic/opaque tinsel.

July 2 - Boiling Springs, 80s, muggy, almost dark. Caught 2 on #26 red brown/rainbow.

July 3 - Boiling Springs, same, 8:45–9:30pm. None on red brown/rainbow or new #26 safari, 2 on #18 spinner brown. Some mayflies coming off.

July 4 - Big Spring, 6:30–9pm, nice 80°. New #26 safari w/ gray thread rib and head is super, caught 7–8, some in slack water, from 6:30–8pm and again at 8:45, good fly, took pictures. Caught only 1–2 on #26 safari/black head or rainbow, but few flies in sample, lots of black-fly larvae, some very dark banded. Caught 11, some big, on #18 gray/silver (black fly?). Several larvae, #18-#20 brownish w/ reddish and grayish touch (took pictures). Caught 3 on gray/white or double gray—not sure.

July 6 - Allenberry, fairly hot, creek low, very cloudy, not from rain, algae?, Yellow Breeches water plant has been having higher than normal turbidity, no rain to speak of. Few fish seen, although Yellow Breeches Anglers recently stocked? Caught 2 on pink shrimp, none on tan or brown caddis/peacock, 6:30–8:45pm, few splashy rises to white midge or caddis.

July 12 - Big Spring, hot, 90°, 6:45pm. None on several patterns, 2 on gray/silver, lots rising at 8:45, could not get good spot, too much algae, left.

July 13 - Big Spring, 6–9:15pm, 90°, cooling quickly. Caught 1 on safari #26/med. black w/ wet black wing, 1 on Orange Dot Shrimp, lost it, 3 on otter cress, lost it, 6–7 on pearl gray/silver (#415), 2 on #22 gray/white on top, started fishing nymphs in film, lots of fish rising, caught 2 on #22-#24 fat white, 7–8 on floating midge pupa #26? The naturals are one color—one of the very lights—light yellow beige looks close, but fly stained w/ algae, could be cream, off-white, pale yellow, or beige. Must try all. Whatever—siliconed, the floating pupa works as well as a dry!

July 20 - Big Spring, nice day. Caught none till outlet, then 15–20 on various colors and sizes, none on safari or red.

July 23 - Boiling Springs, hot, late, 8pm. Caught 5 on #18 old gold light 676/cream 712.

July 26 - Big Spring, 7–9pm, 88°. Caught none, did not fish outlet, used new #24 w/ rainbow tinsel. Should take photos of various tinsel to see difference. Some fish looked at #26 ecru pupa on top, (color? gets stained w/ algae), saw 2 caught on olive gray cress.

August 4 - Fisherman's Paradise, 10am-1pm, 85°, just after rain. A couple on brown/silver, none on most #24s, few fish in stream, low—most in outlet. Caught 12 or more on pink shrimp.

August 6 - Fisherman's Paradise, same as before.

August 7 - Big Spring, 7:30–9pm, went straight to outlet. Caught 2 on new brown/silver, 2 on pink shrimp, moved to corner at 8:30pm, caught 12 or so on #24 light? cream or so, stained green by algae and still works. Caught flies, green ones and reddish brown. Dry appears to be #24 beige gray ultra dark 3790, light legs, maybe a light gray stripe rib—thin, maybe black head.

August 27 - Allenberry, water a little high and cloudy, first chance to go for whitefly, fair hatch. Not as many fish, didn't do well, none on nymph or wet, need a good emerger pattern. Caught nothing from 6:30pm till hatch. Only time I went.

September 29 - Big Spring, nice day, 2–5pm. Caught 1 in slow water on gray-brown cress, caught a few at corner on khaki. Too much algae, didn't fish outlet.

October, 3rd week - Pulaski, New York. Caught 11 salmon, 1 landed, 2 coho, 2 rainbow, 1 parr, most on dark red or fluorescent red/white.

October 24 - Fisherman's Paradise, 4–6pm, cool, at outlet, water coming out of upper outlet. Caught 4 on khaki, 4 on red beads, saw midges—#22 black, #24 yellow. Caught no fish on spinners, but they are rising to something.

1998

January 2 - Big Spring, nice, 50°+, 3:30–530pm, cold at end, lots of people, no fish feeding. Tried gray/white, red black/silver, brown/silver, mink, otter cress, silver, copper, orange/white, #26 dark ones, #18 light–dark gray. At outlet at 5pm, 1 on white/Royal Bonnyl, 3 on cream Glo Egg/orange spot.

January 4 - Big Spring, nice, 60°, 3–5:30pm, same as before, at outlet, 4:30pm. Caught 1 on yellow/brown mono?, 1 on yellow/brown thread, 2 hits on Glo Egg. Got 1 fly pupa, 293A taupe green/safari #26.

January 23 - Boiling Springs. Caught 2–3.

January 31 - Big Spring, 3–5pm, 40°, no hits on 293A/safari, 3 at outlet, 5 on rust/silver #18, a couple on black/silver, brown/silver, took pictures, #26 is beige thread w/ dark brown tying thread under and wrap over small head, rest are #18+ reddish brown, closest is probably 938 coffee brown ultra dark/silver, but fly used was more reddish brown/silver.

February - Mild winter, no time to fish.

March - Big Spring, went 2–3 times in middle of month, nice weather, 85° one day, crowded. Caught either none or 2–3, mostly on #24-54/47 or so. Not many caught. Big mink worked late some.

April 4 - Big Spring, 65°, water up 3–4 weeks and in road. Caught 3 on #24 - 54/47, one big 16"+, eating cress bugs and #24 khaki/black thread bands (may be safari), and #24 light gray or charcoal w/ dark thin bands. Cress are light olive brown w/ light tan underside. Tried gray/white, silver, red bead, otter cress, black/silver, #24 olive/silver, white/Royal Bonnyl, red brown/flash, #24 brown/white, #12 mink, #18 charcoal. Caught 1 or 2 on pink shrimp.

April 10 - Big Spring, nice, 55°–60°, water up from heavy rain yesterday, very cloudy. Caught 14 or so at outlet, 6 on new #24-325A/27 pale gray/smoke head and same but black 8-0 Unithread head, 3 on 102/27 dark linen/smoke, 2 on #24 safari/green beadhead, 1 on safari #24, 1 on silver. From 3–7pm, tried all bead flies, 1 on black, 1 on silver, none on #20 red. Orange Dot Shrimp, gray/white, #24 black/olive, #14 tan, #24 tan/black head, #24 safari/tinsel, 1 on pink shrimp, 2 on 54/47. Saw big caddis, #14 body, wings—rusty. At 4pm, black midges. At 6pm, smaller light midges. Got only 2 pupae, #24s, same as on April 4, but better match may be 293A/347 taupe green/dark linen or 475/126 raisin/khaki—will try tomorrow.

April 12 - Big Spring, 4pm, nice, 65°+, water down 2" and clearer. Caught 4 on red beads, 3 going upstream, 1 at outlet. At outlet, 4 on 475/126, one big, 3 on 293A/347, only 1 on original 325A/27—all #24s. None on brown/silver, #26 safari bead, #26 off-white?, 54/27. Saw big caddis again, wings turkey rusty, body front 1/3 rust, rear 2/3 linen? Fish again stopped taking 6–6:30pm, feeding on something else. Small caddis coming off, very small, light color, and #20 banded—caught no flies.

April 20 - Boiling Springs, 2 hrs. Caught 3 on tan caddis larva/peacock, none on red, gray/white, several other colors, caddis hatching. As of this date, 8" more rain this year than average. Yellow Breeches still up, clearing.

May 21 - Penns Creek, green drakes now, no turkeys.

May 30 - Sawmill Creek, saw beaver dam. Caught one 10" brownie on tan caddis nymph, Goose Gessner got 1 on minnow.

June 6 and 8 - Big Spring, very cool. Caught 10–15 or more, big ones on #18 silver, #18 copper, #12 mink. Most flies are #22–#24 gray-greens, no pictures, too tired. Also caught on gray/white, #24 - 54/47, #24-54/silver, pink shrimp, none on most everything else. Must develop gray-green. Also 1 on olive shrimp.

June 14 - Big Spring, 4–6pm, nothing.

June 21 - Big Spring, 3–7pm, hot, 80s. Caught 30+, 4 on mink 12 up through, 15 on #24-280/rainbow, no hits on same 280 w/ silver or bead, 1 on #24-54/47, 7 on #24 red w/ 1 bead, 2 on #18 rainbow beads, 2 on #24 safari/bead, none on gold, silver, or black beads, none on 47/silver, 5 on #22 yellow/brown rib at 7pm, 2 on pale gray/black thread, no weight, none on #24 khaki on top, one on #18 mink, most at outlet, must try bigger rust/Royal Bonnyl. Took pictures. Flies: #24 gray-green, #22–#24 light gray w/ dark head, shrimp are 1 color, 3827 matches body, 977 back (golden browns), try #20–#22 size. One #18+ appears dark olive brown (rear shell coming off), one #18–#20 greenish mottled w/ rose blotches, one #18 stonefly nymph pale olive, #22 caddis larva green #733, medium olive is close, various gray-greens, one #24–#26 very light, lots of reds and bleached ones.

July 5 - Big Spring, nice, 85°, 7:30–9pm. Caught 1 on 280/rainbow, 5 on #20-762/white (2 before outlet), 2 on new shrimp, 2 on #18-415/silver (light gray), none on #18 red brown/silver, 1 on pink shrimp, 2 big hits on #12 mink at dark, 1 on #18-763/white.

July 11 - Drove to Big Spring, forgot fly box, drove home. Went to Boiling Springs, 7–8:30pm, cool, 70s. Caught 5 on #18 gray/white, 1 on #20 gray/white, none on black/silver.

July 12 - Big Spring, 6–9:15pm, nice, 80°, then cool. Caught 1 on #280/rainbow, none on #20 gray/white. Only 2 spots open. At outlet, caught 6 on #24 red beadhead real quick, none on it after 6:30pm, lots of fish feeding, esp. later, and rising till 9:15pm, then shut down completely. None on #24 cream/brown head, silver, tan and new shrimp, gray/silver, white/Royal Bonnyl, #20 red, #24 gray/cream, #24 safari, brown/silver, 1 on 280/rainbow again, 1 on black/silver, 1 on #18 mink, 2 on #12 mink at dark, 1 on #24 54/47, big one on 47/silver wet (clear wing), 1 on #24 safari beadhead (greenish), 2 on #18 olive/silver, 3 on #18 red beads, 2 on pink shrimp. Others catching well on top using #28 cream, I think. Got flies: black-fly adults, few cress, #20 gray-green w/ thin dark rib, biggest seen yet, smaller gray-greens, new caddis larva #26–#28, olive, lots of them, safari is real close, maybe a little greener, should have worked, maybe fished too deep since there was lots of surface feeding, has small head, 2 larger segments, then 7 body segments same, 1 smaller tail segment. Could rib fine black, head is actually a light brown like Weikert larva.

July 19 - Big Spring, 5–8pm, w/ Ed Koch, hot, 90°, at outlet. Caught 6 on #24 red beadhead, none on gray/white, 3 on #18 silver, none on black/silver, 1 hit on 712/tan shrimp, none on 293A/361, 1 on #24-869/Veniard silver wrapped together, none on #18 same, none on #18 red beads. Sipping at 6:30pm. Caught 1 adult, appeared black, in scope later was #28-126 khaki underside of abdomen, legs and head under same, light smoky wings, top is dark brown, 475 raisin is close, will try to take picture. Caught 10, including 3 big ones, on #24 safari/green irid. beadhead—must tie khaki/same bead, caught these 7:30–8pm, before this, thinking black was correct color, caught 4 on #24-361/gray thread—must try khaki, 2 on 280/rainbow at last, 1 on double gray #18-3021/3787, 6–8 on #26-475 raisin (try black too), 4 on black wet #24—broke it off in nice fish, none on black mono #18, 2 more on #24 red beadhead, 1 on #24 black/silver, try some raisin wets, caught pupae, mostly gray-greens #24–#28, some 361 safari, some #126 khaki, safari ones tend to have thin black rib (thread) and dark head, khaki ones seem to have a darker overall cast—maybe dark head will help. Lots of larvae in khaki and safari, #28–#24, #26 most common, almost like light green olive mono flies, only smaller. Tied some #18 chartreuse thread w/ mono to try, took pictures. One picture was near match, though fly was not used yet—must try #24-102 dark linen tied w/ dark brown 6/0 and covering head. Underthread shows through space between linen wraps as faint rib.

July 25 - Allenberry, 9am–1:30pm, 70° up to 80°, w/ Ed Koch. Caught 1 at dam on pink shrimp, then none on black/silver, 10 on #18 gray-white, most in area above pavilion. Pumped 1 fish: #28 or smaller cream midge adult, wings smoky gray, thorax top had hint of tan, legs white mottled, unusual #24 nymph, took pictures, mottled legs, dark raisin brown wing stubs on sides, 9-segment body, segment color close to #312A, narrow band between close to 543 hemp and very narrow, like 4:1 width ratio of segments to thin band, head is separate? Like praying mantis, each segment had clear paddles sticking out from sides. Correction—cream midge was 530 chamois—use dark gray wet wing?, 3rd insect have no idea, was cigar-shaped hairy, 8 segments white and gold? tinsel and dark head (empty shell?). Another smaller, chamois is close, fat #24 w/ reddish brown ribbing and head. Use floss body, #3827 pale golden brown is perfect, #300 mahogany is close but too red. Must use #319A Spanish tile thread, faint in body. Tied some, did not get back to try. Little craneflies were hatching, uncertain of color, maybe light yellow. Must look up nymph in book—might be damselflies?

July 25 - Big Spring, 6–9:15pm, 80°. Caught 3 on #24 red beadhead, 2 big ones broke off, none on #24 khaki bead, #24 safari bead, 1 on #20 gray-white, at corner, 4–5 on #26-102/brown head w/ weight. At 8pm, 1 on #26 safari dry nymph, lots of fish rising, caught 10 on #26-102/brown head on top, pumped none, rising till 9:15pm.

August 2 - Fishermen's Paradise, 2–8pm, nice day, very few fish in upper part, stream low, no rain, lots of algae slime on bottom. At outlet, 1 on pink shrimp, then nothing most of afternoon, fish feeding, finally several on little wet until poly wing pulled off, #20, body 54 seal brown, must make some more.

August 8 - Big Spring, 4–9pm, hot, 80s, then cool. None on #24 red, 2 on #18 gray/white. At outlet corner, 4 on #24-290/rainbow, 2 on #47 olive/silver, 2 on #22 brown/silver, none on brown/white, red/black, dark gray/silver #22, at outlet, 4 on pink shrimp, 2 on orange shrimp, pumped fish—looked like dark nymphs, 3 on Orange Dot Shrimp, full moon light till 9:30pm. Fish started rising at 8:30pm, caught 3–4 on #18 black mono—no lead, #26-102/brown thread head on top was good, then broke off. In scope, naturals are greenish-reddish—will be hell to match, try 918 red copper dark/921 copper or 371 mustard/921 copper #18–#22, late hatches are khaki type #24s, 1 single red worm, 1 caddis light gray and white banded like black fly—unusual around #22.

August 9 - Big Spring, 80s, muggy, will rain late, heavy cloud cover, dark early, 7:30–8:30pm only. New fly from yesterday, #18 red thread underbody and tail, fluor. yellow mono body, olive brown thread head and finish. Caught 3, very good considering crowd, 3 more at outlet. Tried red head one—no good, chartreuse head one caught 2 in 12 casts—not bad. Fish started rising, broke leader, by the time it was retied in the dark, fish would not take nymph. Had #20 original pattern to try, believe this is better size, must try again. Might not float—must check, maybe why fish did not take it. Took no pictures, yesterday's nymphs faded in alcohol already (red gone).

August 15 - Big Spring, 6–8:30pm, very muggy, 80°, overcast. Caught 2, one big, on new rose-olive, and 2 above corner. Fish rising early, 7:15–7:30pm, little black flies everywhere, even at 6pm. Tried #26 black/white, got 2 hits. Went on top, #26 khaki/black thread head, got 2. Tried black wet white wing under, nothing, too big, esp. wing. Tried #26 safari on top, got 2, then #26 raisin, 6 on top, saved last fly, might have gotten 12. Dark now, rose-olive nymph no good, pumped one fish. Only 6 flies, but good, rose-olive nymphs and dry, must have pattern, some gray-green nymphs and dry, black things that have 2-segment body, all legs on front segment, 4 wings, and head. Looked at them in scope—adult black flies?, #24–#26, 2 body segments, rear banded med. dark gray and ecru or fawn, next is darker, have 6 legs, 4 wings, black head, 2 feelers, some gray-green, some reddish.

August 22 - Big Spring, 80s, 5:45–8:30pm. Caught 5–6, a big one broke off. Then 4–5 more at corner on new #20 olive-rose mono—good fly. Somebody at outlet. Rises heavy from 7:30–8:15pm. Caught one fly, appears to be #26 thin black midge. New wet raisin sunk doesn't work, none on #26 raisin on top like last week, 2–3 on #26 cream/thread, then 5–6 on raisin wet fly on top. Peg Myers caught 12 on peacock. All shut down at 8:30pm, no fish pumped.

August 29 - Big Spring, hot, muggy, 80s, 6:30–8:15pm. Caught 2–3 on rose olive, most fish don't look but caught 6–8 at outlet. Hatch over but still good fly. One on olive/silver #18, 2 on #24 black/white, none on new ant dry, 2 on #26 raisin dry. Took pictures—#20-102A w/ thread rib 287, make some, black-fly larvae?, w/ enlarged part—rib brownish #840 w/ maybe cream, #28-#102, #28 cream w/ gray thread—make, #28 gray-white—make some.

September 10 - Allenberry, first time out for whiteflies, 6:30–8:30pm, lower dam section, Ed Koch was there. Caught 3 on pink shrimp, fair number of whiteflies from 7:30–7:45pm, 2 missed on Ed's #14 white hackle fly, 1 on spinner, didn't try foam emerger, fair number of fish.

September 12 - Big Spring, 6:30–7:45pm, forgot fly box, no light, 88°. Found a few flies in pouch. None on #18-831/silver, pink shrimp, #24 red bead. Caught 5 at outlet on #24 red bead?, no rises till late, not as good as 2 weeks ago, 1 on #24-475 raisin, lots of refusals. Pumped 1 fish, #20 red worm, #22 olive brown.

September 21 - At Yellow Breeches water plant, lots of #24 black midges and #22 yellow mayflies.

September 22 - Big Spring, 6–8pm, low 80s, muggy, overcast, sprinkled at 8pm. Caught none till near end, 1 on 950/off-white shrimp, many feeding, picking off cress tops, none on black/red, #20 gray/white, red beads, a few rising at 7:15pm, not many, 2 on black wet w/ white wing—not right. At 7:45pm all rising stopped. Pumped 1 fish, 1 snail about #24, one #26–#28 shell only, one #18 appears dark brownish w/ thin rose rib, partially emerged (3 sections). Maybe dark brick—try brown mono and red thread.

September 28 - Big Spring, muggy, 90°, 6:30–7:30pm. Fished at corner with Ed Koch, caught none. Thunderstorm coming, windy. Tried #26-102 beadhead, #24 red bead, #18-3371/3777, #26 peacock dry, 1 miss, #26-126. Only a few rising early and quit early, thunderstorm 5 miles up I-81.

October 11 - Big Spring, 70°, clear, windy. One hit on pink shrimp, 1 on #22 black/silver, none on #18-831/silver, red bead, gray/silver, 1 on #18-762/white, few feeding 1–5pm. At outlet caught 10 on #18-762/white, 5 on #24-475/361, pumped 1 fish, took pictures, #26-3023 brown gray/#361 safari (make these), #28-102/brown head—need medium brown, not reddish, one #24 red, one #18 reddish tint olive, but darker than last month and brownish, some #28 nearly yellow with smoke cast, pale safari larvae #20ish, dry #24 is tannish/dark brown head—543 hemp very close—make some, few black flies #32, one #20-3906B 831 olive gold.

October 13 - Little Lehigh at Allentown Park, 10am–4pm, cool and windy early, cleared up, 60°, water slightly cloudy from yesterday's rain. Went up left side first, caught 1 on #24 red bead in slow water, 2 others looked, none on 18 gray/white. In deeper water and slight riffle, none on 54/27, 3 on #18-831/silver, none on #22 black/silver. Across bridge and down other side, at deep run below rock dam, 2 on #26-3023/361. At hatchery outlet, 6 more on same, then 5 on #26-475/361, 2 more downstream in deep flat, 1 just above bridge in slow water. Below bridge, caught none.

October 25 - Boiling Springs, 70°, nice, 5–6:30pm. None on #18 gray/white, #22 olive/silver, #26-102/brown head, raisin/361, 3 on #18 pink shrimp—1 big, 3 on #24 red bead—2 big.

November 29 - Big Spring, record temp. 70°, fair wind till late, 1–4pm. None on #24 red bead, #18 gray/white. Fairly crowded at outlet, 4 pm, 1 on 831/silver, none on olive mono, #24-102/brown head, #20 gray/white, 4 on pink shrimp, shut off at 4:30pm. Pumped 2 fish—2 red worms, 1 about 3/4" long (San Juan Worm), several brownish black-fly larvae w/ multibranched feelers #22 fat, try darker beige brown 840 and ecru. Took pictures—most are #26-102 dark linen/Unithread, 8/0 dark brown is close but need dark smoke—try to find. Will tie these to try. One nice adult #24-102 dark linen w/ faint body marks, legs same w/ dark dun/smoke cast, same with wings, some brown on head, 2 black eyes. Also same in #32.

December 20 - Big Spring, 2:30–4:30pm, 50s, went right to outlet. Caught 7 on new #26-102/dark brown Unithread head during three periods of use, 4 on new #22-840/ecru, 1 on red San Juan Worm, 2 on #24-50/silver, none on #20 gray/white, #24 red bead, 318 olive/silver, #26 safari, #24 safari bead. All nice fish, brookies, brilliant colors. Pumped 1 brookie—#18 cress bugs, very light, 2 black-fly adults, one #18 red worm, black-fly larvae not brown this time as in November but more charcoal—must try. One #26 or #28-102, almost no rib or head color—just 102, #26-102, but smoke or charcoal rib or head color—must get thread, though dark brown works well—1 every 12 casts—one #18 brownish olive maybe—hard to tell, one #20 olive rose, drys are #26–#28, appear black, are really gray-brown w/ brown legs—smoke is too green, muskrat about right.

1999

January 17 - Big Spring, 4–5:30pm, 50s, 4" snow, iced over, lots of people. Caught 3 on new #26-102/iron gray head and 8X, none on #18 gray/white, 2 on #938/silver at corner, 2 more on #26-102/iron gray on 7X. Dark at 5:30, no more hits. Pumped 1 fish—got 1 larva, #18 or #20-3021 brown gray very dark/869 hazel nut brown very dark. Try this and also 3021/silver. If not, try 1 shade lighter hazel nut. Caught 1 adult midge in air—body dried looks black or charcoal, legs goldish.

February 15 - Big Spring, nice, near 50°, 2–5pm, crowded. None on #18-543/712, #24-54/47, one at bend on #24 red bead, finally 6 at outlet on #18 gray/white at 4:30–5pm. None on #16 mink, #20 black/silver, #18 red bead, #26-102/iron gray, #24 khaki bead, pink shrimp, otter cress. Pumped 1 fish—small cress #20, #18 black-fly larva, dark, try 3787 or 3022 w/ 613 or 3032, #22 pale green larva, 295A lemon is close w/ white thread spaces, rust head. Also small dark browns (pieces), caught drys in air, must remember to look at before they dry out. Most common was #22, black or charcoal thin body, same legs, feather antennae. Other was #28, brownish gold body and legs, 2 distinct segments plus head w/ large eyes, 6 legs on front segment. Almost no rises but left early, saw few caught.

February 21 - Big Spring, cold, 3–4pm. Nothing on new flies of 15th, no midge adults, 4 at outlet on #26 black thread/white poly wet. Pumped 1fish—mostly #22 gray-greens, try 102 and 295A w/ black and brown thread, also retie last week larva w/ rust head—too big a head.

February 27 - Boiling Springs, rainy, fished a half hour. Caught 1 on new #295A/brown head. Pumped 1fish—full of bread and lg. #18 yellowish nymph.

February 28 - Big Spring, rained, up some, fairly clear, 40s, 3–5:30pm. Tested patterns at outlet, #22s, 1 on 102/iron gray, 9 on 295A/iron gray, 3 on 102/dark brown, 3 on 295A/dark brown, 3 on new 295A larva w/ small 65 rust head inc. 1 big, 3 on #18 543/712, none on #22 black/CDC wing. Pumped 1—mostly same as 15th, esp. 295A. Took pictures.

March 20 - Big Spring, 3:30–6:30pm, 40s, crowded. Caught 6 on #20-762/white below dam—one 20". At corner, 2 on #18-3024/silver, 2 on #18-543/712. At outlet, 3 on #22-295A/iron gray Uni, none on 54/47, 54/silver. #22 drys are black w/ golden legs.

March 28 - Fisherman's Paradise–Spring Creek, 3:30–6:30pm, nice day, 50°, water up some. Caught 6 along side on #18 and #20-762/white, 6 at outlet on same, 3 at outlet on #18-438/cream and 1 on side. Small flies coming off. Pumped 3, took pictures—1 black-fly larva 646 or 47, mostly #18-840/thin rib cream, one #26-293A/102 is a fair match, 2 black unknowns, several mayfly nymphs #18-474/17?

April 3 - Big Spring, 3:30–6:30pm, 70°. Nothing in 2 lower lots, 4 below dam on #18-762/white, 1 big. Nothing on 762/white, #24 red bead, #18-840/yellow thread, #18 silver, #18-950 shrimp, 1 on #26-102/dark gray thread. Only saw 2 caught. Water looks very dingy like last time? None at outlet—strange.

May 20 - Boiling Springs, nice, lots of flies. Caught 6 on #18 white/Royal Bonnyl, none on pheasant tail. Caught no flies, sulfurs at dark?

May 23 - Boiling Springs. Caught 10 on #18-762/white. Caught 1 fly, not cahill, wings mottled #12–#14.

May 30 - Big Spring, 94°, 5–8:30pm. At corner, saw 4 caught on tan chenille worm w/ brown thread rib, about a 3X #8 curved. Caught 15 or so at outlet, 1 on #18-938/silver, 3 on #18-762/white, 4 on #20-762/white, 3 on #26-102/dark brown head, 3 on #26 raisin, 6 on #18 orange/white, 1 on Orange Dot Shrimp, none on 950 tan shrimp or brown/cream. Pumped 4 fish, 3 empty, fourth had #18 greenish, #18–#20 olive, 1 larva pale olive w/ reddish under, one #18 adult olive brown. Drought conditions fairly severe up north, limestone streams here affected slightly.

May 31 - Boiling Springs, 8–9pm, nice. Caught 10 on #18-842/white.

June 5 - Boiling Springs, 8–9pm, nice. Caught 8–10 on #18-842/white, same hatch, small then lg. cream ones.

June 11 - Boiling Springs, 7–9:30pm, nice. Caught 10 on #18 silver/red head in fast water, none on silver/black head, copper, 3 on #22-842/white, 10 on #18-842/white during early hatch up to about 9pm, then lg. cream flies coming off. None on light Cahill wet, 10 on #16 red-brown spinner. Caught flies—#18 BWO duns, 3782 looks same as 842—check.

June 12 - Boiling Springs, 75°, 8–9pm. Caught 8 on #18-842/white, 3 on #16 red-brown spinner.

June 13 - Boiling Springs, 70s, 7–9pm. Caught 10 on #18-842/white, also some on 3782/white, 3–4 (1 big) on #22-840/white, 1 on red beads, 1 on #18 brick red, 2 on #16 BWO nymph, none on 762/white, 5–6 on #16 BWO spinner.

June 19 - Boiling Springs, 6:30–9pm, 70°. Caught 5 on #18-842/white, 3 on #22-842/white, fishing not as good as before, #28 black beetle coming off, #18 mayfly, BWO? Caught 10 on #18-676 light old gold through hatch, larger cream fly coming off too, lots of fish rising to spinners at 9pm, didn't try.

June 20 - Boiling Springs, 70° and cooler, nice, 6:30–9pm. Caught 12 on #18-841 at upper dam, lost fly, several on #18-842/white, #22-840/white, #18-676, larger flies cream? coming off, may be switching to them. At 8:45pm, fish rising to spinners, 8 on #16 BWO spinner.

June 26 - Big Spring, 93°, 7–9:30pm, muggy. Caught 5 below dam on #20-762/white, caught 1 fishing upstream, 1 at corner on #24-745/brown, 3 at outlet on #18-762/white, none on safari bead, black/silver. Pumped 1 fish, not much, small cress and one #26-102/brown.

June 27 - Big Spring, 91°, muggy, 7–8:30pm, storm coming. Caught none on 762/white, red bead, pink shrimp, cress, mink. Saw others caught on unknown flies.

July 3 - Boiling Springs, hot. Still hitting #18 BWO spinner but only at dark, lg. light-colored fly on.

July 10 - Big Spring, 7–9pm, 80°. None below dam, fewer fish everywhere, lots of grass, elodea, crowded. At outlet, 3 on #18-415/silver, lots of casts though, none on #18 black/silver, 762/white, #24 red bead, #24-54/47, #26-361/light gray, #26-361 and 126/iridescent bead, 1 on #24-47/silver wet and 293A/361 wet, 2 on #26-102/dark brown, 4 on #26-475. Pumped 2 fish, took pictures—mostly #26–#28 102/dark brown or safari, lots of black-fly adults, black-fly larvae dark brownish bands.

July 11 - Big Spring, 7–9pm, 85° down to 70°, nice, lots of people earlier. Went right to outlet, none on #18-842/712, 102/dark brown, #24-918/silver, 1 on #20-415/silver, 1 hit on 102/dark brown, 4 on 475 and 475w/ silver. Pumped 1 fish, took pictures—1 red, several 102/dark brown #26–#28.

July and August - Drought, 90s, miserable.

August 28 - Big Spring, 9:30am–12n, nice, windy. Caught 6 on #20 olive mono/red thread under. Pumped 1 fish—361 safari #24–#26 w/ gray or brown head.

September 4 - Big Spring, 10am–2:30pm. One 20" rainbow on #18 red beads, 3 on #20 olive/red mono, 3 on #22-3078 pale yellow/319A red brown head, 1 on 2–3 others and cress, none on gray/white, shrimp, #26 safari bead, 2 on #18 copper. Pumped big one—nothing.

September 6 - Big Spring, 4–7pm, rainy, remnants of Hurricane Dennis. Caught 2 on #20 olive/red mono, 1 big, 1 on #18 red beads, also big, none on olive cress or yellow/red-brown head or copper.

September 12 - Big Spring, nice, 80° and cooler, 5–8pm, went right to outlet. Caught 3 on new #20 Light Tangerine Shrimp but many casts, very few fish at outlet, heavy weeds downstream, none on new #18 red/green beads, 415/silver, 831/silver, brick red/silver, copper, 2 on #24 brown/yellow, 1 on #26-102/brown head, none #26-361/iridescent bead, #18 mink, 1 on #24 red bead, few rises near dark, 1 on #26-361 on top, pictures of 102-361 pupa, brownish black-fly larva.

September 18 - Big Spring, 75°, nice but windy, 12n–2:30pm. Caught 8 on new #26-47/Unithread dark brown head, fishing upstream through and at outlet, this is a super fly. None on #20 olive/red mono at outlet, 2 on 831/silver. Pumped 3 fish—nothing.

September 19 - Big Spring, 70°, nice, little wind, 5–7:30pm. Few fish feeding, 1 hit on new #26-47/dark brown Unithread, few rising at 6:45, caught 7 on #26-361 safari dry. Done by 7:20pm.

September 26 - Boiling Springs, 6–7:30pm, nice, cool. Caught 1 on new #26-47/dark brown Unithread, hatch started same as Friday night, fewer flies but still good, unknown fly, appears #14 cream, 6 on #18-841 or 842/white.

October 2 - Big Spring, nice, 70° down to 50°, 5–7:30pm. Caught 2 below dam, 1 up through, 5 at outlet on #26-47/dark brown

Unithread, 2 on #26-475/361, very little rising. Pumped 3 fish, most #26-295A lemon yellow is close, 72A primrose too light, some #20-295A caddis larvae w/ red brown head, black-fly adults, some #18—try olive mono w/ Danville med. brown under and head, few #26-102/dark gray, gray is wide, most cross between safari and lemon yellow, primrose a little light, jungle gold a little dark but try w/ iron gray Uni wide or 475 raisin—a little dark, but try.

October 9 - Big Spring, rainy, overcast, 5–6:45pm. Caught 1 on #26-47/dark brown Uni, 1 on pink shrimp. Pumped 2 fish—nothing. No rises from 6:30–6:45pm.

October 31 - Boiling Springs, 5–6pm, nice. Caught none, no hatch, tried several midges.

November 7 - Big Spring, 50°, 2–4pm, nice. Caught 3 on #22-840/ecru at parking lot, 4 on #26-475/gold, at outlet 4 on #18-3787/3032, 2 hits on 475/primrose. Pumped 2 fish—one #18–#22 cress, mostly #30-475 (too dark)/thin Uni tan, #26 light steel, #26 khaki, #26 pale green caddis.

November 12 - Big Spring, 2:30–5pm, cool. Lost 2 on #26 ?, none of other new ones worked, foul-hooked 1 and pumped it—#28–#32 adults jungle gold too dark, lemon yellow too light, dark brown or gray thread head and rib (top only), bottom solid gold/yellow, legs same as rib/head, cress-tan, #16 caddis hatching, body yellow/rib brown, wings med. brown, mottled on top, legs golden.

December 31 - Big Spring, 45°, nice, tons of people, 2:30–5pm. Caught 1 at lot on #24 med. beige brown/white, 1 at outlet on #26-102/dark brown. Pumped 1 fish—one #20 cress and one #26-102/dark gray thin rib. None on other patterns on list for this time period.

2000

January 2 - Big Spring, nice big crowd. Caught 1 at lot on #18-415/silver, 1 fishing upstream on #26-102/dark gray. Got cold, left.

February 20 - Big Spring, nice but cool, about 40°, 3–5pm. Hooked 4, landed none, 2 on #18-762/white.

February and March - Went 3 times to Big Spring, windy but generally nice, 4–6pm. Caught none, tried all on hatch list.

April 1 - Big Spring, 3–6pm, nice, 70°, windy. Caught 6 fish, 2 on #24 red bead, 2 on 102/dark gray, 2 on pink shrimp, one 20", one 17", both on the 102 fly. Pumped one, took pictures—#18–#20 dark reddish brown, half emerged, #898 is dark band, #28-309A/dark brown Uni thread, #18 cress bugs. Stopped by Boiling Springs on way home, caught 2 on pink shrimp. Try a 474/dark brown thread.

April 2 - Boiling Springs, 2–3:30pm, nice, 60°. Caught 1 on 54/47.

April 7 - Yellow Breeches water plant, some #20 adult gray 18A taupe clair/light gray, #28 adults 56B/471, #18 cranefly 530 body, 543 head, yellow in wing and 56B/309A or 531 good—#28.

April 12 - Yellow Breeches water plant, cold and windy, #16 craneflies 309A camel, #18 medium brown, 593 close, thin tan rib, rest are #30 and down including safari, dark grayish brown, dark with tentlike wings, #32 raisin or dark gray with thin 47 rib. Cranefly head same color as body—camel, gray stripe on top only, legs camel.

April 15 - First day at camp, cold, Penns Creek a little high and cloudy. Didn't fish, black flies and black midges bad, big caddis hatch, only saw flies above water, no rises, #16 dark brown with turkey tail wings, gold legs, rear half of body has tan stripe.

April 16 - Big Spring, 6–8pm, nice. Caught 5 fish, 3 on #26-102/iron gray. Pumped one—2 midges, #24-126/56B (took picture with fly), other #28-#30 brown w/ tannish bands, no picture.

April 19 - Yellow Breeches water plant, cool, rainy, windy, #30 medium brown/chamois tan, close to picture taken of fly from Big Spring on 16th.

April 23 - Big Spring, 4–8pm, cold, 50°, windy, cloudy. Caught 5 on otter cress, 1 on pink shrimp at outlet. Peg and Barry Myers stopped at 7pm. Peg caught 5 on top in 30 minutes. Pumped 1 fish—#24–#26 361/iron gray head and thin rib 99%, few risers, missed one at dark on #102/dark gray. 361 color is close in microscope, should be more yellow green, head definitely gray, brown head is too far off, 102 and 126 too white, as are granite and natural. Ecru is close. Fly has a touch of tan with the green. Also #22 caddis larvae—try pale yellow beads or thread.

April 29 - Boiling Springs, nice, 55°, 6–8pm. Caught 2 on #18 copper mono, large mayfly #12 light/brown bands on back, #16 blue wing?, body reddish quill (light reddish brown, tan edge).

April 30 - Big Spring, 7:30–8:30pm, very cold. Hatch of #20 dark midges at 8pm. No fish on new flies.

May 1 - Big Spring, 7pm, 15 minutes—storm coming. Caught 1 big one on new #22-474/dark brown. Pumped fish—nothing—quit.

May 4 - Penns Creek, 7:30–8pm, watched march brown spinners up high in the air, #12, some fish rising to caddis.

May 6 - Big Spring, 7–8:30pm, nice. Caught 3 on pink shrimp, 3 on #22-126/iron gray, fished on top.

May 14 - Big Spring, 6–8:30pm, 65°, cold at dark. At outlet, 1 on #20-762/white, 1 on #18-762/white, 1 on #18 copper mono, 1 on pink shrimp, 1 on #18-918/silver, none on orange/white, lost 2 big ones. Mayflies, #14, a half dozen or so, appear very light. Caught spinner—whitish. Pumped 2 fish—#24-102 or #18 dark brown.

May 21 - Boiling Springs, 7–8:30pm. Caught 7 on #18 orange/white, 1 on #18 medium brown/silver. Nice hatch of sulfurs. Tied emerger wet—old gold light body and blue wing #18.

May 28 - Big Spring, 4–8:30pm, very cold, stream up from rain but crystal clear. Caught 1 on #24 red at corner, none on 938/silver, new glass caddis, #26-102/gray, #24-54/47, 762/white, olive w/ red under, 1 on pink shrimp, 2 on orange/white, 1 on cress, 2 on #18 tan fur caddis (1 big brown). Pumped one fish, took pictures—#18 light brown/thin cream rib, #28 medium gray mottled, #24-309A/brown head BCS65, most are 347 and 309A and #18-3827 light brown.

May 29 - Boiling Springs, 7:30–8pm, nice, 70°, caught 6 on orange/white. Hatch of sulfurs right at dark, 8:40pm.

June 3 - My birthday. Boiling Springs, nice, 70°, 8–8:40pm. Caught 7 on #18 orange/white, 1 on #18 red brown fur, 1 on #18 green metallic. Hatch heavy 8:45–9pm, fish will not hit orange/white anymore. Caught 1 fly, red eyes, blue wings, #18, light gold yellow body, ruddy thorax.

June 4 - Big Spring, 6–9pm, 60s, cool, nice, storm coming later, dark clouds. None fishing upstream on new 3827/116 or 309A/medium brown at outlet, none on brown caddis, #20-762/white, 1 on #18 beige/white, 2 on #26-347/medium brown, not many rises. Pumped 2 fish, took pictures—lots of #24–#28 thin midge larvae, most straw color or pale yellow w/ lightest brown head, 295A/light brown BCS94 Unitan (underthread 8/0 bright yellow silk BCS53), 1 fish had about 100 flies, most #24s and down, lots of midges, same color as above caddis, head light brown and light gray or body color, some black-fly larvae, dark gray and dark beige #18, some #28-127A/116, #24 golden brown (same as #26 or 543/dark brown), some of the 102 and 347 flies, some adults, black flies, and what appear to be adults of 127A/116 pupae.

June 17 - Big Spring, 6–9pm, 90° till 8pm, then cooled off. Caught 2 fishing upstream on #22-762/white and 2 at outlet, none on 415/silver, black/silver, brown/silver, #24 red, 54/47, 47/silver, 102/brown, taupe/khaki, 16 on #26-309A/dark brown head. Rises at 8:45pm, fog/mist at 9, caught 4 on #18 black mono before this. Pumped 2 fish—lots of black-fly larvae, #16 down to #22, most light beige, some darker. Lots of reddish caddis #18 and down, most olive tint, pale yellow w/ spots on back, #26 gray-green pupae and adults, #28-531 saffron adults, head and legs lightest brown BCS55 Unitan. Lots of emergers #26–#28 light yellow, medium gray, light brown head as adults. Lots of #24–#26, bottom 309A, light brown head, top dark gray, others are lighter, toward khaki–pale green, 102. Lots of sizes of caddis, many pale colors, black flies that are 840/3047, #18 reddish-greenish, some very dark black-fly larvae.

June 23 - Boiling Springs, 7:30–8:30pm, nice, 80°. Caught 5 on reddish brown sulfur nymph, none on silver, beige/white, tan caddis. Caught 2 flies—#18 blue wing, body orange-gold, legs cream/pale yellow.

June 24 - Big Spring, 7–9pm, 94° at house, cooler here, water nice. None on new #18 white beads at lot. Switched to new #26-309A, none till near corner, nice brown broke off. Ed arrived. At outlet, 7 or 8 on #26-309A, 5 on #24 light yellow/brown head, none on #18 brown/silver, #18 beige/white. Pumped 2 fish. A few rises at 9. Caught 1 on #26 floating (close to 309A). Lots of #18 dark brown w/ touch of olive, #28 green w/ yellow flecks, (3012 is close), #18 light brown, almost light straw 3822 w/ light brown head and some shading, #26 light khaki 3013 w/ dark gray thin rib and head, #18+ light tan or cream caddis larvae, #26 light khaki adults, lots of #18 black-fly larvae dark gray and white, #18 black-winged ant, only one 309A type.

June 30 - Big Spring, 80°, nice, cool at 8, 7–9+pm. At outlet, none on #18 white bead, beige/white, 1 on black/silver, brown/silver, 361 bead, 309A, several on #26-293A/347, almost no rises. Pumped 3 fish, took pictures—mostly dark beige black flies, plus 1 odd thing, #20 adult medium brown w/ straw legs and head blotches and thin rib.

July 1 - Big Spring, 7:30–9pm, 90s in afternoon, 80° now. Fished at bend, 2 on 293A/347, 2–3 more on top near dark, 1on cream shrimp, none on new light brown head w/ yellow beige #18 body, didn't try other 2 new flies. Should try #24-27/17 instead of 293A/347 or 475/361.

July 2 - Big Spring, 7:30–9pm, hot, muggy, water a little cloudy. At corner, 2 on 293A/347, missed several on top, not much going on, got tired, left.

July 4 - Big Spring, 6:30–9pm, 80°, nice, nobody here. At outlet, 8 or so on new #18 reddish brown beads, 6 on #24 red bead, 4 on new white bead, 3 on old #22 pale yellow/rust rib thread, 3 in a row on new #18-3045/silver, 4 hits on new #18-610/silver, only 1 on 293A/347. Not many rises, but some caught on black. Took pictures. Most appear to be black-fly larvae of several color types. Red-green caddis, cream and orangish, or reddish brownish, #28s assorted linens, 102 safari, some #24s, lots of black flies, especially darker. Tie some dark gray and dark beige.

July 8 - Big Spring, 6:30–8:45pm, nice, 70°. One riser, some on cress. At outlet area, 1 on 841/ecru, 1 on 762/white, 1 on 3045/silver, 6 on #24-54/47 wet, none on new reddish brown bead, Ed caught 5 on black wet. Pumped 2 fish—#18 light brown like 3045, 309A #24s, #28s like 54/47 only lighter, #28 like 102/dark brown or gray, #24—try a pale yellow/light brown thread, most caddis are very pale green, yellow, reddish olive, #32 pale yellow adult, dark brown or black adult #28, #26 adult dark brown or gray/silver white—both bands wide.

July 9 - Allenberry, 89°, 6:30–8:30pm. Caught 9 on #18-762/white, 1 on #18 tan peacock caddis, water low, only rises are splashy.

July 12 - Boiling Springs, nice, 8–9pm. Caught 4 on #18 olive/silver, none on gray-white, 1 on cream shrimp, not much coming off, fish rise like they're after caddis, 2 more nights about the same, 15th and 20th.

July 22 - Big Spring, 6:30–9pm, nice, cool. Caught 1 on #18-762/white at lot. At outlet, 1 on #18 reddish brown beads, 3 on #18 gold, few other hits, none on 54/47 wet, 361/green bead, new #18 light yellow, white shrimp, beige/white, 475. Sipping rises from 8:30–9pm, 102/dark brown on top, only 1 hit, landed none.

July 23 - Big Spring, 6:30–9pm, cool, nice, 70°. Only 1 on medium beige/cream, not much moving, none on #20 red olive mono, #20 red, cress, pink shrimp, dark gray/white, #20 orange shrimp, #26-347, #26 black wet, #26 black/yellow, few rising.

August 6 - Fisherman's Paradise, 1 hour in afternoon. Caught 2 on #18-762/white, rain all the way up, stopped 1 hour, then poured. Midges hatching, lots of rises at outlet.

August 9 -Fisherman's Paradise, 11:30am–2pm, hot. Caught 8 or 9 on #18-762/white, some on #22 same, better as it stained greenish, 2 on #24 dark beige/white, hit hard. Pumped several—cress bugs, adult black fly, #18 pupae medium brown, #24 camel/dark brown, #28 pale cream larvae, #14 reddish brown/dark cream and some adults 840/841, #18 red larvae, 1 snail and some odd things, lots of #24–#26 khaki types, #24-977/dark brown.

August 12 - Big Spring, nice, cool, 70°, 7–8:30pm, dark earlier. At outlet, 6 on new #24-977/dark brown, 3 on #18-840/841. Pumped 1 fish, took pictures—1 pupa and 1 adult, #26-530/iron gray.

August 13 - Big Spring, nice, cool, overcast, 6–8:30pm. Nothing at lot with 977/dark brown, near outlet, nothing on 762/white, new #18 browns, new #26-530, 5 at dark on #12 mink, 2 over 16". Pumped 2—#24 midge larvae, pale yellow beads, #26 medium gray/cream, #18 thin 3821 straw, no rib, #26-337/iron gray a little dark.

August 20 - Big Spring, cool, 3–7pm. Caught 3 on olive/silver, not many feeding, few rises, tried 15 patterns. Pumped 1fish—3 black-fly larvae, brown.

August 27 - Big Spring, 80°, 6–8pm. At outlet, 1 on #18-842/white, several on old #18 bleached mole pattern, a couple big. Pumped 2 fish—big #18 light brown caddis, lots of black-fly larvae and adults, #24 green metallic adult, lots of #26–#28 pale yellow, camel or hemp close, #24 safari, light tans, cream w/ fine brown ribs, linen, #22 adult had light gray body, rose thorax, pale green larvae #22, #32s.

August 30 - Boiling Springs, hot, muggy, 80°+. Caught 1 on new black-fly larva, none on pink shrimp.

August 31 - Boiling Springs, hot, muggy. Caught 2 on shrimp, 1 on beige/white, saw #14 light-colored flies, mottled wings.

September 3 - Big Spring, 6:30–7:30pm, very muggy, cloudy, water up and slightly cloudy, fog coming in. Caught 2 at outlet on #18-840/543, none on red bead, #26 brick/silver, 762/white, #14 mink, 1 on silver, lost all 3.

September 11 - Big Spring, 10am–2:30pm, rainy, got wet 3 times. Caught 4 at outlet on #28 dark brown, only pumped up 1 insect, #24-102/dark gray.

September 21 - Big Spring, 5–7pm, cool, nice, cold at 7pm. Caught 12 on #26-47/dark brown from dam to near corner, 4 are 15"+. From 5-6:15pm, some chased fly, then none till 7. Tried outlet at 7, nothing. Pumped 3 fish including 1 big—found only 1 cress bug. Caught adult, #24, body black and white, wings palest gray and long.

September 23 - Big Spring, 6–7pm, cool, cloudy, storm fronts, area shocked. No fish at outlet, 2 on #26-47/dark brown.

September 24 - Big Spring, 5–7pm, cool, overcast, sprinkles. Few fish at outlet, 3 fishing upstream on #26-47/dark brown, 1 on #24 olive/silver, 1 on #18-762/white, none on shrimp, pink or zebra. Caught drys, took pictures, #22 adult dark brown striped body, silverish look, #20–#22 flying ants, dark brown, 2 body segments, small head, #20 dry, dark brown, thin gold bands, #18-733 green/light brown head, Unicamel, excellent match, black flies grayish dark, #24-573/dark brown not bad, #22 reddish brown, olive greenish tone, #18 medium brown, lots of these.